D1307923

Mobsters, Gangsters and Men of Honour

Pierre de Champlain

Mobsters, Gangsters and Men of Honour

CRACKING THE MAFIA CODE

HarperCollins*PublishersLtd*

National Library of Canada Cataloguing in Publication

Champlain, Pierre de, 1946–
Mobsters, gangsters and men of honour : cracking the Mafia code / Pierre de Champlain. – 1st ed.

Includes bibliographical references and index.
ISBN 0-00-200668-5

1. Mafia – Canada. 2. Mafia – United States.
3. Organized crime – Canada. 4. Organized crime – United States. I. Title.

HV6441.C443 2004   364.1′06′097   C2003-905645-7

RRD 9 8 7 6 5 4 3 2 1

Printed and bound in the United States
Set in FF Quadraat

To my nieces,
Isabelle and Julie,
two lovely young women
to whom I wish the best in the accomplishment of their lives.

"The Mafia is oppression, arrogance, greed, self-enrichment, power and hegemony above and against all others. It is not an abstract concept, or a state of mind, or a literary term. . . . It is a criminal organization regulated by unwritten but iron and inexorable rules. . . . The myth of a courageous and generous 'man of honour' must be destroyed, because a mafioso is just the opposite."

—Cesare Terranova, Italian Magistrate,
murdered in 1979 by Cosa Nostra

Contents

Figures

Introduction

The idea of writing a book on the rules and protocols used by the Mafia has been with me since 1990. I had read hundreds of books on the history of the American and Sicilian Mafia, biographies of mobsters and studies on the social impacts of the Mafia. Throughout all these readings, there were allusions to rules and protocols by which members of the Mafia were expected to abide, but without any details. During my research, I discovered I was more interested in confirming the existence and purpose of these rules than I was in studying organized criminal activity itself. So far, I have not encountered a study that deals with this precise question.

Back in 1975 I had attended the public sessions of the Quebec Crime Probe on organized crime, held in Montreal. Aside from examining criminal activities, the commission was studying the inner functions and structure of the Montreal Mafia family, led at that time by the Calabrese-born Vincenzo Cotroni and Paolo Violi. I learned that this small, regional group of mafiosi took directives from the New York–based Bonanno crime family. For instance, the Montreal faction had to seek permission from New York to make new members. I also learned that the Cotroni-Violi group had within its ranks members of the Sicilian Mafia—the Rizzutos and the Caruanas—who had settled in Montreal during the 1960s. However, the Sicilians were subject to strict rules regarding their right to participate in criminal activities on their own. Disputes over this right would lead to several killings within the Calabrese faction in the years that followed.

Thus began my interest in the rules and protocols of the Mafia. I chose to study the American Mafia—known by its members as Cosa Nostra ("Thing of Ours")—because it is a highly structured organization whose ranking hierarchy has a profound effect on its daily operations, and because rules and protocols have played an important role in shaping its organization and function. But while the American Mafia is the focus of this book, I will also refer to cases in the Sicilian Cosa Nostra and the Canadian-based Sicilian Mafia.

The nucleus of both the American Mafia and the Sicilian Mafia is the family. All members are related, either by blood or by marriage alliances. Fathers, sons, brothers, uncles, nephews, cousins, godsons, brothers-in-law and fathers-in-law work together in criminal relationships based on trust, mutual respect and silence. These bonds give the Mafia an aura of impermeability.

Relationships within the family and between members and outsiders—other Mafia families and criminal entrepreneurs who are not part of the Mafia—are governed by rules of conduct. There are two distinct levels of authority among family members: those who command and those who obey. At the top of the pyramid there is a boss who controls every aspect of the lives (including the private lives) and criminal activities of his family. He is assisted by captains, who, in turn, command an army of soldiers. Elaborate sets of rules serve to maintain this hierarchy. There are rules dictating the moral conduct of a mafioso—silence (never talk to police), discipline (strict obedience to the boss) and respect (for other members and their wives)—and there are rules on the scope and type of criminal activities that members are allowed to engage in. These rules are, of course, unwritten. They are learned in an environment in which family members must show they are willing (and not afraid) to commit acts of violence, including murder, to prove themselves worthy.

While Cosa Nostra may be a disciplined organization, it is nevertheless an organization made up of men who, quite frequently, transgress their own rules. When such situations occur, the organization allows the hearing of charges against members. Depending on the gravity of the offence, sanctions may vary from a fine to suspension or expulsion to the death penalty. The killing of a Cosa Nostra member is one of the most strictly controlled actions, without exception requiring authorization by the boss of a family.

For more than half a century, federal and state authorities have considered the American Cosa Nostra the backbone of organized crime in North America. A study of its rules and structure provides a glimpse at the rationale behind the conduct of its members, and, in particular, behind their perpetration of murder and other crimes. With this book, I hope to present a new approach to understanding this complex criminal organization.

Chapter 1

The Birth of a National Criminal Organization

The Mafia first emerged as a powerful criminal organization in the middle of the nineteenth century, taking shape in the rural areas of Western Sicily. When the Italian feudal structure began to be abolished in the early 1800s, the barons who were Sicily's landlords retreated to Naples. Their place was quickly filled by a new middle class of estate managers—the *gabelloti*—who exploited not only the peasants but the barons as well. The *gabelloto* evolved into the "mafioso," who asserted his position using violence and, at the same time, acted as a mediator between the baron and the peasants. The Mafia protected the poor against the abuses of the state and against banditry, both of which were common in rural areas of Sicily. The Mafia dispensed justice, through intimidation and violence, for people who could not get it by legal means. The word "mafia" was first used in 1838 in a police report by law enforcement authorities in the province of Trapani.[1] With a small "m," it is used to describe someone who displays courage or pride. When it has a capital "M," it refers to the criminal organization.[2]

As the nineteenth century came to a close, social and economic hardship forced more than two million people from Southern Italy, most from Sicily, to leave their country for the United States and Canada. They were told the living conditions would be better. These immigrants, unfamiliar with the English language and culture, were met with hostility from already well-established English, German and Scandinavian immigrants, who looked down on these dark-haired, Catholic, agrarian immigrants.[3]

The massive waves of immigration, which peaked during the first decade of the twentieth century, carried with them people of dubious reputation. As early as 1878 the Italian government made an attempt to break up the Mafia by forcing mafiosi to immigrate to the United States. Like immigrants from Ireland, China and Eastern Europe, the Italians settled into exclusive ethnic areas in large cities such as New York, Philadelphia, Chicago, New Orleans, San Francisco and Los Angeles. At the turn of the nineteenth century, New York City was the second largest "Italian City," after Naples. Southern Italians and Sicilians settled mainly on the Lower East Side, beneath the Brooklyn Bridge. Half a million people strong, they comprised one-fourth of the city's population.[4] While the Sicilian Mafia reigned mostly in the rural areas of Sicily, the American Mafia took shape in urban ghettos.

Illiterate and ill-informed, immigrants were naturally suspicious of police officers, who did not understand their language. Poor communication between immigrants and police and overcrowding in ghettos made for ideal conditions for the development of criminality that would favour the growth of the Mafia. The so-called patriotic Mafia, which in the motherland had protected people from the injustice of the state, soon turned to preying upon and exploiting its own people. Unlike dominant ethnic groups such as the Irish, Jews or Eastern Europeans, Italian immigrants were defenceless on United States soil, and the Mafia knew the immigrants would never dare complain to the police.[5]

But the Mafia was not the only game in town. Italian immigrants were suddenly met with a wave of extortion letters demanding money. The amount depended upon the victim's status and wealth. These letters, written by freelance criminals, were invariably signed with a hand print, or with sketches of skulls, coffins or crossed daggers. If the person dared to refuse or ignore the threat, he was killed, or his house or business blown up. The extortions, which peaked in the late 1880s and were common not only in New York City but in Chicago and Kansas City as well, came to be known as "Black Hand" operations. Soon all crimes committed in Italian ghettos were attributed to the Black Hand (La Mano Nera), reinforcing the distrust of other ethnic groups towards Italian immigrants.

According to Giuseppe "Joe" Petrosino, the first Italian member of the New York City Police and one of the most knowledgeable experts on the

Italian underworld at the time, Black Hand activities were the same as "those committed at one time by rural outlaws in Italy; and the victims, like the killers, come from the same ignorant class of people. In short, we are dealing with rural banditry transplanted to the most modern city in the world."[6] Petrosino was convinced that members of the Black Hand were not part of the Mafia or the Camorra (a criminal organization with roots in Naples), but acted on an individual basis. He claimed that because the drawings within these letters of extortion varied in style and execution, they were clearly written and sent by individual criminals: ". . . if we were really dealing with a single organization, the symbol too would be a single one."[7]

Members of the Mafia and the Camorra had a deep disdain of the Black Handlers, who operated beyond the rule of the underworld. Because many victims had received letters signed "The Mafia," Black Hand activities had given the Mafia a bad reputation. Black Handlers had even sent letters to the Mafia itself. Surprisingly enough, these leaders of organized crime did not hesitate to report the extortionists to the police. This was in clear violation of the Mafia credo of honour against inform-ing.[8] But it was the only way for the Mafia to get rid of these extortionists over whom it had no control, and who were not abiding strictly by the underworld's conventions.

Benito Mussolini, the leader of the Italian Fascist Party, had his first encounter with the Mafia when he visited Sicily for the first time in May 1924. His visit to Piana dei Greci, a small village near Palermo, was a revelation. Il Duce was asked by Ciccio Cuccia, the mayor and *capomafia* of the village, why he was surrounded by so many policemen. "I have the whole of this district on my orders. Your Excellency has nothing to fear when you are by my side," declared the mayor. The remark shocked the Fascist leader, who realized that he, a statesman who fought the Mafia as one of the state's worst enemies, would not need any physical protection while he was travelling in Mafia territory. Cuccia was later put under arrest during anti-Mafia operations.[9]

Upon returning to Rome, Mussolini appointed a special prosecutor, Cesare Mori, an ex-police officer, to fight the Mafia. Thousands of people, many of whom had nothing to do with the Mafia, were sent to jail and tor-tured. In 1925 elections were abolished, and the Mafia lost its privileged alliance with the Social Democrat Party. A ferocious campaign against the Mafia and mafiosi ensued that did not end until 1928. By that time, Mori had succeeded in eradicating the Mafia—for a time. The Sicilian Mafia remained inactive for over a decade, until it was revived by the Allied Force command during the Second World War. When the Allies landed in Gela and Licata, Sicily, in July 1943, all of the cities' mayors, most of them full-fledged Mafia members, were reappointed by the military.

While hundreds of mafiosi had been convicted in Mori's campaign, others managed to flee to America. Criminal fugitives used a number of routes to enter the United States. They would land in Canada, and then travel to Buffalo or Detroit, or go directly to New York City. They would also enter from the south, through New Orleans, Miami or Tampa. These fugitives, many of whom came from Castellammare del Golfo, a small village in the province of Trapani in western Sicily, would later form the core of the American Mafia. Among them were Salvatore Maranzano, Joseph Bonanno, Michael Coppola, Vincent Mangano and Joseph Magliocco, all in their twenties when they fled Sicily.[10]

THE CASTELLAMMARESE WARS OF 1929 TO 1931

From 1929 to 1931 the streets of New York were the main battleground of a fratricidal war, the result of opposing views on the organization of the Mafia. The "Castellammarese Wars," some of the most dramatic confrontations in the history of Italian organized crime in America, played a profound role in shaping the American Mafia's family structure, ranking positions and code of conduct. The wars would lead to the creation of the Commission.

Giuseppe Masseria was born in Marsala, in the province of Trapani in 1879. In 1903 he fled to the United States to escape a murder charge in Sicily. He settled in the Mulberry Bend District of New York City, where the Sicilian Mafia was already well established. The group, which operated in the Lower East Side, was led by the Morello brothers, Giuseppe and Nicholas, their half-brother, Ciro Terranova, and Terranova's brother-in-law, Ignazio Saietta. Masseria joined the group in 1907. Masseria saw the Mafia as autonomous, able to function without alliance to other ethnic crime groups, such as Jewish and Irish gangs. (The Irish were already predominant in certain areas of organized crime, such as gambling.)

The main opponent to Masseria was Salvatore Maranzano. He believed that to survive and operate efficiently in America the Sicilian Mafia needed radical transformation in its structures and modus operandi. Maranzano judged it was necessary and advantageous for the Mafia to make alliances with other criminal gangs. He strongly opposed the idea that full control of the Mafia over New York City should rest solely in the hands of one man. He wanted this power to be shared among other family leaders.

Maranzano had made few incursions in the United States before he settled for good in New York in 1927 at age forty-three. Born in Castellammare del Golfo in 1868, and raised in an upper-class environment, the well-educated Maranzano spoke several languages. He had studied to become a priest, but becoming a member of the Mafia was more appealing. He was a fervent admirer of the Roman emperor Julius Caesar, and would later model his campaign against Masseria on Caesar's military tactics. Maranzano came to America not as a fugitive but as a representative of Don Vito Cascio Ferro, with the assignment to organize the American Mafia families under an exclusive command.[11]

Before 1920 Italian groups had some control in various areas of the city, extending from the Lower East Side to Uptown, in Italian Harlem. But no one group had full hegemony over the others. Paul Vaccarelli and his Five Points Gang had a stronghold in the Bowery. Ciro Terranova had influence in Harlem and in the Bronx.[12] In 1913, for unknown reasons, Masseria broke with the Morellos. The same year, he ordered the murder of a Morello cousin, Charles Lamonti. Six months later, Lamonti's brother was also killed. In 1914 Masseria was sentenced to a four-year term in Sing Sing for burglary.[13] After a series of gangland killings among the Morello group, Masseria become the undisputed leader of the gang, and his leadership was not challenged until 1929.

By the late 1920s, there were five Mafia clans in operation in the five boroughs of New York City. The Masseria clan was the most influential. It included Sicilians who were well established in the United States—Peter Morello, Salvatore Luciano, Joseph Doto, Michael Coppola and Anthony

Carfano—and the Calabrian-born Frank Costello. Another group was led by Albert Mineo, and included Vincent Mangano, Frank Scalice and Albert Anastasia. These two families had interests in Manhattan and Brooklyn. The Bronx family was led by Gaetano Reina. Gaetano Gagliano and Gaetano "Thomas" Lucchese were its most prominent members. A fourth family, led by Joseph Profaci, controlled part of Brooklyn. The fifth, under the command of Salvatore Maranzano, had interests in Brooklyn and Manhattan.[14] The Maranzano faction included several mafiosi who had been born in Castellammare del Golfo and had fled their country to escape the Mussolini campaign against the Mafia. Stefano Magaddino, Joseph Magliocco, Joseph Profaci, Joseph Bonanno and Salvatore Maranzano were among them.

Confronted by a flood of Sicilian mafiosi who entered the United States under the protection of Maranzano during the late 1920s, Masseria soon felt his authority threatened. To make it clear that he was the undisputed boss of Italian organized crime in New York City, he ordered Maranzano to pay the pizzu (literally meaning the beak of a small bird), a practice initiated by Vito Cascio Ferro. When you are ordered by a Mafia boss to pay the pizzu or "wet the beak," you have an obligation to acquiesce.[15] But Maranzano refused to comply.

On January 20, 1920, the United States Congress had sanctioned the Volstead Act, the 18th Amendment to the Constitution of the United States of America, which forbade the production and sale of any alcoholic beverage where the grade was more than half of one percent. (The Act was abrogated nearly fourteen years later, in December 1933.) Prohibition became the springboard that allowed the American Mafia to organize and to dominate competing criminal gangs.

Criminal organizations saw in the Volstead Act a unique opportunity to respond to a formidable demand for a product that had become illegal overnight. No one could manufacture, sell or buy alcohol in large enough quantities. The Mafia held several meetings to plan how to meet the overwhelming demand, as did other criminal organizations.

Prohibition was also an opportunity for Masseria to test Maranzano's tolerance. Masseria ordered the killing of an important Detroit Mafia figure, Gaspare Milazzo. Milazzo, also born in the village of Castellammare del Golfo, was responsible for the supervision of Maranzano's interests in the Midwest. Maranzano did not respond to that killing. Then, on February 26, 1930, Masseria moved to kill Gaetano Reina, a prominent gang leader in the Bronx, who had recently joined the Maranzano group. The killing stirred the wrath of all the Italian gangsters in the city, and Masseria felt compelled to justify the murder. He said that Reina had betrayed him in merging forces with Maranzano.

After the Reina murder, Masseria appointed his lackey, Joseph Pinzolo, to supervise the Reina group. But Gaetano Gagliano and Thomas Lucchese did not accept this intruder and called upon Maranzano to get rid of Pinzolo. A deal was arranged. To show their mutual trust, both Maranzano and Gagliano agreed to kill two important members of Masseria's group. Gagliano would hit Pinzolo, while Maranzano would get rid of Peter Morello, Terranova's brother-in-law. Masseria had just appointed Morello boss of all Italian crime families in New York City, answering to Masseria. Masseria was known as the "Boss of all Bosses." The move was seen by Masseria's opponents as a manoeuvre to control the rackets in New York, in particular the sale and distribution of alcohol, and gambling and extortion.[16]

Maranzano struck first by having Peter Morello slain in his office on August 15, 1930. Three weeks later, on September 9, 1930, Pinzolo was shot to death in his Manhattan office. As previously agreed, Gagliano became the leader of the Reina faction.

After these two losses, Masseria officially decreed a death sentence against all the Castellammarese. On October 23, 1930, Joseph Aiello from Chicago, Maranzano's ally and an ardent enemy of Al Capone, was killed. Maranzano made his mind up to kill Masseria as soon as possible. A plan was set to kill Masseria on November 30, 1930, as he left an apartment where he was holding an important war meeting with his lieutenants. But when the meeting over, Masseria stayed behind when his cohorts left. Two Masseria men, Steve Ferrigno and Albert Mineo, were shot to death.[17]

After a year of war, mafiosi from Cleveland called for a special meeting of all Mafia families of the United States. The meeting was held in Boston. A five-member commission was set up to ask Maranzano to engage with Masseria on a peace truce. Maranzano refused to meet the delegation. In the face of Maranzano's unwillingness to negotiate, another special meeting was called, in New York. This time, Maranzano showed up; Masseria did not. Maranzano then stated that the conflict would end only with Masseria's death.[18]

Masseria's main lieutenants—Salvatore Luciano, Vito Genovese and Meyer Lansky—realized their boss was losing the war against Maranzano. They secretly engaged in negotiations with Maranzano to have Masseria killed.

On April 15, 1931, Masseria was having lunch in a Coney Island restaurant with Luciano. Luciano left the table to use the bathroom, leaving Masseria alone. By the time Luciano came back, four gunmen had erupted into the restaurant and killed Masseria.

After Masseria's execution, Maranzano called for a meeting in a Bronx hotel. To a gathering of between four and five hundred mobsters, Maranzano explained that Masseria had been murdered because "he killed people without justification." He went on to lay out a new structure for the crime families of Cosa Nostra, establishing chains of command and communication and formalizing the rules of conduct: never talk about the existence of the organization, even to a wife or children; never seduce the wife or girlfriend of a fellow member; obey without question all orders of one's leaders; never assault or charge falsely any other member, no matter what the provocation. All past grievances were to be forgiven and a total amnesty for past deeds granted.

The New York Mafia families would be merged and realigned. Salvatore Luciano would take over Masseria's family, with Vito Genovese as underboss. Luciano would control Manhattan and the waterfront. Gaetano Gagliano was to lead the former Reina family, seconded by Thomas Lucchese as underboss. Gagliano would keep the Bronx as his territory. Assisted by Albert Anastasia, Vincent Mangano would share Brooklyn with Joseph Profaci, who had been neutral during the war.[19] Finally, Joseph Bonanno would head the former Maranzano group. Maranzano named himself *Capo di tutti capi*—"Boss of all Bosses"—of the American Cosa Nostra.[20] With Luciano, he got a piece of criminal activities in Manhattan and other boroughs.[21] (The structure of the New York Cosa Nostra remains the same today, aside from the elimination of the position of "Boss of all Bosses" and the addition of a sixth family in New Jersey in 1931, under the leadership of Steve Padami.[22])

Maranzano called another meeting at a Catskills resort hotel near Wappingers Falls, in upstate New York, to which the New York Italian underworld was invited, as well as other Mafia leaders from outside the city. Maranzano explained how the situation stood in New York City, and how strong his power was.[23] Maranzano reaffirmed Capone's position as the boss of the Chicago underworld, while Capone agreed to recognize Maranzano as *Capo di tutti capi* of the Italian Mafia throughout the United States.[24]

But the new structure imposed by Maranzano worried Luciano and his non-Italian associates. Luciano feared that a new war would burst out with the non-Italian criminal organizations if Maranzano acted like a dictator. Mafiosi of the younger generation such as Luciano and Vito Genovese, along with Jewish gangsters Meyer Lansky and Benjamin Siegel, were criminal entrepreneurs; they were willing to do business with other criminals, no matter what their ethnic origin, provided profit was the reward. This philosophy, one that would shape the next half century of American organized crime, was not entirely shared by Maranzano.[25]

On September 10, 1931, Maranzano was killed at his Park Avenue offices by four gunmen posing as Internal Revenue Service investigators. As a symbol of co-operation between Italian and non-Italian gangsters, most of the gunmen were non-Italians.[26] Maranzano's murder was seen as the beginning of the "Americanization" of Italian organized crime.[27]

Following Maranzano's murder, a meeting was called in Chicago in November 1931 to give Luciano the opportunity to explain and justify the Maranzano slaying. A triumphant Al Capone hosted the meeting, held at the Congress Hotel. Luciano told participants that Maranzano had plotted his death, as well as those of Genovese and many others.[28] Delegates urged Luciano to abolish the position of "Boss of all Bosses," which he did. In its place, a commission of six was established: the leaders of the five New York Mafia families plus the head of the New Jersey family. Later, following the meeting at the Congress Hotel, Al Capone of Chicago and Frank Milano of Cleveland were allowed to sit on the Commission.[29] (Capone's leadership was short-lived; late in 1931 he was sentenced to an eleven-year jail term for tax evasion. He was succeeded by Paul Ricca.[30]) Luciano also created a national crime syndicate board, in which Italian crime families would be associated with Jewish and Irish gangsters. The Benjamin Siegel–Meyer Lansky connection would become an important ally for Cosa Nostra.[31]

Luciano had come to realize that, within a family, a boss could use his power indiscriminately against the low-ranked and defenceless soldiers. He therefore created for each family the position of *consigliere*, whose role and mandate was to arbitrate disputes between soldiers and the upper-echelon family members and to advise the boss. Under Masseria's and Maranzano's tenures, soldiers had had no protection if the *caporegime* (captain) to whom they reported had a more-or-less well-founded grievance against them. With the establishment of the *consigliere* position, a *caporegime* could not have one of his soldiers killed or punished without the approval of the family. The *consigliere* acted as a protector for the soldiers, enabling them to speak and defend themselves without fear of reprisal.[32]

Luciano also established a "Council of Six," whose main role would be to hear and decide on matters involving the conduct of members or grievances between the five New York families and the one in New Jersey. The council was made up of one representative from each of these families who had the rank of *consigliere*. Similar local boards were later instituted in the Chicago and Detroit families.[33] The *consiglieri* would hear grievances or charges against members of these families, and decide on sanctions where rules had been violated. When there was a tie vote, the boss of the concerned family would have a casting vote. A soldier would not be punished before being given the chance to defend himself before the council.[34]

Salvatore Luciano's goal was to get the Cosa Nostra out of the ghettos and into the modern world, where it would join forces with other non-Italian criminal organizations, becoming a powerful national crime syndicate that would look beyond racial and ethnic differences to engage in joint criminal ventures.[35] Other criminal organizations would soon follow Cosa Nostra's example. When Prohibition was repealed by the 21st Amendment to the Constitution on December 5, 1933, underworld leaders went looking for other means of diversifying their sources of illegal revenue.[36]

THE CREATION OF "MURDER INC."

Not very long after the establishment of the American Cosa Nostra in 1931, an enforcement branch, labelled "Murder Inc." by the press, was formed to carry out death sentences ordered by Cosa Nostra. The Brooklyn-based organization worked exclusively for Cosa Nostra, and was not affiliated to any specific family. It was created to maintain an equal balance of power in the hands of the Commission, to prevent open violence and to reduce gang warfare and the perpetration of impulsive crimes by independent crime groups.[37] Albert Anastasia acted as liaison between Cosa Nostra and Louis Buchalter, a Jewish labour racketeer responsible for Murder Inc. operations. The organization undertook executions that Cosa Nostra did not want to be involved in. The hired killers were Italians, Jews and Irishmen. They were not allowed to work for outsiders, nor could they perform murders for fees or for revenge or other personal reasons. Murders were restricted to those for business purposes.[38]

In 1940 Murder Inc. came to an end with the arrest of one of its professional killers, Abe Reles. Faced with multiple first-degree murder charges, Reles told the police everything he knew about the organization. His revelations led to the arrest of six other accomplices, who, to avoid the electric chair, revealed what they knew. On November 12, 1941, Reles, who had been held secluded under close police watch in a hotel room in Coney Island, met his fate: his body was found six floors below on top of an extension of the hotel. Despite Reles's death, the District Attorney succeeded in convicting Louis Buchalter, who was electrocuted on March 2, 1944. Buchalter became the first and only American underworld leader to be executed after a murder conviction.

UNDERWORLD MEETINGS

The history of American organized crime, and especially of the Italian mob, is filled with underworld meetings, many of them either monitored or interrupted by police (thus giving us information about what went on in them). As with those of legitimate businessmen, underworld meetings are called to discuss specific problems: the settlement of disputes; the appointment of a new leader; the allocation of territories. They provide opportunities for making new contacts or forging alliances between criminal groups.[39]

Two major underworld meetings were held during the 1920s, the first in Cleveland in December 1928, and the second in Atlantic City in May 1929. Prior to these, a peace conference was held in Chicago on October 20, 1926, at the Hotel Shermann. The purpose of this meeting, which gathered together Al Capone's gang and his main Irish rival, George Moran, was to divide Chicago and Cook County into trade areas between the gangs of Chicago. Capone got the lion's share. He would keep the West Side from the Loop to Cicero, the most important sectors for bootlegging and prostitution. Participants agreed on the terms of a peace treaty, and a general amnesty was declared. No more murders or beatings were allowed. All previous shootings or murders were to be regarded as closed incidents. Leaders of factions would be held responsible for any breach to the pact.[40] Two months later, however, Capone broke the treaty by trying to establish a "benevolent monopoly."[41]

The Cleveland Meeting, 1928

The first known meeting of the American Mafia was held in Cleveland, Ohio, on December 6 and 7, 1928, at the Statler Hotel. The host was Cleveland's top bootlegger, Giuseppe Porrello, the head of the so-called Mayfield Road Gang. Twenty-seven delegates came from as far as New York; Brooklyn; Buffalo; Newark; Detroit; Boston; Chicago; Gary, Indiana; Philadelphia; St. Louis; Tampa; Miami; Hot Springs, Arkansas; Kansas City and New Orleans. The conference, from which non-Sicilians such as Al Capone were excluded, was described by the *Cleveland Plain Dealer* as a meeting of the "Mafia Grand Council of America." The New York delegation was the most important, and it was led by Joseph Profaci. One of the purposes of the meeting was to ensure the continuation of a steady supply and uninterrupted distribution of corn sugar, an indispensable component to whiskey production. Participants placed Frank Milano, from Cleveland, in charge of distribution. Among other matters on the agenda, participants were asked to elect Joseph Aiello from Chicago as the new leader of the Unione Siciliana;[42] Antonio Lombardo, the former president, had been murdered in September 1928. Just as the crime leaders were about to set up their strategy for the forthcoming Atlantic City convention, scheduled for May 1929, the Cleveland police raided the hotel and arrested them. All were later released and fined $50 each.[43]

The Atlantic City Meeting, 1929

The Atlantic City conference was the most important multi-ethnic gang conference ever arranged by the American underworld. Some thirty racketeers met at the President Hotel, in Atlantic City, from May 13 to May 16, 1929. Enoch Johnson, a local gambling and political kingpin, hosted the conference.[44] Participants came mainly from the East coast. New York City again had the most important delegation, led by Salvatore Luciano. It included Frank Costello, Joseph Doto and Johnny Torrio, and many Jewish gangsters such as Meyer Lansky and Arthur Flegenheimer, better known as Dutch Schultz. Chicago was represented by Al Capone, Frank Nitti and Jake Gusik. Detroit, Philadelphia, Cleveland, Kansas City and Boston also sent representatives. Notable absentees from the meeting were Giuseppe Masseria and Salvatore Maranzano.[45]

The Atlantic City conference had been called by Frank Costello and Johnny Torrio, two peace-minded and widely respected underworld leaders. One of the topics on the agenda was the excessive use of violence by Al Capone. New York City gangsters were especially upset by the amount of publicity prompted by Capone's violent activities. The

Valentine's Day bloodbath that had occurred three months earlier was horrific to the gangs. Capone had unilaterally ordered the killings of seven members of the North Side Moran gang, thus violating the 1926 Chicago peace treaty. On May 7, just a few days before the Atlantic City meeting, three long-time Capone associates, John Scalice, Joseph Giunta and Albert Anselmi, whom Capone suspected of plotting to over-throw him, had been savagely killed by Capone himself during a ban-quet.[46] Delegates at the Atlantic City meeting asked Capone to withdraw temporarily from the scene while things cooled off. (A few days later, Capone was arrested in Philadelphia for illegal gun possession.[47])

The delegates agreed that no boss could be killed without the consent of the National Crime Syndicate.[48] A special committee, consisting of the Sicilians, the Irish and the Neapolitans, was created to arbitrate important disputes in Chicago.[49] Prices of goods and services were to remain the same all over the country. No one would be killed or disci-plined without being tried. Funds were allocated to ensure the elections of complacent politicians on a national scale.[50] These agreements reached at the Atlantic City convention would later determine the organ-ization of criminal activity in the United States.

The New York City Meetings, 1933 and 1934

In 1933 the New York police broke up a meeting of major Jewish organized-crime figures at the Franconia Hotel. Among them were Benjamin Siegel, Louis Buchalter, Jacob Shapiro, Joseph Stacher, Harry Teitelbaum, Harry Greenberg and Louis Kravitz. All were arrested and booked. The purpose of that meeting was apparently to discuss the impact on organized-crime groups of the repeal of the 18th Amendment to the Constitution.[51]

A second meeting was held the following year, at the Waldorf Astoria Hotel, for the leaders of Italian and non-Italian criminal organizations from across the country. Johnny Torrio, Meyer Lansky and Frank Costello outlined the highlights of what was to be known as the "Big Six": Salvatore Luciano, representing Cosa Nostra, Meyer Lansky, Benjamin Siegel, Louis Buchalter, Jacob Shapiro and Abner Zwillman, from New Jersey. This national crime syndicate would be governed not by one leader but by regional boards, headed by local bosses. The Big Six would control all criminal activities. The country was divided into geographic regions. A commission of national crime leaders would hear and arbitrate disputes arising between local bosses. Each leader reigned absolutely in his territory. His authority was to be unchallenged, and no murders could take place without his permission.[52]

The gang leaders also set up a "kangaroo court of the underworld," which would hear only those charges considered serious enough to carry the death penalty against top-echelon gang members. Its decisions were final and could not be appealed. (Well-known Jewish syndicate members Dutch Schultz and Benjamin Siegel would be sentenced and executed by this court.[53]) Delegates also gave their consent for the formation of an enforcement arm to carry out death sentences decreed by the kangaroo court. This decision would lead to the creation of the infamous Murder Inc.

In 1935 another meeting was called in Kansas City to get the approval of underworld leaders from Chicago, Cleveland and Detroit for Torrio and Costello's plans.

From then on, gangland wars stopped. New territories were allocated according to everyone's specialities. Meyer Lansky was given Florida and the Caribbean. Benjamin Siegel got California and Nevada for gambling operations. Frank Costello received the slot machines, Buchalter the garment centre, Luciano narcotics and prostitution, and Michael Coppola the numbers racket. The Cleveland syndicate, headed by Moe Dalitz, was given the Midwest outside of Illinois, where Capone reigned.

The Havana Meeting, 1946

Salvatore Luciano was deported from the United States to his native Italy, in February 1946. Less than eight months later, he secretly moved to Havana, Cuba, with the help of Meyer Lansky. In December 1946 he presided over an important meeting attended by several prominent Cosa Nostra figures, most from New York. Among them were Frank Costello, Joseph Doto, Albert Anastasia, Carlo Gambino, William Moretti, Vito

Genovese, Joseph Profaci, Meyer Lansky, Vincent Mangano, Anthony Carfano, Michael Miranda, Joseph Bonanno, Joseph Magliocco, Thomas Lucchese, Anthony Accardo and Charlie Fischetti from Chicago, Carlos Marcello and Phil Kastel from New Orleans and Santos Trafficante from Tampa. Frank Sinatra, who had a close relationship with Fischetti, was present as an entertainer.

The purpose of the Havana meeting was to discuss the sharing of casino gambling operations and the establishment of new routes for the supply of drugs into the United States. The fate of Benjamin Siegel was discussed as well. Siegel was suspected of diverting funds from the construction of the Flamingo Hotel in Las Vegas for his personal use. He was to be murdered in his Los Angeles home in June 1947.

In February 1947 the Federal Bureau of Narcotics and Dangerous Drugs, known today as the Drug Enforcement Administration (DEA), learned about Luciano's presence in Cuba. Strong pressure was brought to bear on the Fulgencio Batista regime to have Luciano expelled to Italy, which was done on February 23, 1947.

The Apalachin Meeting, 1957

On November 14, 1957, a New York State trooper, Sergeant Edgar Crosswell, observed an unusual amount of activity surrounding Joseph Barbara's residence in an isolated area of Apalachin, New York. Crosswell knew that Barbara had strong organized-crime connections with the Stefano Magaddino family of Buffalo. A number of cars bearing licence plates from New York, New Jersey, Florida, Missouri, Pennsylvania, Illinois and California were seen parked in the driveway of Barbara's residence. Crosswell called in reinforcements, and a roadblock was set up. A number of guests who tried to evade the roadblock were caught in the woods. A search of all guests, as well as their cars, revealed that none of them had firearms or were the subject of warrants in the state of New York. Upon questioning, the men all said they had come to pay a visit to their friend Barbara, who had been ill. While there were insufficient legal grounds to detain them, the state police believed they had met for unlawful purposes.

An investigation was ordered into the activities and associations of the individuals found at Barbara's home. It was estimated that about sixty-three people attended the meeting. However, there are no exact figures on the number who succeeded in evading police roadblocks. Out of twenty-seven participants who were served with subpoenas to appear before a grand jury, twenty refused to answer questions regarding the purposes of that meeting. Several were indicted for contempt.

The investigation revealed that the Apalachin meeting had been planned for a long time: dozens of hotel rooms in the area were reserved, large amounts of food were ordered and many of the attendants arrived by plane. Twenty-five of the guests were related by blood or marriage, and others were related to other well-known underworld figures. Half of the attendees were native-born Americans, while the remainder had been born in Italy, the majority in Sicily. Investigations disclosed that attendees were known to be involved in criminal activities such as drug trafficking, illegal gambling, contraband of illicit alcohol, and labour union activities.

While the press speculated that the Apalachin conference was motivated by the murder of Albert Anastasia, who had been killed three weeks earlier in Manhattan, police surmised that the large contingent of mobsters had gathered to discuss the division of territories, the division of crime proceeds, labour racketeering activities and corruption of public officials.

The startling discovery of the Apalachin meeting forced law enforcement agencies, especially the FBI, to reconsider its policy of ignoring or refuting the existence of this secret society that had been in existence on the American continent for half a century. In 1961 the FBI initiated the "Top Hoodlum Program," which focused primarily on participants of the Apalachin meeting. Despite various investigations, grand jury panels and legislative and senatorial hearings held on this meeting,[54] none of the delegates would reveal the true intentions behind it.[55]

La Stella Restaurant Meeting, 1966

The meeting at La Stella restaurant was dubbed "Little Apalachin" by the press. On September 22, 1966, the New York police interrupted a lunch in a private dining room in the basement of La Stella, in Forest Hills, Queens. Two alert policemen had noticed an unusual number of black limousines parked in front of the restaurant. Thirteen high-ranking members of Cosa Nostra families were arrested. From New York were family boss Carlo Gambino and two of his *capiregime*, Joseph N. Gallo and Aniello Dellacroce; Joseph Colombo, who had recently been appointed boss of the former Profaci family; Thomas Eboli, acting boss for the Genovese family; Michael Miranda, *consigliere* and host of the meeting; and soldiers Dominick Alongi and Anthony Carillo. From Louisiana came brothers Carlos and Joseph Marcello, Anthony Carollo and Frank Gagliano, and from Florida, Santos Trafficante.

All of the men were charged with "consorting with known criminals" and released on $100,000 bail each. A grand jury was called to inquire into this secret meeting. An FBI investigation revealed that it was a meeting of the Commission. The main item on the agenda was the settlement of a dispute between the Marcellos and the Carollos of the New Orleans family, concerning Anthony Carollo's future role in the sharing of proceeds in New Orleans' criminal activities. A second item of discussion was the designation of a successor to the ailing family boss, Thomas Lucchese, who had brain cancer. (He died on July 13, 1967.) Carmine Tramunti was selected as the new boss. (Tramunti's tenure was short: he was indicted on a conspiracy charge to traffic heroin. In 1973 he was sentenced to life imprisonment, and died in prison in 1978. Anthony Carollo replaced him as boss.) The final item on the agenda was the confirmation that the triumvirate of Thomas Eboli, Michael Miranda and Gerardo Catena would run the Genovese family.

The Miami Meeting, 1969

Intelligence from the Pennsylvania Crime Commission revealed that major crime figures of the Sebastian LaRocca family of Pittsburgh, the Genovese family and the Kansas City family attended a meeting in Miami in March 1969. The purposes of that meeting were to discuss the appointment of a successor to Vito Genovese, who had died a month earlier, and to consider the opportunity of establishing a casino in Anguila, a British Caribbean island.[56]

The Acapulco Meeting, 1970

On February 16, 1970, the Mexican police, acting on tip from the Royal Canadian Mounted Police and the FBI, broke up an important meeting that gathered major American and Canadian organized-crime figures in Acapulco, Mexico. It was the first meeting of American and Canadian mobsters held outside the United States. In attendance were Moses Polakoff, a criminal lawyer who had represented Salvatore Luciano in the 1930s and 1940s, and Meyer Lansky, who allegedly hosted the conference. From Canada came a large contingent of delegates, among them Montrealers Vincenzo and Frank Cotroni, Paolo Violi and Irving Ellis, and from Hamilton, Ontario, brothers John and Rocco Papalia.[57] While not much was revealed about the purpose of the meeting, indications were that Lansky wanted to move on a campaign to legalize casino gambling in Atlantic City and to find a way to infiltrate the casinos through union employees.[58] The Canadian mobsters wanted to discuss their possible involvement in the Quebec government's project to open casinos in Montreal.

THE MEANING OF "COSA NOSTRA"

It was in 1963 that the words "Cosa Nostra" were used in public for the first time, when Joseph Valachi, testifying before a Senate subcommittee, revealed the name of the organization to which he belonged. Valachi, a long-time soldier in the Genovese family, became the first member of Cosa Nostra to defect and agree to testify against the organization.[59] When asked what Cosa Nostra meant, Valachi said, "'Our Thing.' I don't know what they called it in Italy. I know this thing existed a long time, but in my time I have been with this Cosa Nostra and that is the way it was called."[60]

Federal law enforcement agencies, the FBI and the Federal Bureau of Narcotics and Dangerous Drugs were already familiar with the term. In his book *Theft of the Nation*, Donald Cressey says the term was already in use in 1961 and 1962 by these federal agencies, although it was misspelled phonetically: "causa nostra."[61] An electronic wiretap placed in the office of the National Cigarette Service, in Providence, Rhode Island, from March 1962 until July 1965 monitored the conversations and criminal enterprises of Raymond Patriarca, the Cosa Nostra boss of New England. On October 20, 1964, Patriarca was heard saying that if he was called to be questioned about the Mafia or Cosa Nostra he would reply that "the only Mafia he ever heard of is the Irish Mafia the Kennedys are in charge of," and that he would deny that he knew about Cosa Nostra.[62]

While "Mafia" and "Cosa Nostra" were used indiscriminately by media and government agencies speaking of the American Mafia, Joseph Valachi stated that the word "Mafia" had never been used by members of Cosa Nostra to refer to the American organization.[63] In New York City the expression "Cosa Nostra" has been used by its members since at least the Second World War.[64] In other U.S. cities, Cosa Nostra is known by different names: in Buffalo it is called "The Arm"; in New England, "The Office";[65] in Chicago and Kansas City, "The Outfit" or "The Clique";[66] in Cleveland, "The Combination."[67] The latter has been used by New Jersey mobsters, who also sometimes used "*combanische*."[68] Many of these terms were learned from electronic surveillance.

According to Tommaso Buscetta, a former member of the Porta Nuova family who defected from Cosa Nostra in 1984, the word "Mafia" is pure literary creation. True mafiosi call themselves "men of honour" and their criminal organization "Cosa Nostra."[69] On the evening of his initiation, Antonino Calderone, from Catania, Sicily, learned for the first time that Cosa Nostra was the name of his new organization, not the American Mafia, as he often heard through the media: "There is no such name as Mafia, explained the presiding officer of the initiation ceremony, only cops and papers call it Mafia."[70]

Chapter 2

The Structure and Organization of Cosa Nostra

The American Cosa Nostra has been described by many experts as a national criminal organization, consisting of a confederation of around twenty families, each operating with similar organizational structures and using similar methods for its criminal enterprises. Most of its members reside in the New York City area.[1] The most significant and still active U.S. Cosa Nostra families operate in the following states:

California: The Los Angeles family is headed by Peter Milano, and is represented on the Commission by the Chicago family.

Florida: The Trafficante family, based in Tampa, is currently run by Vincent LoScalzo, and is represented on the Commission by the Chicago family. It also uses Miami as a base for its operations.

Illinois: The Chicago family is headquartered in Chicago and operates in Chicago and surrounding areas, in northeastern and other areas of Illinois, and in various locations in Florida and the western part of the United States. The Chicago family is run by Jimmy Marcello and has a seat on the Commission.

Louisiana: Headquartered and operating in New Orleans, for several decades the boss of the Louisiana family's organized-crime activities was Carlos Marcello. The current boss is Anthony Carollo, who reports to the Chicago family.

Michigan: The Detroit family is headed by Jack William Tocco. It also operates in various other locations in the state but no longer has a seat on the Commission.

Missouri: The Kansas City family is allegedly run by Anthony Civella, son of Carl Civella, and operates in Kansas City and surrounding areas. It is represented on the Commission by the Chicago family. The St. Louis family operates in areas surrounding St. Louis, and is represented on the Commission by the Chicago family.

New England states: Massachusetts and Rhode Island have been controlled by the Patriarca family for several decades. The leader is Luigi Manoccio. The New England family is represented on the Commission by the Genovese family of New York.

New Jersey: The DeCavalcante family is headed by John Riggi, and is based in northern New Jersey. The DeCavalcante family reports to the Genovese family.

New York City: The Bonanno family (approximately 100 members), the Colombo family (approximately 90 members), the Gambino family (approximately 130 members), the Genovese family (approximately 150 members) and the Lucchese family (approximately 110 members) each control an area of operations in New York City.[2] The New York families all have seats on the Commission.

New York State: The Todaro family is headquartered in Buffalo, and has influence over several other areas, such as Toronto, Hamilton and Niagara Falls, Ontario, Canada.

Ohio: The Cleveland family is run by Joseph Iacobacci and reports to the Genovese family.

Pennsylvania: William D'Elia, from Scranton, is the current boss of the former Bufalino family, based in Philadelphia and Atlantic City. It is represented on the Commission by the Genovese family. The Pittsburgh family is currently headed by Michael Genovese, and is represented on the Commission by the Genovese family.

Wisconsin: The Milwaukee family is represented on the Commission by the Chicago family.

THE COMMISSION

The Commission, sometimes called the "High Commission," "Grand Council" or "Administration," is the highest ruling body of Cosa Nostra. Its function is mainly judicial. The Commission hears complaints about the conduct of Cosa Nostra members and arbitrates disputes over control of criminal and legal activities. When appropriate, it imposes disciplinary measures. Its rulings are final, with no recourse for appeal. It also promotes joint ventures between and among Cosa Nostra families, approves and recognizes newly elected bosses, and authorizes the admission of new members.[3]

There have been up to nine members sitting on the Commission: representatives of the five New York families, plus the Buffalo, Detroit, Chicago and Philadelphia families. Small crime families from Kansas City, Pittsburgh, Tampa and New Orleans do not sit on the Commission, but are represented by a member of the Commission who looks after their interests. He is called *avvocato* or *rappresantante*.

All family bosses are given the same respect and are regarded as equals, even those who do not sit on the Commission. The Commission will arbitrate disputes to maintain stability and cohesion among Cosa Nostra families, but if two families want to resolve a difference among themselves, the Commission will not intervene unless asked. The Commission does not get involved in the internal affairs of a family, as each family is independent. If a family boss wants to murder a member of his own family, he does not need permission from the Commission. However, if the intended victim belongs to another family, or is an associate of another family, a boss must get permission from the family to which the intended victim belongs.[4]

The Commission ratifies any dealing or treaty that Cosa Nostra might conclude with another criminal organization. It looks after Cosa Nostra's interests on matters regarding criminal operations or joint ventures with other criminal groups in territories over which it has jurisdiction, or shares authority. It also establishes and maintains peaceful coexistence among Cosa Nostra families, as well as with other criminal groups.

Membership of the Commission

The Commission was set up in 1931 by Salvatore Luciano after the Castellammarese Wars. Over the decades, Commission membership has fluctuated constantly. At the beginning, it consisted of six members: the heads of the New York and Newark area families. It later extended membership to the families of Buffalo, Detroit, Chicago and Philadelphia.[5]

Cosa Nostra families that do not have a seat on the Commission nevertheless have representation before it. All families west of the Mississippi are heard through the Chicago representative. Families east of the Mississippi are represented by New York,[6] including Cleveland, which had its own seat on the Commission until its number of family members decreased.

According to Joseph Bonanno's biography, Philadelphia and Detroit were allowed to sit on the Commission following a decision reached at a national meeting of the Commission held in 1956.[7] It was decided that Commission members elected at that meeting were to hold office for a five-year term, and would surrender their mandate in 1961. Beyond 1961, Bonanno claimed, it was an "unauthorized Commission."[8] Sam DeCavalcante, a Cosa Nostra family boss in New Jersey, shared that opinion.[9]

In the late 1970s, according to a taped conversation with John Rosselli, a high-ranking member in the Chicago family, the Commission membership was reduced to six members—Chicago and the five New York City Cosa Nostra families. When Joseph Zerilli, the head of Cosa Nostra in Detroit, died in October 1977, his family lost its seat on the Commission. The same thing apparently happened to the Philadelphia family when its leader, Angelo Bruno, was killed in March 1980. As well, family bosses of Buffalo and Cleveland were excluded.[10]

The Commission's Powers

In the event that a boss is suddenly arrested or imprisoned, he may not have time to appoint someone to replace him, and the family administration may be unable to reach an agreement on whom to appoint. The Commission may then be called to select an "acting boss"—someone who will be vested with the full authority of a boss, but for a limited period of time. In January 1987, when Phil Rastelli, the boss of the Bonanno family, was sentenced to a twelve-year prison term following his conviction for labour racketeering, he was replaced by Salvatore

Farrugia, a *caporegime*, by order of the Commission. The Commission decree helped keep peace among dissenting factions of the family during Rastelli's imprisonment.[11]

The Commission may sometimes ratify the decision of a family's choice of a leader, in particular when the family leader is a member of the Commission. In May 1978 Joseph Colombo died, seven years after he had been shot in the head at a June 1970 rally in New York City. During these years, while the elder Colombo was on life support, the family was run by several different members. When Colombo died, Vincent Aloi became the acting boss. Aloi was later sentenced to a jail term, and was replaced by Carmine Persico, a long-time member of the family. Persico himself faced criminal charges over a hijacking case, so he appointed Thomas DiBella as acting boss. Carmine's brother, Alphonse, became the family's *consigliere*. Later, Carmine Persico appointed his brother acting boss, which gave him a voice on the Commission's board. This nomination did not please an old *caporegime* of the family, Anthony Abbatemarco, who complained to the Commission. The Commission ruled that Alphonse Persico was to be recognized as the acting boss, thus reinforcing Carmine Persico as the true leader of the Colombo family.[12]

The Commission can intervene in the appointment of a boss to avoid warfare. After the murder of Philadelphia Cosa Nostra boss Angelo Bruno, in March 1980, Phil Testa, then underboss, was in line to succeed Bruno. Testa, however, was detested by most of the family *capiregime*. Sensing conflicts within the Philadelphia family, the Commission intervened, confirming Testa's nomination as the new boss. This action, which mitigated potential clashes, allowed Testa to appoint Nicodemo Scarfo as *consigliere*.[13] In July 1984 the Commission appointed Raymond Patriarca Jr. as the successor to his father, Raymond Patriarca Sr., the long-time boss of the Cosa Nostra family in New England, who had recently died at age seventy-six. Patriarca's position should have been filled by Angelo Angiulo, the eldest ranking member of the family, but he was immensely disliked by the family soldiers.[14]

Sometimes a Cosa Nostra family may simply disappear because its membership has declined over the years and no potential leader is powerful enough to become the family boss. The Bufalino Cosa Nostra family, for instance, had its stronghold in northeastern Pennsylvania. The family's leader, Russell Bufalino, was released from prison in May 1989 at the age of eighty-six after serving almost nine years in prison for conspiracy to murder Jack Napoli, a principal witness against him in a trial for extortion. Because of his poor health, Bufalino stepped down, and Edward Sciandra, then *consigliere* of the family, assumed the acting boss position. The Commission decided that the family would be absorbed by the New York families. No new members would be admitted, and there would be no official boss. The New York Genovese and Gambino families were given permission to take over Bufalino's already existing operations in New York City, and eventually moved into northeastern Pennsylvania.[15]

In February 1985 the entire membership of the Commission was faced with a racketeering trial. The United States Attorney General for the Southern District of New York, Rudolph Giuliani, unsealed an indictment under the Racketeering Influenced and Corrupt Organizations (RICO) Act that charged four of the five bosses of New York City's Cosa Nostra families, and associates from all five families, with participating and operating a "commission," a criminal enterprise under the provisions of the Act. Giuliani based his indictment on Joseph Bonanno's autobiography, *A Man of Honor*, in which the former boss described in detail the functioning of the Commission.

The defendants in that case were Paul Castellano, boss of the Gambino family (his name was removed from the indictment after his murder in December 1985); Anthony Salerno, boss of the Genovese family; Anthony Carollo, boss, and Salvatore Santoro, underboss, and Christopher Furnari, *consigliere*, of the Lucchese family; Carmine Persico, boss, of the Colombo family (who assumed his own defence); Gennaro Langella, underboss, Ralph Scopo, soldier, and Anthony Indelicato, *caporegime*, of the Bonanno family.

The trial started in September 1986. During the trial the defendants admitted, for the first time in the history of the Mafia, the existence of Cosa Nostra and its Commission. They contended that the Commission was not involved in any racketeering activities and that being a member of Cosa Nostra was not a crime per se. The "Commission Trial" proved the existence of Cosa Nostra, its rules and its criminal activities.[16] On

November 19, 1986, after six days of deliberation, the jury found the defendants guilty. With the exception of Indelicato, who was sentenced to forty years in jail, all of the defendants were sentenced to one hundred years in jail and fined $240,000 each.

The defendants appealed their convictions and sentences, but they were upheld. Only Furnari, Persico and Langella are still alive and serving their sentences in a federal prison. Indelicato was released in 1998, then was sentenced to a two-year jail term for parole violation.

Status of the Commission

According to various law enforcement sources, it appears that the Commission has been more or less inactive since 1996. Its jurisdiction is mostly confined to the New York area. One of the main reasons for the Commission's decline was the conviction and imprisonment of the Genovese, Lucchese and Colombo family bosses and acting bosses. The New York families are now run by acting leaders or by committees.[17]

The Colombo family has been suspended from the Commission since 1993, when it appears the family ignored a moratorium on killings imposed by a 1992 Commission edict. During 1991 and 1992 an internecine war among two Colombo factions over the family leadership left almost a dozen victims on the streets. In 1993 the Persico faction was alleged to be responsible for the murder of Joseph Scopo, a *caporegime* in the Colombo family.

According to underworld sources, at the beginning of 2000, the Commission reconvened for the first time under the initiative of Joseph Massino. The meeting was held in an eatery in Queens that Massino used as his base of operation. It gathered representatives from the five New York families.[18]

THE CHICAGO COSA NOSTRA

The Chicago Cosa Nostra is run rather like a corporation. Some believe that the Chicago Outfit, as it is usually known, is the successor to what was referred to as the "Capone Gang." The structure of the Chicago Outfit is dissimilar to that of the New York families, mainly because the Chicago family is not of Sicilian origin. When the Commission was formed after the Castellammarese Wars, the Chicago family was officially recognized as part of Cosa Nostra. Still, it remains a very fluid organization.

The Chicago Outfit is divided into six street crews: Taylor Street, Grand Avenue, 26th Street, the North Side, Rush Street and the suburb of Chicago Heights. The West Side crew, which is part of the Taylor Street crew, has the most power, because most of the "made" members (those officially inducted into a crime family) live and work in that area. Each crew has its own specialization, or area of criminal activity—burglary, truck hijacking, prostitution, pornography, extortion. All crews are involved in gambling activities.

The Chicago Cosa Nostra is governed by a boss, seconded by underbosses, advisors, street bosses and lieutenants. Each crew has a street boss, who makes sure the leaders of the Outfit receive a share of the proceeds. A crew is composed of made members, also referred to as soldiers, and associates, who are known as "connected."[19]

The Chicago family is currently headed by Jimmy Marcello, and the family membership is about two hundred made members, including seventy-five made members and associates in their sixties or seventies. Despite several RICO indictments on its members, the Chicago family has proven to be one of the most stable Cosa Nostra groups in the United States because of its experienced leaders, who managed to stay away from heroin trafficking.

THE SICILIAN MAFIA

The pyramid structure of the Sicilian Mafia was suggested to its leaders by their Italian-American counterparts during a meeting in Palermo in 1957, at which time the Sicilian Cosa Nostra had some difficulties in the management of its internal affairs.

According to Tommaso Buscetta and other *pentiti* (former members who have defected from Cosa Nostra and have chosen to co-operate with police and prosecutors), the family (also known as *cosca*) is the base of the Sicilian Cosa Nostra. Today there are nearly two hundred Mafia families throughout Sicily, with an approximate membership of six thousand. In the province and city of Palermo, there are about one hundred Mafia clans.[20] A family controls a village or an urban zone (this applies particularly to Palermo), and takes the name of the city or the village it controls. For instance, Buscetta belonged to the family of Porto Nuova, a district of the city of Palermo. The leader of the family is elected by the soldiers. The leader selects an assistant and a *consigliere*, who appoints the *capodecina* or "chief of ten." The *capodecina* leads a group of soldiers.

A system of Provincial Commissions was created to settle disputes between families and their leaders and to regulate the criminal activities of all Mafia families. There is a Provincial Commission in each of the nine provinces of Sicily: Palermo, Trapani, Agrigento, Caltanissetta, Ragusa, Catania, Enna, Messina and Siracusa. Families are represented at Provincial Commissions by a *capomandamento* or "district leader," who defends their interests at the provincial level. In the province of Palermo—and in the city of Palermo in particular, where several dozen families operate within a small area—the *capimandamento* represent three contiguous families at the Provincial Commission.

At the top of the pyramid is the Inter-Provincial Commission, also known simply as the Commission or the Cupola. One *capomandamento* from each province sits on the Cupola. The Cupola coordinates the Provincial Commissions and facilitates the circulation of information.

Cosa Nostra does not have complete hegemony in Sicily. A dissenting group known as the Stidda (meaning "star") surfaced in Agrigento and Caltanissetta in the mid-1980s, when some families split from Cosa Nostra to oppose the tyrannical management of the Corleone family, then led by Salvatore Riina. Members of the Stidda are known as *stiddari*. The existence of the Stidda first became known in 1989, during the interrogation of Francesco Marino Mannoia, a former Mafia boss of Caltanissetta.

Italian authorities have identified Bernardo Provenzano, of Corleone, Sicily, as the current boss of Cosa Nostra. Provenzano has been a fugitive since 1963. He became boss after the capture of Salvatore Riina in January 1993. Riina has been since sentenced to life imprisonment for the murders of Sicilian judges Giovanni Falcone and Paolo Borsellino, both of whom were killed in 1992.

Structure of a Cosa Nostra Family

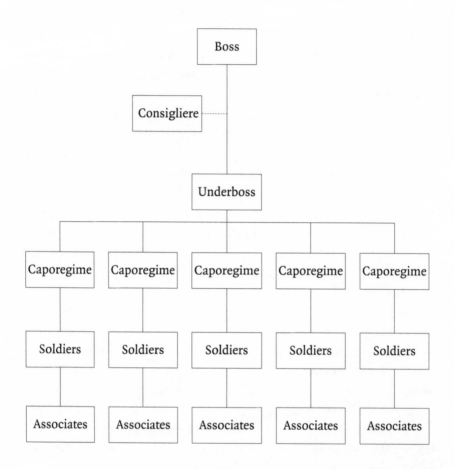

THE HIERARCHY OF A COSA NOSTRA FAMILY

Cosa Nostra is based on a hierarchy of command that resembles a feudal system: members (vassals) are obedient to a "lord," the leader of the family.[21] Its ranking members define and enforce its policies, allocate territories to families, arbitrate and rule on disputes among members, establish mechanisms for succession of leadership and control its membership.[22]

It is not firmly established whether ranks existed in American Cosa Nostra families before the Castellammarese Wars. In 1930 Salvatore Maranzano implied that ranks already existed, during a speech he gave before a crowd of four hundred mobsters in a Bronx hotel, following the execution of Masseria. In his testimony before a Senate committee, Joseph Valachi observed, ". . . at that time, during the troubles [the Castellammarese Wars], there is nothing like lieutenant or anything like that."[23] On the other hand, capidecina were being used by the Sicilian Mafia as early as the 1870s, according to Nicola Gentile, a ranking member of the Sicilian Mafia who was living in New York City at the time of the Castellammarese Wars.[24]

Cosa Nostra families, which are sometimes referred to as borgata in the American Cosa Nostra, operate within a defined geographical area. All Cosa Nostra families operating across the United States have a similar structure. Each family has a boss, who is seconded by an underboss. Each boss also has a consigliere who acts as his advisor. Below these positions are the captains or "section leaders," better known as capiregime. Each caporegime commands a regime—a group of ten or more soldiers, depending on the size of the family. (In Sicily the regime is known as decina, "group of ten.")

Soldiers hold the lowest rank in a Cosa Nostra family. A soldier usually has a number of people working for him, known as associates. While subject to the same set of rules as the initiated members, associates— who may not be of Italian descent—cannot be made, or initiated into the family.[25] In some crime families, particularly those with a 'Ndrangheta structure, there may be a position of treasurer, whose function is to collect from members annual dues that will be used to pay legal expenses or for flowers at funerals.[26] (The secret criminal society known as the 'Ndrangheta, or Calabrian Mafia, has its roots in the Calabria province in Southern Italy. There are several cells of the 'Ndrangheta in activity in Canada, and particularly in Toronto and Hamilton, Ontario. The most influential is the Commisso group, based in Toronto, which has its roots in Siderno, Calabria.)

Joseph Bonanno referred to the *capo consigliere* or chief counsellor position. Also in use in Sicily, it is an informal position held by a boss who carries much prestige and power. Before Giuseppe Masseria's murder in 1930, the position of *capo consigliere* was held in New York City by Toto Aquilla and by Gaspare Massina of Boston. These men derived their power from their influence over the other families' bosses and their ability to keep the peace between the upper ranks and the soldiers.[27]

The ranks in Cosa Nostra's hierarchy are strictly observed. Members involved in dealings with another family will communicate only with a counterpart of equal rank. A boss deals with a boss, an underboss with underboss, and so on. Within a family, the boss confers only with his underboss and/or *consigliere*. *Capiregime* receive communications and orders from the underboss.[28] If a Cosa Nostra member is incarcerated, he does not lose his rank, but he is replaced by a substitute.[29]

In Cosa Nostra, as in any large corporation, formal communications and meetings between soldiers and high-ranking members must be prearranged. For example, if a soldier wants to talk to the boss or the *consigliere*, he must follow the established chain of command by making an appointment through his *caporegime*.[30] However, a boss is free to speak with anyone he chooses to, even with an associate. No made member is obliged to pay respect to someone who is not a made member.

The Boss, or *Capo*

A boss is chosen by a consensus of all the *capiregime* of a family—more a "proclamation" than an election. A *caporegime* asks or "feels out" the opinion of his crew's members, and casts his vote on their behalf. The selection of the boss reflects a consensus of the capiregime.[31]

It is rare that someone emerges as the family boss by only a few votes over his opponent.[32] He would then command a split family, as was the case for Paul Castellano, who became boss of the Gambino family after his cousin, Carlo Gambino, died in October 1976. Paul Castellano's tenure as boss of one of the most powerful Cosa Nostra families in the United States was not an easy one. Aniello Dellacroce, an old and experienced member, was the underboss of the family. He was the natural choice as the next boss, but Gambino chose Castellano before he died. Castellano's appointment caused dissatisfaction among the family. The "Manhattan faction," which included Carmine Fatico and John Gotti, remained loyal to Dellacroce.

If a family is left without a successor, the members meet and reach a consensus of one person, whose name is submitted to the Commission for approval. When the leader of the Lucchese family of New York, Thomas Lucchese, became seriously ill in 1967, the Commission finally approved Carmine Tramunti to succeed Lucchese, who died not long after. In some instances, a boss may be appointed on a provisional basis. After the murder of Albert Anastasia in October 1957, Carlo Gambino took over Anastasia's family. He was appointed for a period of three years, subject to a review by the Commission. When the probation period ended, Gambino was confirmed as the head of the former Anastasia family.[33]

In Sicily, if there is only one candidate for boss, each member of a family casts his vote publicly by raising his hand in favour of the candidate. If there is more than one candidate, the election is done by secret ballot. In larger families, the *capidecina* confer with their crew members and then relay the results to a secretary.[34]

Succession in a Cosa Nostra family is based more on a candidate's merit than on blood relationships. While a family boss can recruit close relatives, he cannot unilaterally appoint his son as boss of the family. Each time a boss has tried to prepare a son as his successor with quick promotions within the family hierarchy, it has caused a great deal of turmoil among family members. When Joseph Bonanno elevated his son, Salvatore, to *consigliere* in 1964, many senior members of the family complained to the Commission about Bonanno's nepotism. In the end, the Commission did not recognize the appointment. In the Gambino family, several senior *capiregime* took offence to John Gotti appointing his son, John Jr., barely in his thirties, as acting boss. In November 1991 Joseph Sodano, a *caporegime* in the Philadelphia family, spoke frankly to his boss, John Stanfa, saying, "It is an insult to people who are knowledgeable and who have been around you for twenty-five years. Does [John Junior] have the ability to guide people?"[35] When Carmine Persico, serving a life sentence since 1986 for murder and racketeering charges, appointed his son, Alphonse, as his successor in 1994, it triggered a bloody war between two factions of the Colombo family. One of these factions was led by Victor Orena, who struggled with the idea that the elder Persico, from his cell, would command the family through his son. In 1994, a truce was arranged, and Alphonse Persico was recognized as the acting boss of the Colombo family.[36] Raymond Patriarca's succession by his son, Raymond Jr., left the New England crime family in a state of disarray and stirred up a lot of dissatisfaction among the family members because of Raymond Jr.'s alleged incompetence. The only exception to the rule has been in the case of the Tampa family, which was run through the 1950s to the mid-1980s by Santos Trafficante Sr., and then competently run by his son, Santos Jr., who died in 1987.

Ralph Natale, former boss of the Philadelphia family, rose to power in a very unusual way. Natale was the government's main prosecution witness against Joseph Merlino, the current Cosa Nostra boss, and six co-defendants at their trial in March and April of 2001 on a thirty-six-count racketeering indictment.[37] Natale became a turncoat in 1999 when, as boss, he was arrested on drug trafficking charges. He pleaded guilty and admitted to his involvement in eight murders and four attempted murders. During his testimony, Natale told the court that in 1990, while he and Merlino were both in jail, they plotted to overthrow John Stanfa, then boss of Philadelphia. Shortly after Merlino was released from jail in 1994, in a ceremony that took place in a hotel suite in Philadelphia, Merlino "made" Natale and, immediately after that, Natale became the new boss, with Merlino as underboss. Natale said he had gained the support of the New York families in his takeover of the Philadelphia family.[38]

A boss remains the boss, even if he is in jail, until he dies or resigns. Aware of police surveillance, jailed bosses have sometimes used an unscrupulous lawyer or family relative to relay messages to leaders on the outside. (The lawyers enjoy immunity—their relationships with their clients cannot be monitored by prison authorities.) Rarely, though, a boss will step down voluntarily. In 1931 Salvatore Sabella, the first boss of the Philadelphia family, resigned at the age of forty after he was arrested for "atrocious assault and battery with an automobile."[39]

Over the last decade, law enforcement officers have exerted strong pressure on family bosses by closely monitoring their actions and meetings with their confederates. To elude police scrutiny, some crime families are run by a committee of *capiregime*. The Genovese family, for example, has a long tradition of running its criminal operations through a committee of high-ranking members. During the incarceration of Vito Genovese from 1959 until his death in February 1969, the family was ostensibly run by Gerardo Catena, then the underboss; Michael Miranda, the *consigliere*; and Anthony Strollo, a *caporegime*. In reality, these three were "front bosses." Front bosses are used to deceive law enforcement by focusing surveillance away from the real leader of the family. According to Vincent Cafaro, a former soldier in the Genovese family who later became a government witness, the real boss was Philip Lombardo, to whom Genovese relinquished leadership. Lombardo led the Genovese family until he retired in 1981. Then Vincent Gigante took over, with Anthony Salerno acting as front boss, stepping down temporarily when he suffered a stroke in 1981.[40] Vincent Gigante, at age seventy-six, is now serving a twelve-year sentence following his conviction in 1997, and the Genovese family is run by a two-man committee known as "street bosses."[41] They advise and assist the family's captains in their daily operations.

The Role and Power of the Boss

The boss's most important function is to maintain order within his family. He is the final arbitrator on all internal matters pertaining to his family. Though he may be overruled by the Commission, a boss has absolute authority over his family and the territory he controls, provided his actions do not bring him into conflict with another boss.[42]

The boss acts as a head of state as well.[43] He may be called on to negotiate with bosses of other families about criminal operations in an "open territory," or to arbitrate a dispute between two families. Thus, a boss must maintain good relations with his peers. Bosses have access to each other at any time since they know each other personally. Alliances and agreements concluded among bosses are formal. A boss also makes agreements and alliances with "outsiders," or non-members of his family, to operate illegal rackets in his territory. These agreements must be approved by the Commission.[44]

A boss devotes most of his time to the daily operations of his family. All matters are cleared through him. Requests from his lieutenants or associates come to him through the underboss or the *consigliere*. He refers each matter to a person capable of handling the problem. All decisions made by the boss become "law," and must be enforced.[45]

A boss has the responsibility to protect and save the reputation of his family. He is called upon to resolve the personal problems of his family members. He may have to solve a marital problem or discipline a member for misconduct. Joe Sferra, a *caporegime* in the New Jersey family of Sam DeCavalcante, had a drinking problem, and publicly insulted the mayor of Atlantic City while attending a convention. During a conversation recorded by the FBI, DeCavalcante said to Sferra, "I can't let you get away with things where it reflects on the group of people. There have been several complaints. Joe, you're a *caporegime*—you're supposed to set an example."[46] A few weeks later, Sferra was demoted to soldier.

As the leader of a small world, the boss is often called on to mediate and render justice. The boss's prestige and power are recognized by people of his neighbourhood, who go to him because he has the power to fix problems fairly and quickly. If someone has a legitimate grievance, the boss will rule to have the grievance addressed.[47] From time to time, he will hold court in the back room of a restaurant. People line up at the entrance with their grievances. Carlo Gambino, for example, would listen patiently to old women in black shawls, old men in black hats, housewives with aprons on, storekeepers, landlords and tenants on various problems, ranging from a father's distress to learn of his daughter's pregnancy to a husband's inability to pay doctor's bills. He would direct one of his subordinates to arrange for a solution to each problem.[48]

Gambino, born in Palermo, was continuing a tradition begun by old-guard Sicilian Mafia bosses such as Calogero Vizzini[49] of Villalba and his successor, Genco Russo of Mussomeli. They were powerful *capimafia* and mayors of their villages during the 1940s and 1950s. They would grant favours, help a victim of a theft through mediation between thief and victim, find a job for a family father and so forth. Although Vizzini and Russo did not expect immediate payment for their services, months or years later villagers might be asked to return the favours done so graciously. Remittance might involve, for example, hiding a fugitive or a firearm from police.

The boss of a family has demonstrated a capacity to instil fear in his underlings, who are dependent on him for protection and assistance.[50] Dominick Napolitano, a former *caporegime* and powerful Cosa Nostra member in the Bonanno family, once remarked that rising in Cosa Nostra depends on "how strong you are and how much power you got and how fucking mean you are—that's what makes you rise in the mob. Every day is a fucking struggle, because you don' know who's looking to knock you off, especially when you become a captain or boss."[51]

In the world of Cosa Nostra, power is not necessarily demonstrated by muscle, but rather by a willingness to use violence when required to enforce rules. Frank Tieri, the former boss of the Genovese family, was an eloquent example. A frail man in his seventies, weighing at the most 140 pounds, Tieri had a share in a flea market with Joseph Cantalupo, an associate of the Colombo family of New York. The flea market was operated by Louis LaRocca, a stocky, six-foot-two, 280-pound man. One day in April 1976, Tieri asked Cantalupo how things were going with the market. Cantalupo answered that LaRocca was five thousand dollars behind on rent. Enraged, Tieri told Cantalupo to make sure LaRocca found the money or "he would have his balls cut off." Cantalupo reported to LaRocca what Tieri had said. LaRocca "turned absolutely white. He stood there for maybe a minute and began trembling. Then, without another word, he left. He came back a short time later. With him, he had the five thousand dollars. We paid the rent that day."[52]

Tieri's power and authority were so firm that nobody around him would think of running rackets of any kind without first asking for his authorization. His home was located in the neighbourhood of Bath Beach, Brooklyn. People living in that vicinity never bothered to lock their doors at night, as the area became free of breaks and enters while Tieri lived there.[53] In November 1980 Tieri became the first American Cosa Nostra boss to be convicted under the RICO Act for racketeering, fraud and tax evasion. He died in March 1981, at age of seventy-seven.

The Conduct of the Boss

Cosa Nostra functions best when it carries out its business in total secrecy. A boss must protect his image and conduct himself accordingly. At all costs, he must avoid publicity and the company of public figures such as politicians, entertainers, journalists or reporters. To elude police surveillance, Mafia bosses are even encouraged not to attend the funerals of their members. Carlo Gambino was a model of discretion. Though very powerful, he lived in a modest house and avoided displays of opulence. Because of Gambino's low profile, law enforcement ignored him for several years. Angelo Bruno, boss of the Philadelphia family, practised the same philosophy. He dressed simply and expected the same from his underlings. He once ordered one of his *caporegime* who had bought a Lincoln Continental to return it and buy a less eye-catching car.[54]

But Gambino's and Bruno's examples were not always imitated. Salvatore Luciano, Frank Costello and Joseph Colombo from New York and Sam Giancana from Chicago attracted a lot of publicity for themselves and therefore for the Cosa Nostra organization. Costello, the acting boss of the Genovese family in the 1940s, was known as the "Prime Minister" of New York's underworld. He was often seen with politicians, judges and entertainers. Luciano was always surrounded by women.

In 1970 Joseph Colombo, boss of the former Profaci family, engaged in a campaign to denounce the use of stereotypes of Italian-Americans by federal and state authorities. He founded the Italian American Civil Rights League. Colombo made many appearances on TV shows and demonstrated in front of FBI headquarters in New York to protest the arrest of one of his sons, who had been accused of melting down coins for their silver content. Colombo succeeded in having the labels "Mafia" and "Cosa Nostra" removed from government reports, from TV series such as *The Untouchables* and from the movie script of *The Godfather*.

However, Colombo's public appearances triggered a series of investigations by federal, state and local authorities. Other Cosa Nostra bosses were furious, especially Carlo Gambino, who reminded Colombo to stay away from public controversy. Colombo did not listen. In December 1970 the FBI arrested Rocco Miraglia, one of Colombo's bodyguards, and seized an attaché case in which was a list of names of those who had contributed to the Civil Rights League. Carlo Gambino's name was on the list. On June 28, 1971, Colombo was shot and critically wounded as he was participating at the second anniversary rally of the Civil Rights League in Columbus Circle. The hit man, Jerome A. Johnson, was immediately killed by one of Colombo's bodyguards. Colombo had committed two cardinal sins: drawing the attention of the FBI to Cosa Nostra, and embarrassing Carlo Gambino, his mentor, who had favoured him as the head of the former Profaci family and a member of the Commission.

Chicago boss Sam Giancana also had a strong inclination to make headlines. Giancana, who for some time shared a mistress, Judith Campbell Exner, with President John F. Kennedy, could hardly restrain himself from talking to members of the press. He would openly display his frustrations against the FBI agents who followed him constantly. In an unprecedented act, Giancana sought and won an injunction against the FBI that prevented its agents from following him closely. (The injunction was overturned on appeal.)

Giancana was extravagant and sometimes outrageous when in public with women. His lack of humility and inattention to his criminal businesses irritated Chicago's crime leaders, who felt that Giancana did not project an image in keeping with his status in the Chicago family. He was summoned before the Chicago Grand Council to defend himself on charges of having attracted too much public and media attention.[55]

Giancana displayed his wealth at his daughter's wedding. He never paid his traffic tickets. He discussed his appearances before the

McClellan Committee with reporters.[56] Worse, Giancana committed a breach of security when he identified Frank Sinatra as the intermediary to look for if you wanted to speak to President John F. Kennedy.[57] Giancana's conduct angered members of the Grand Council of Chicago. He was ordered to step down when lieutenants questioned his ability to run the family's rackets. Giancana was replaced by Sam Battaglia, a former member of the 42 Gang.[58]

When John Gotti took over the leadership of the Gambino family in December 1985, he instantly turned into one of the most high-profile Mafia bosses in North America. His fame made him as popular as Al Capone at the height of his career in the 1920s. Born in 1940 in the Bronx, Gotti was labelled the "Teflon Don" for his apparent invincibility when he was acquitted of racketeering charges in 1987 and again in 1990. It was discovered that in the 1987 trial, the foreman of the jury, George Pape, accepted a bribe of $60,000 to influence the jury. Pape was sentenced to three years in jail for obstruction of justice in November 1992. Gotti loved the attention the media directed at him. "Are you the new boss?" a reporter asked Gotti at a court appearance in 1986. "Yes," replied Gotti, "I am the boss of my wife and kids." He liked to dress in expensive suits, he dined at luxurious restaurants and, above all, he liked to talk to the press. For some years, until Mayor Rudolph Giuliani put an end to it, Gotti hosted the Fourth of July fireworks display in Howard Beach, Queens, where he lived. The event gained him the support and veneration of the neighbourhood.

At the other end of the spectrum of attention-getting behaviour, a more conservative and old-school Mafia member, Vincent Gigante, the boss of the Genovese family, pretended for three decades to be mentally disturbed, in a ploy to elude racketeering indictments by United States authorities. Gigante, known as the "Oddfather," was often seen walking on the streets of Greenwich Village in a bathrobe, speaking to himself, accompanied by his brother. On April 7, 2003, Gigante finally admitted he had feigned insanity and pleaded guilty to obstruction of justice. He was sentenced to a three-year jail term in addition to his twelve-year sentence for 1997 racketeering charges.

Doing Business with The Boss

A Cosa Nostra boss is treated like a king. He is surrounded by people who make every aspect of life easy for him. He is assisted by an army of *capiregime*, soldiers and associates who make sure that he is well protected, that he gets his share of the proceeds of crime and, above all, that he will not be subject to a plot to remove him, either from inside or outside the family.

In principle, the boss is not to be approached or spoken to by family members at any time, unless he has already established or developed a privileged relationship with them. When a boss goes to a restaurant, Cosa Nostra members do not sit at his table unless invited; when a boss is conferring with other people in a restaurant, members are expected to stay outside unless they are called in. Carmine Galante took this approach when meeting with Cosa Nostra members,[59] as did Paul Castellano, who allegedly perceived members as a "lower class," and would lunch with them only for business purposes.[60]

From 1976 to 1982 FBI agent Joseph Pistone successfully infiltrated the Colombo and Bonanno families. He gained the confidence and even respect of many members of those families. Pistone's success was such that he was able to meet members of other families in Tampa and Pittsburgh. One of Pistone's FBI colleagues was working on an operation involving black gang members engaged in political corruption, and wanted to make a favourable impression by seeming to have powerful connections with members of Cosa Nostra. He asked Pistone to pose as a Mafia member and show the gang how to approach a Mafia leader. Pistone met the men in a Los Angeles hotel suite and taught them the etiquette of dealing with a boss: when a boss arrives in a room, everybody must stand up; they must speak slowly "because he doesn't want to have to ask for anything to be repeated, and he's not used to talking to blacks or hearing black street talk." The gang members were also told not to shake hands with the boss, either at the beginning or at the end of the meeting, and not to touch him in a friendly manner. They were not to address the boss unless invited to do so. The boss would speak only to the person he had done the favour of coming to meet.[61] These manners of conduct are well known among Cosa Nostra members and show how much respect and deference are given to a family boss.

The Underboss, or *Sottocapo*

The underboss is appointed by the boss.[62] The person holding this position is usually a long-standing made member of the family. However, it occasionally happens that a member who has never before held a ranking position in the family may be appointed. Peter Casella was a soldier when, after a long-term incarceration for narcotic trafficking, he was appointed underboss by Phil Testa, himself former underboss of the Bruno family.[63]

The underboss does not necessarily become boss when the boss dies or resigns. Sometimes the *consigliere* may oppose such a promotion and will choose instead to appoint an "acting boss," who will manage operations while the *capiregime* meet and reach a consensus on electing a new boss.[64]

The Role of the Underboss

The position of underboss is essentially that of a vice president. He relays messages to and collects information for the boss, and passes down orders to *capiregime*.[65] He acts as deputy of the family when the boss is absent or in prison. He supervises all legal and illegal operations of the family. He has direct access to all of the family's *capiregime* and receives their reports from field operations. (There are a very few *capiregime* who may report directly to the boss.[66])

The underboss also acts as a buffer or "screen" for the boss. If a problem arises at a lower echelon of the family—for instance, a dispute between two soldiers—a *caporegime* will take the matter to the *consigliere* or the underboss. The problem will be taken to the boss only if the case is serious.[67]

Bosses of the Five New York Families Since 1931

(As of January 2004)

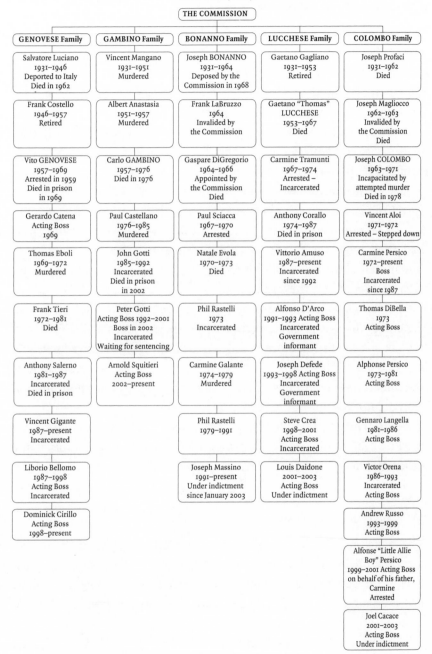

THE COMMISSION

GENOVESE Family	GAMBINO Family	BONANNO Family	LUCCHESE Family	COLOMBO Family
Salvatore Luciano 1931–1946 Deported to Italy Died in 1962	Vincent Mangano 1931–1951 Murdered	Joseph BONANNO 1931–1964 Deposed by the Commission in 1968	Gaetano Gagliano 1931–1953 Retired	Joseph Profaci 1931–1962 Died
Frank Costello 1946–1957 Retired	Albert Anastasia 1951–1957 Murdered	Frank LaBruzzo 1964 Invalided by the Commission	Gaetano "Thomas" LUCCHESE 1953–1967 Died	Joseph Magliocco 1962–1963 Invalided by the Commission Died
Vito GENOVESE 1957–1969 Arrested in 1959 Died in prison in 1969	Carlo GAMBINO 1957–1976 Died in 1976	Gaspare DiGregorio 1964–1966 Appointed by the Commission Died	Carmine Tramunti 1967–1974 Arrested – Incarcerated	Joseph COLOMBO 1963–1971 Incapacitated by attempted murder Died in 1978
Gerardo Catena Acting Boss 1969	Paul Castellano 1976–1985 Murdered	Paul Sciacca 1967–1970 Arrested	Anthony Corallo 1974–1987 Died in prison	Vincent Aloi 1971–1972 Arrested – Stepped down
Thomas Eboli 1969–1972 Murdered	John Gotti 1985–1992 Incarcerated Died in prison in 2002	Natale Evola 1970–1973 Died	Vittorio Amuso 1987–present Incarcerated since 1992	Carmine Persico 1972–present Boss Incarcerated since 1987
Frank Tieri 1972–1981 Died	Peter Gotti Acting Boss 1992–2001 Boss in 2002 Incarcerated Waiting for sentencing	Phil Rastelli 1973 Incarcerated	Alfonso D'Arco 1991–1993 Acting Boss Incarcerated Government informant	Thomas DiBella 1973 Acting Boss
Anthony Salerno 1981–1987 Incarcerated Died in prison	Arnold Squitieri Acting Boss 2002–present	Carmine Galante 1974–1979 Murdered	Joseph Defede 1993–1998 Acting Boss Incarcerated Government informant	Alphonse Persico 1973–1981 Acting Boss
Vincent Gigante 1987–present Incarcerated		Phil Rastelli 1979–1991	Steve Crea 1998–2001 Acting Boss Incarcerated	Gennaro Langella 1981–1986 Acting Boss
Liborio Bellomo 1987–1998 Acting Boss Incarcerated		Joseph Massino 1991–present Under indictment since January 2003	Louis Daidone 2001–2003 Acting Boss Under indictment	Victor Orena 1986–1993 Incarcerated Acting Boss
Dominick Cirillo Acting Boss 1998–present				Andrew Russo 1993–1999 Acting Boss
				Alfonse "Little Allie Boy" Persico 1999–2001 Acting Boss on behalf of his father, Carmine Arrested
				Joel Cacace 2001–2003 Acting Boss Under indictment

The Counsellor, or *Consigliere*

In the Sicilian Mafia, the *consigliere*, as a rule, is elected by the "men of honour" (soldiers) of the family;[68] in the American Cosa Nostra, the *consigliere* is usually appointed by the boss,[69] but may be elected by the *capiregime* of a family.[70] The boss, however, always has the right of veto. In 1977 Phil Testa, then underboss of Bruno family, nominated Nicodemo Scarfo as the new family *consigliere*, to replace Joe Rugnetta, who had died. Testa's recommendation was rejected by boss Angelo Bruno, who found Scarfo "too young and hotheaded."[71]

The most controversial *consigliere* nomination was certainly that of Salvatore Bonanno, the eldest son of Joseph Bonanno. At that time, Joseph Bonanno was at war with the members of the Commission, who had tried unsuccessfully to summon Bonanno. They had heard that Bonanno had cooked up a plot to have three members of the Commission murdered, but they wanted to give him a chance to tell his side of the story. The Commission had also heard of Bonanno's plans to depose Frank DeSimone, a crime leader in Southern California, and replace him with Salvatore. While in hiding, Bonanno appointed his son *consigliere*. The nomination was an encroachment on tradition, as the underboss should have been appointed. In any case, the Commission did not recognize the appointment because of the father-son relationship. The nomination of Salvatore as *consigliere* caused a split within the Bonanno family. Some supported the boss, Joseph Bonanno, while others did not.

The Role and Power of the Consigliere

The *consigliere* is on the same level as the underboss, although he has no direct authority over the *capiregime* and soldiers. The *consigliere* has often been portrayed as an elder family member in semi-retirement.[72] Today, however, members holding the *consigliere* position are often very active in criminal affairs.

The duties of the *consigliere* are critical to the survival of the family and its boss. He is chosen for his vast knowledge of precedents, his ability to render sound advice and especially his qualities of diplomacy. A close confidant of the boss, he advises the boss on all matters, and particularly on violations of the rules of conduct by family members or members of another family. In Sicily, a family boss does not take the responsibility of making a decision without having consulted with the *consigliere*.[73] Though he is supposed to act as a neutral advisor, the *consigliere* often finds historical precedent to justify the wishes of the boss. His role is to ensure the boss always saves face. The boss cannot be placed in a situation where his words or actions might be questioned. The *consigliere* will always make sure that the boss is right.[74]

The *consigliere* also serves as a mediator between the *capiregime* and the soldiers when a dispute occurs. If the *consigliere* resolves the problem, it does not go any further.[75] If a soldier is not satisfied with a decision made by his *caporegime*, he is entitled to ask the *consigliere* for a remedy. "I have the authority to overrule him," explained Joseph Russo, the *consigliere* for the Patriarca family, to Vincent Federico, a new inductee in the family, during his initiation ceremonial.[76] When a soldier is in trouble with the police, his *caporegime* will obtain the *consigliere*'s advice on whether the soldier should be helped or simply murdered lest he pose a security risk for the family.[77] Vincent Cafaro, a former soldier in the Genovese family, described the *consigliere* as the "powerhouse."

Typically, the *consigliere* has no subordinates who report to him. But the Bruno family provides an unusual exception. The family had within it two factions: the Calabrians and the dominant Sicilians. To avoid a feud, it was decided that the Calabrian faction would be headed by a *caporegime* who would simultaneously hold the *consigliere* position, thus giving the Calabrian members access to the family boss.[78]

In some powerful families, such as the Gambino and Genovese families, the *consigliere* is called on to play an important function. In January 1986 long-time Gambino family *consigliere* Joseph N. Gallo (no relation to Joey Gallo) tried to stop the brutal ascension of John Gotti, who had plotted the murder of his boss, Paul Castellano, and underboss, Thomas Bilotti, in December 1985. While the family was without a boss, seventy-seven-year-old Gallo found himself temporarily at the head of the family.

His role was to oversee the election of a new boss from among the twenty-three *capiregime* of the Gambino family.[79] Gallo, a man of the old Mafia guard, disliked Gotti. He had no respect for a man he viewed as a mere hoodlum.

At an important meeting of all the *capiregime* of the Gambino family, Gallo hoped to rally the *capiregime* behind him by asking them to resign; he would then immediately reappoint those who sided with him against Gotti. As acting boss, Gallo believed he had the power to demote all the *capiregime*, even the underboss. "I'm right," Gallo said. "I can break [demote] the captains, I can break the underboss anytime I want." But Gotti, who was present at the meeting, foresaw the manoeuvre. He had killed his boss, apparently with the Commission's approval. He felt he was now the new boss, and was only awaiting the moment when, with the approval of the family's *capiregime*, he could place the crown on his head. Gotti said to Gallo: "I'll getcha voted in or voted out. Joe, you think you're dealing with a fool. I break them twenty-three captains. I put in ten captains that I promote tomorrow . . . they vote you down. I break them, put my original captains back and you ain't no *consigliere*."[80]

Following that dramatic confrontation, Gallo lost his position and was replaced by Salvatore Gravano, a forty-one-year-old long-time associate of John Gotti.[81] The appointment of such a young *consigliere* pleased all *capiregime* and soldiers. Many felt it was difficult to communicate with Gallo, a man too old to understand the reality of the lives of a younger generation of mafiosi.[82]

The Captain, or *Caporegime*

The *caporegime* is appointed by the family boss. The number of *capiregime* varies depending on the size of the family.[83] At the end of the 1980s, the Gambino family had about twenty-five functioning *capiregime*.

When a new boss takes over a family, he typically expects the resignation of all the family's captains. When John Gotti took command of the Gambino family, he felt that the *capiregime* were part of the old cabinet: "I could break every one captain now . . . a new boss does that as soon as [he is elected]."[84]

The Role and Power of the Caporegime

Also known as *capo*, lieutenant, captain, skipper and *capodecina* (mainly in Sicily), the *caporegime*'s position is similar to that of a supervisor in a business. The *caporegime*'s main functions are to oversee street-level operations, receive orders from the boss and make sure the boss's wishes are complied with. He is responsible for enforcing and protecting the criminal activities in his crew's territory.[85] A *caporegime*'s stature is not related to the number of soldiers who report to him. *Capiregime* all share equal status.

A *caporegime* is a close confidant of his soldiers, and is the intermediary between them and the upper levels of the family. He protects and defends his soldiers when they are in trouble with the law or with another Cosa Nostra member. He resolves administrative matters and avoids getting his boss involved. John Gotti was once approached by Angelo Ruggiero, who had recently been appointed *caporegime*. Ruggiero came to Gotti with a small problem regarding a loan shark. "I don't deal with this anymore," said an irritated Gotti.[86] When Paul Castellano led the Gambino family, the *capiregime* needed special authorization to attend a sit-down with Castellano at his home in Staten Island. Only the *consigliere*, Joseph N. Gallo, had unlimited access to Castellano.[87]

According to a New York City criminal lawyer who acted as counsel for many Cosa Nostra defendants, the *caporegime* is not directly responsible for the commission of murders. These orders are given by the boss or the underboss, who then directs a *caporegime* to choose a soldier to perform the task.[88]

The *caporegime* must at all times have control over his soldiers' activities. Anthony Gaggi, a *caporegime* in the Gambino family, experienced serious problems with one of his soldiers, Roy DeMeo. The impulsive soldier was responsible for a large car-theft ring in New York City. The stolen cars were dismantled, and their parts sold throughout the world. DeMeo suspected that an associate and his girlfriend were informing the police about the operation. DeMeo ordered the couple murdered without telling his *caporegime*. When Castellano read the news in the paper, he summoned Gaggi. Gaggi was forced to admit that he did not know about the murders. But he was obliged to defend his soldier's action lest he implicitly admit he was incapable of controlling DeMeo's actions or those of any other soldier on his crew.[89]

A *caporegime*'s power derives from the perception of his soldiers that his orders reflect the will of the boss. He can rule on the territory of activities and the sharing of proceeds of every one of his soldiers. He may also set the percentage on returns of moneys made by his soldiers.[90] The *caporegime* must be informed of all his soldiers' street actions. He needs to be told in advance of any planned or forthcoming criminal operation. In return, he has a duty to keep the boss informed of all the activities of his regime. John Gotti did not fuss over that particular rule, though. When a soldier asked Gotti whether he needed the permission of his *caporegime*, who lived in Queens, to run a gambling operation in that area (where Gotti also lived), Gotti said, "No big deal." "But he is a captain!" remarked the soldier. "I'm your boss," shot back Gotti.[91]

A *caporegime* cannot appoint a soldier as acting *caporegime* without going through the proper channels, that is, through the underboss and then the boss. Michael Caiazzio, a Gambino *caporegime*, made Buddy LaForte acting *caporegime* without seeking permission from Aniello Dellacroce, the underboss. Caiazzio was subsequently demoted to soldier and assigned to James Failla's *regime* along with LaForte.[92]

Several prominent Cosa Nostra families have developed a special body called the "administration," consisting of the *consigliere* and *capiregime* of the family. The administration hears and arbitrates minor disputes and advises the boss on important matters affecting the family. Its decisions are not final and can be overturned by the boss. The existence of such administrations was not known until June 10, 1969, when the government released taped conversations from an electronic device installed in the Kenilworth, New Jersey, office of Cosa Nostra boss Sam DeCavalcante.[93]

The Conduct of the Caporegime

As the leader of a crew, a *caporegime* must exhibit model conduct, both with his peers and with outsiders and citizens. (Mafiosi draw a clear line between themselves and the rest of the world. An "outsider" is someone who may be engaged in criminal activities but does not belong and is not connected to a Cosa Nostra family. A "citizen" refers to the general public, people who have nothing to do with crime and criminals.)

Mike Sabella, a *caporegime* in the Bonanno family, went to a local garage to pick up a new Oldsmobile he had purchased. The garage owner handed him a bill for fifteen dollars for light repairs. Sabella threw it back and refused to pay. The incident occurred in New Jersey, a territory ruled by Sam DeCavalcante. Joseph Zicarelli, a soldier in the Bonanno family, lives and operates in New Jersey. He answers to Mike Sabella. During a casual conversation between Zicarelli and DeCavalcante (they had known each other for many years), Zicarelli talked about Sabella's bad conduct towards the garagist. At that point DeCavalante asked Zicarelli to tell Sabella "that he couldn't act this way."[94]

Another example of bad conduct is reported in a taped conversation from June 1965 between Sam DeCavalcante and Lou Larasso, a soldier for DeCavalcante. DeCavalcante told Larasso that Joe Sferra, a *caporegime*, was driving his daughter and three other girls home from school. He was following a teenager who was driving his car very slowly, with his girlfriend sitting close to him. Sferra became upset and went around the boy, cutting him off. The teenager then chased Sferra. When both were stopped at a light, Sferra and the teenager got out of their cars. Sferra allegedly berated the young man and pushed him. The teenager was enraged and pushed Sferra so hard that he fell and broke his foot. When asked by DeCavalcante about his foot, Sferra said he had fallen. But DeCavalcante later learned about the incident. "Is this any way for an *amico nos* [friend of ours] and a *caporegime* to act?" lamented DeCavalcante. "No," replied Larasso.[95]

The Soldier, or *Soldato*

The *soldato* is the lowest rank in a Cosa Nostra family. "Button men," "good fellows" and "wiseguys" are all terms for a soldier. "Wiseguy" is commonly used in New York City, while in Chicago "street man" or "operator" is preferred.[96] In Sicily, soldiers are called "men of honour." Although soldiers are all of equal status, some of them may command more respect or prestige than others. However, any soldier carries the full authority of his family when representing them.

The Role of the Soldier

A soldier is not obliged to engage in criminal activities. But whether his activities are legal or illegal, he must report on a regular basis to his assigned *caporegime*.[97] Accountability is one of the most important obligations of a soldier. This rule is strongly stressed to new members during the initiation ceremony. "You must go on record with your *capo*" before getting involved in a criminal activity with other members, whether or not they belong to the same family, warned Joseph Russo, the *consigliere* in the Patriarca family in Boston.[98] The soldier must inform his *caporegime* of all his comings and goings, whether they are for business or for vacation, and must give his *caporegime* a telephone number where he can be reached at any time. If a Cosa Nostra member in a position of command cannot reach soldiers wherever they may be, it appears that he has lost control over his men and he therefore loses prestige.

A soldier who is not satisfied with his *caporegime*'s decision on a particular matter may approach the *consigliere*. "It is your privilege to come to me," explained Russo to a new inductee. But a soldier has the duty to meet with his *caporegime* first: "Whatever you do, you must see him first because you are responsible to him. You must obey and honour your *capo*."[99]

Soldiers Who Answer Directly to the Boss

Before the early 1960s, soldiers could not directly reach the underboss or the boss. They had to go through their *caporegime* first. Since then, the rule has changed and, in some families, a boss may have two or three soldiers who report directly to him.[100] This was the case for Lou Larasso, who answered to Sam DeCavalcante;[101] for Robert DiBernardo, who was actively involved in the distribution and the sale of pornographic materials and had direct access to Paul Castellano concerning matters related to a Teamster local;[102] and for Michael Clemente, who was accountable only to Frank Tieri, the boss of the Genovese family in the late 1970s.[103]

Some soldiers, for many reasons, acquire a certain prestige and become highly regarded by their superiors. One of them was Vincent Rizzo, a soldier in the Genovese family. Rizzo had privileged contacts with international networks and controlled the distribution of stolen and counterfeit American securities.[104]

There are also a few examples of associates who reported directly to a boss. One was Hugh McIntosh, who had a close relationship with Carmine Persico, boss of the Colombo family. Another was Joe Watts, who made a fortune in loansharking activities, and reported to John Gotti.[105]

"Plant" Positions

Around 1950 a new position, called a "plant," was created. Cosa Nostra members used as plants are carefully selected and kept out of any criminal activities until they reach senior positions and attendant respectability in the world of business or politics. One such plant was Anthony Scotto, a *caporegime* in the Gambino family, whose father-in-law was the brother of Albert Anastasia, a family leader in New York. Scotto was the president of Local 1814, the International Longshoremen's Association. He was twice appointed delegate to the International Labor Organization, an international association of labour unions, by presidents Lyndon Johnson and Richard Nixon. As a presidential appointee, Scotto had entry to the White House, thus gaining considerable influence in labour unions.[106]

Another typical example of a plant was John C. Montana, a well-known Buffalo businessman who had been "man of the year" of that city. The police discovered him among the nearly sixty attendees at a national convention of Cosa Nostra held in November 1957 in Apalachin, New York, at the residence of Joseph Barbara.[107] Montana had been an important *caporegime* in the Magaddino family of Buffalo since 1931.

"Acting" Positions

The New York families in particular use "acting" positions to fill in for high-ranking members. For example, when a family boss is imprisoned, he may appoint an acting boss. The acting boss looks after the daily criminal activities of the family and resolves minor problems. However, he is not allowed to make major changes to the family's administration—such as appointing a *caporegime* or admitting new members—or to authorize a murder. He must first consult with the boss, who holds his position of authority for as long as he is recognized as the official boss.[108] When a family member, usually a ranking member, is appointed acting boss, he carries the full authority of the family boss and is entitled to respect from all family members. There can also be acting under-bosses, acting *consiglieri* and acting *capiregime*.

In the Sicilian Mafia, the term *reggènte* designates someone who temporarily holds a ranking position on behalf of a Cosa Nostra member who is incarcerated or a police fugitive.

Associates

As a rule of thumb, Cosa Nostra members trust only men of Sicilian descent when engaging in criminal activities. However, throughout its history, Cosa Nostra has called upon Jewish, Irish and black gangsters for their expertise or skills. These associations can be episodic or can last for years. Meyer Lansky was in close association with the New York–based families, especially the Genovese family, for several decades.

Before being formally introduced to the inner circle of criminals, future associates are scrutinized for their manners, their way of speaking and their reactions to certain situations. An individual who is quick to meet or deal with members of a crime family is marked as an infiltration agent for the police. The associate must play by the rules of the streets and give Cosa Nostra members an opportunity to check on him.[109]

Although criminal associates work in inner circles, they are subject to strict rules concerning their level of acceptance and their conduct with members. Accepting an associate into a crime family is always a risk. In most cases, the associate cannot expect to enjoy the same privileges that made members do. Moreover, if an associate is not of Italian descent, at least through his father, he cannot expect to become a made member. The associate, as the weak link of the chain, is most likely, if arrested, to be pressed by police into becoming an informant.

Types of Associates

It is estimated that each Cosa Nostra soldier has between ten and fifteen people working for him. Sociologist Annelise Anderson has categorized four types of active associates: close associates, associates, businessmen and professionals.

The close associate is always a man of Italian descent. He is likely to one day become a made member of the family when there is a vacancy. He may have been proposed for membership in the past. The close associate is deeply involved in criminal activities as well as in legal activities. He may answer to one or two Cosa Nostra members, but he works for the family as a whole rather than for a particular member. He is known as "registered." The close associate may have developed expertise in an area that is lucrative for the family. He is held in high esteem by the members, and benefits from the protection of the family in cases of police intervention.[110] Law enforcement and state agencies describe a close associate as "constantly in the company of several Cosa Nostra members, or someone who has been in some business dealings with Cosa Nostra members in the recent past, or someone who has been in business with them, whether legal or illegal."[111]

The associate can be from any ethnic background. He works for and answers to only one member. He is usually involved in criminal activities such as loansharking or illegal gambling. He enjoys the protection of his mentor, but not of the family.[112] He is accepted and trusted by the family after a certain period of time. "He can be part of the family as long as he is a money maker and brings money to the crime group. But he will be always looked at as an outsider despite years and years of close relationship with the family," said Martin Light, a former criminal lawyer who represented members of the Colombo family and who was sentenced to fifteen years for possession of heroin.[113]

Businessmen are mainly individuals who do not fulfill basic Cosa Nostra membership requirements. They are used by Cosa Nostra members to operate legal or illegal business fronts. They are not regarded as gangsters.

Professionals are usually corporate and criminal lawyers, accountants and bail bondsmen whose main clients are members of a crime family.[114]

Chapter 3

Becoming a Made Member

Soldiers are the backbone of a Cosa Nostra family. They represent the power base and the continuity of the family. Older soldiers carry with them experience and expertise in the business of Cosa Nostra. The recruitment of young and capable men is very important, but a family must be careful not to admit too many people at one time, as some seek admission to Cosa Nostra only to gain power and prestige.[1] To be admitted, a prospect must fulfill certain conditions or qualifications, be sponsored by a member, go through a long screening process, submit himself to a probation period and, finally, go through an initiation by taking an oath to the organization.

CONDITIONS OF ADMISSION

Historically, only white males of full Italian heritage could be admitted to Cosa Nostra. But in the early 1980s the rule was loosened to allow the admission of other valuable candidates. Men whose father was of Italian descent but whose mother was from another ethnic group could be accepted, as could men married to non-Italian women. The patrilineal requirement is strictly observed, though. Hugh McIntosh, whose non-Italian father was married to an Italian woman, was a close friend and bodyguard of Carmine Persico, the boss of the Colombo family, and served him faithfully. But McIntosh could not be admitted into the family, even though he may have been a valuable candidate.[2] Jimmy Burke and Henry Hill, close associates in the Lucchese family, met with the same obstacle because their fathers were Irish. The Chicago family does accept non-Italians as members; however, they are not involved in the highest level meetings or decisions.[3]

Men admitted into Cosa Nostra once had to be related by blood or by alliance in marriage to someone who was already a member. In Sicily, where this rule was strictly followed, the importance of bonds and kinship were more important than respect and money. Around 1920, due to heightened emigration to America, the Sicilian Mafia families broadened their membership criteria. Membership was open not only to Sicilians, but to Italians born in regions of mainland Italy, such as Naples. Kinship bonds were also extended to individuals such as godparents, godchildren and best men at the weddings of sons or nephews, because they were tied to the family through their part in a religious ceremony.[4] In a taped conversation recorded by the FBI in the early 1960s, Angelo De Carlo, a New Jersey *caporegime* for the New York–based Genovese family, voiced his regret that the strict rule of admission was no longer observed: "Before, it was more relationship. All the bosses—it was through relations—cousins. That's the way this thing—Cosa Nostra—was supposed to start. All relations. That's the way it started in Italy. That's the way it should have been kept. You had it for your son to get in, brother, son-in-law. You had to be in the family to get into it."[5]

Being the son of a Cosa Nostra member is always a guarantee of eligibility.[6] But, in Sicily, a man cannot become a member of the same family that his father, brother or uncle belongs to. This rule exists to prevent a concentration of power against members of the family who are not affiliated by blood. In the United States, this rule has not always been observed. The Gambino, Genovese and Profaci families include men of close lineage.[7] Joseph Profaci, boss of his family until he died in June 1962, had his brother-in-law, Joseph Magliocco, as underboss. His niece was married to Salvatore Bonanno, son of Joseph Bonanno. In Detroit, a prospective candidate is required to be Sicilian on both sides, and the Zerilli and Tocco families have for decades allowed very strong lineages among their members. Canadian Mafia groups based in Toronto and in Montreal, particularly the Caruana, the Cuntrera, and the Rizzuto crime families, are also closely interrelated.

In Sicily, prospective candidates are refused admission if one of their kin—a father, son or brother—has been killed by Cosa Nostra. If the candidate became a man of honour, he would be entitled to learn the names of his kinsman's killers. This rule was established to prevent any act of retaliation.[8]

A candidate usually cannot be admitted to Cosa Nostra if his father, brother or uncle is a police officer. But there are always exceptions. John Robilotto, a Joseph Valachi associate in the 1940s, ran into a roadblock because his brother was a member of the New York City Police Force.[9] Robilotto was connected to Anthony Strollo, a *caporegime* in the Genovese family. When he was refused membership in that family, Robilotto switched his allegiance to Albert Anastasia, who overlooked the rule and took Robilotto in.[10] In Chicago, John Matassa was made a member of the Northside crew. His father was a Chicago detective who was known to have close links to Sam Giancana.[11] In the early 1990s the family of John Stanfa of Philadelphia had as an associate Ronald Previte, a former member of the Philadelphia police.

In Sicily a recruit may not have any relationship to a police officer, *carabiniere* (a member of an Italian army corps) or public figure. But exceptions are made when breaking the rule is to the advantage of Cosa Nostra. Aurelio Ocelli was made into the Vicari family even though his father was a *carabiniere*, because Ocelli Sr. allegedly enjoyed privileged relationships with influential politicians such as Vito Ciancimino, the former mayor of Palermo.[12]

A member of the Sicilian Cosa Nostra does not automatically inherit membership in the American organization. The member must be recommended and sponsored before he is admitted.[13]

Finally, when an aspiring candidate is under the protection of a *caporegime*, he cannot be recruited by another family. Carmine Galante, at that time underboss in the Bonanno family, learned this rule when he first met John Gotti in the 1970s. Gotti had just been sent to the Lewisburg penitentiary for a two-year sentence. Galante liked Gotti and wanted to recruit him into his family. But Gotti already "belonged" to Carmine Fatico, an important *caporegime* in the Gambino family who had extended protection to Gotti. Fatico, by vouching for Gotti, was not only responsible for any of Gotti's actions, but claimed Gotti as "his property."[14]

RECRUITMENT AND SCREENING

Before hiring anyone, prestigious business enterprises expose candidates to a thorough selection process, checking references, interviewing and testing skills with written examinations. The process of hiring may take weeks or even months. Cosa Nostra's selection process is even more rigorous, and the selection of candidates may take several years. In Sicily, according to Buscetta, a prospective candidate is "carefully observed and screened for a period of time without knowing it."[15]

Cosa Nostra looks for candidates born and raised in ghettos, where poverty and continuous unemployment contribute to very strong antisocial feelings, particularly against law enforcement. For many of the youngsters living in these neighbourhoods, joining an established and solid criminal organization is a rare chance at a better life. They are prepared to do anything to be called by the elders they venerate.[16] Recruiters are particularly interested in youngsters who will recognize the organization as the sole authority, which they will put above society and their own family, and for which they are ready to commit crimes.[17]

Members of Cosa Nostra are likely to approach a gang of boys who have committed or are involved in some kind of criminal activity where firearms are used, for instance in robberies or hijackings. They observe how the job is performed and how the boys react to a stressful situation. They automatically exclude impulsive and frightened individuals in favour of those who accomplish their jobs with self-confidence and calm.[18]

It is not essential for a new recruit to have a criminal record. Indeed, it is preferable that police have no photograph or fingerprints of the recruit. However, it sometimes happens that prospective recruits are arrested, convicted and sentenced to a prison term during their criminal apprenticeship. This is a critical test for candidates—their reactions to police interrogations and behaviour towards other inmates while serving their sentences will be closely monitored.[19]

When he joins Cosa Nostra, a member continues whatever criminal activity he had been involved in before joining. If he was a fencer, he remains a fencer; if he was an auto thief, he remains an auto thief. Cosa

Nostra makes a point of using and benefiting from talent and expertise. Thus, the organization also recruits members who have a practical skill or, even better, a college or university education. They may be businessmen, accountants, lawyers, doctors. They generally have no criminal records and hold positions of confidence and trust in their communities. The Sicilian Cosa Nostra has experienced great success in enlisting people who possess strong influence over ordinary citizens.[20]

Before a man is admitted to Cosa Nostra, he must submit to an investigation of his past, his family background and his friends. When Michele Greco, a powerful member of the Sicilian Mafia during the 1980s, was on the verge of being admitted into the Sicilian Cosa Nostra, he was asked why his father had told a criminal court, in the 1930s, that he would seek justice for the murder of his brother. (His statement went against the rule that a Sicilian, whether a mafioso or not, does not go to authorities or police to get justice, but retaliates himself.[21]) A prospect will also be asked if he has had any drug convictions. Individuals who are known drug users are not easily accepted into Cosa Nostra. Joey Gallo, for example, caused the Commission to hesitate before allowing him into the Profaci family, as he was suspected of being a "drug user and a lunatic."[22]

THE PROBATION PERIOD

Once a recruit has been accepted and assigned to a Cosa Nostra member, he is regarded as a close associate, and is subject to the strict rules of the code of conduct. He is not, however, entitled to the privileges conferred on made members. The new recruit will be tested for his value and skills during a mandatory period of probation. The length of the probation may be affected by vacancies created by retirements or deaths. Sometimes it may be up to ten or twelve years. In a conversation recorded by the FBI in October 1964, Anthony Santoli, a long-standing member of the Philadelphia family, explained to Sam DeCavalcante how long he'd had to wait before getting inducted in Cosa Nostra: "I worked! I've been—we've been—doing favours for the organization thirty years! How long am I made now? Eight years? Ten years?"[23]

Under Carlo Gambino's leadership, prospective members had to serve a long period of probation before being officially inducted. Gambino believed that an aspirant should not be formally inducted until he had mastered all aspects of organized crime. He held his *capiregime* responsible for any inducted member who later revealed himself not sufficiently acquainted with all the rules and facets of the organization. Recruits have to show patience and cannot expect to be quickly awarded with membership. "You gotta be patient," Carmine Fatico once said to his protégé, John Gotti, who complained he had been working faithfully for the family for almost fifteen years.[24]

Older Mafia members complain that young recruits are in too much of a hurry to be made. Angelo De Carlo once criticized a new recruit who wanted to be introduced to the other members of the family. "How can I introduce you when I don't know you myself?" he said, alluding to a rule that a Cosa Nostra member cannot introduce someone he does not know, whether that person is made or not.[25] Veteran members also resent that young recruits know too much about the organization's structure before being admitted. "My nephew talks about *caporegime*. You know, years ago, when you was made, they didn't tell you nothing until the last day. Today they tell you a month in advance," said Angelo De Carlo.[26] De Carlo also deplored the admission of people who were good earners for the family but "never broke an egg."[27]

Recruits cannot take for granted that they will be made. If they prove themselves, they may someday be "invited" to join. Paul Gulino, an overzealous wannabe who had killed on orders of Anthony Spero, then acting boss for the Bonanno family, desperately wanted to be made. In July 1993 he showed his impatience and asked Spero directly when he would be made, thus violating protocol. Spero ignored him, and a frustrated Gulino plotted to kill Spero. But Spero got word of Gulino's plans and had him murdered.[28]

Each recruit starts at the bottom. He is required to execute various jobs that require violence or intimidation, such as the collection of debts. Recruits are anxious to impress their bosses, to prove that they are good candidates, that they have the necessary qualifications and especially the ability to earn money for the family. As time goes on, recruits will be tested for their loyalty and competence by being asked to perform more daring criminal assignments. While some Cosa Nostra members are accepted for specific skills, such as being a money maker for the family, most prospective members are expected to participate in a murder before being inducted into Cosa Nostra. Tommaso Buscetta insisted on this prerequisite.[29] However, according to Vincent Palermo, a ranking member in the DeCavalcante family who became a turncoat, Sam DeCavalcante ignored the rule.[30] Salvatore Gravano, former underboss of the Gambino family, states in his autobiography that "committing murder was not a prerequisite for induction into Cosa Nostra, but more often than not, it would happen."[31] By killing someone, a future candidate shows his willingness to perform any job Cosa Nostra requires of him. It also assures to a certain extent that the member will never cooperate with police, although in recent years several turncoats have admitted their participation in committing a murder.

In his book *Quitting the Mob*, Michael Franzese, a former Colombo family member, revealed that when Cosa Nostra was in a rush to recruit a large number of candidates to rebuild the Colombo family membership the prerequisite to kill was waived, as the number of recruits to be made far exceeded the number of persons who needed to be killed. But the new inductees were eventually requested to kill for the family.[32] "Participating in a murder is the primary ingredient to being a member of Cosa Nostra. It is the most important thing you must do," said former Philadelphia boss Ralph Natale, testifying against Joseph Merlino in April 2001.[33]

Before being admitted into Cosa Nostra, a novice must be sponsored by a member of the organization. The sponsor takes full responsibility for his protégé's conduct. Should the novice reveal himself to have been a bad candidate, the sponsor is responsible for carrying out his death.[34] Similarly, if a made member introduces an outsider to the family, he is responsible for the outsider's actions. Dominick Napolitano, a *caporegime* in the Bonanno family, was killed for committing a serious breach of security to the family by introducing FBI agent Joseph Pistone to his peers.[35] After the Bonanno family learned that Pistone had infiltrated their family and others, the Commission reactivated the requirement that a prospective member must commit a murder. The rule was designed to prevent any infiltration by law enforcement into the organization. Future candidates would have to be sponsored by two made members who had known them for at least fifteen years.[36] Pistone would have been the very first police officer to be offered full-fledged membership in Cosa Nostra had he agreed to kill Anthony Bruno Indelicato, one of the gunmen who had participated in the murder of Carmine Galante in July 1979. Indelicato was marked for death by the Bonanno family after his fingerprints were discovered on the getaway car from Galante's shooting. Before the murder was carried out, the FBI withdrew Pistone from the streets and put an end to the undercover operation, in accordance with its policy that undercover agents cannot participate directly in a criminal act.

In New York City, it is customary for a family that intends to induct new members to circulate a list of their names to the other families to make sure none of the proposed candidates has a "beef" (a pending problem) with a Cosa Nostra member or with an associate connected to a Cosa Nostra family. Once a person becomes a made member, it is forever. If it is learned afterwards that a candidate has problems with other members, it poses a very serious issue that needs to be resolved through formal channels. The only way to "unmake" someone is to murder him.

In 1991 James Ida, the *consigliere* for the Genovese family, handed to other New York families a list of prospective members that the Genovese family wanted to initiate. When Anthony Baratta, the acting underboss for the Lucchese family, saw the list, he expressed concerns about one name, that of Ralph DeSimone, an associate. "He is a rat. He has been a government informant," claimed Baratta. Further discussions and meetings between the administrations of the Genovese and Lucchese families were held. Baratta was asked to provide evidence. He later produced minutes that proved DeSimone's co-operation with authorities. On June 13, 1991, DeSimone's body was found in the trunk of his car at the LaGuardia airport.[37]

INITIATION RITES OF THE SICILIAN COSA NOSTRA

When a new candidate has proved himself of value to the organization, he is then officially invited to join the family. The initiation ceremony has remained essentially the same since the beginning. In a book he wrote in 1900, Giuseppe Alongi, a police commissioner in Palermo, described initiation rites practised by an *associazione di malfattori* in 1860. A candidate would be taken by two members to be introduced to the heads of the Mafia in the territory in which he lived. Before the ceremony began, the aspirant was asked if he still wished to be admitted. If he decided he did not (which was unlikely), he had the opportunity to walk out. Otherwise the initiation proceeded. On a table in front of him, the aspirant would see the image of a saint, a dagger and a candle. One of the members would ask the candidate to present his right hand and would then pierce a finger with the dagger, drawing enough blood that it would drip onto the image. Then the inductee would swear an oath to the society:

> I pledge my honour to be faithful to the Fraternity [Fratellanza], as the Fraternity is faithful to me. As this saint and a few drops of my blood were burned, so will I give all my blood for the Fraternity, when my ashes and my blood will return to their original condition, as it will not be possible for me to leave the Fraternity.[38]

The new member was asked to burn the image with the flame of the candle. From then on he was a member of the society.

Some initiations involved the firing of a pistol at a statue of Jesus Christ. This ritual was practised at the end of the nineteenth century by the Association of *Stoppaglieri*, a criminal society in Monreale, near Palermo. Adherents to the Camorra, a Mafia-like criminal organization with roots in Naples, would fire shots at a crucifix.[39]

Antonino Calderone, a former member of Cosa Nostra in Catania, in western Sicily, who became an informant in the 1980s, described to the late Sicilian judge Giovanni Falcone how the ceremony of initiation has been conducted for several decades. When the ceremony is about to take place, the candidates are taken to a secure location, where the representatives of the family and a few men of honour are waiting. For some time, the novices are left alone in a room, where they wait until they are called one by one. The leader of the family presides over the initiation. He tells each neophyte that what is labelled by public, media and police as "Mafia" is in reality called Cosa Nostra or "Thing of Ours." He explains that there is still time to leave the room if the novice wishes to do so. He then enumerates the various rules of the organization: never touch the wife of a man of honour; never steal from a member; never engage in prostitution; never kill a man of honour; always behave correctly; never talk about Cosa Nostra's activities and members to strangers; never introduce yourself directly to other men of honour, but only through a member known to both parties.

Once the rules have been explained, and the applicant has made it known that he still wants to be inducted, he is invited to choose a sponsor from among those present. The novice is asked which hand he fires a pistol with. The master of the ceremony pierces the index finger of that hand with a knife, or sometimes a needle, and blood falls over the image of a saint the novice holds in both hands. (The image of the Madonna of Annunciation, whose commemoration is on March 25, is often used, as she is regarded as the patron saint of Cosa Nostra.) The leader tells the novice that "one comes in Cosa Nostra by blood and we leave it only by blood." The image is then burned, and the candidate solemnly swears that he will never betray the rules of Cosa Nostra, lest he burn like the image. Then the new member is taught the structure and levels of the family of the region or province where he lives. He is assigned to a *capodecina*, to whom he must always report or go through should he wish to see the family leader.[40]

According to the Sicilian Cosa Nostra rules, once someone has become a made member, he cannot be part of another organization such as the Masonry. However, around 1977 a Cosa Nostra leader, Stefano Bontate, persuaded the Cupola to authorize Sicilian Cosa Nostra members to join the Masons. Bontate saw great benefits for Cosa Nostra, as influential Masonic lodge members could use privileged channels to intervene on behalf of Cosa Nostra in pending judicial proceedings against several Mafia leaders.[41]

INITIATION RITES OF THE AMERICAN COSA NOSTRA

According to various members of Cosa Nostra, initiation rites in the American Cosa Nostra have changed very little over the past century, although a few variations are practised in certain families. The use of the image of a saint, a dagger, the piercing of a finger and the flame of a candle are mentioned in almost all initiation accounts,[42] but a piece of tissue was used instead of the image of a saint in the initiations of John Gotti and Nicholas Caramandi.[43]

As with the Sicilian Mafia, a new recruit must be voted on unanimously by all members. Any member can oppose the admission of a recruit.[44] All initiations are presided over by the family boss or, at least, by the highest ranking member present at the ceremony. Nicodemo Scarfo, boss of the Philadelphia family, made a point of presiding over all initiations in his family, so Nicholas Caramandi, a future member and later a defector, had to wait until his boss had been released from jail to become made.[45]

The most vivid initiation account on record was related by Joseph Valachi, the first member in Cosa Nostra's history to defect, in his testimony before the United States Senate Permanent Subcommittee on Investigations of Government Operations, on October 1, 1963. Valachi's initiation occurred in 1930, when the Castellammarese Wars were raging in New York City. It took place in a private house, where about forty people gathered around a long table on which lay a piece of paper, a knife and a gun. The ceremony was guided by Salvatore Maranzano. Taking the oath, Valachi repeated after Maranzano, "This is the way I burn if I expose this organization," while holding a burning piece of paper in his hands that represented the image of a saint.[46] Maranzano then asked each individual present (there were thirty-five to forty people in the room) to hold up his right hand and indicate a number from zero to five with his fingers. Maranzano counted the numbers of raised fingers and reached a number—say twenty-eight. He started counting from the person sitting at his left around the table until he reached person number twenty-eight, who happened to be Joseph Bonanno. Bonanno thus became the *gombah* or "godfather" of Joseph Valachi, which meant that he was responsible for Valachi. Bonanno pricked Valachi's forefinger with a pin. Valachi was told the blood that came from his finger signified that everybody in the room was bound by blood. Valachi was then taught two important rules: Cosa Nostra must be kept secret and sexual involvement with the wife, sister or daughter of another member was prohibited. A breach of these rules meant death for the culprit, without trial. As the ceremony had to be done very quickly because it was "wartime," Valachi was told that other rules would be explained to him at a later date.[47]

Angelo Lonardo, the former Cleveland underboss, provides an interesting account of his initiation, which occurred in the late 1940s. He was asked several times if he "knew and understood" what would happen to him once initiated. Lonardo was also asked, "Do you want to become a member? You still have a chance to refuse or to become a member." If he had refused admission, he would have had to leave the room immediately.[48] There are no known cases of individuals who have refused to go through an initiation. However, there have been cases where a soldier has refused to be promoted to the rank of *caporegime*.

On October 29, 1989, the FBI succeeded in taping an entire induction ceremony, thus bringing convincing proof of the presence of Cosa Nostra in the United States. The ceremony was held in the basement of a house that belonged to the sister of one of the new inductees, in Bedford, near Boston. Seventeen members of the Patriarca family met in the house to induct four new members into the family: Vincent Federico, Robert DeLuca, Carmen Tortora and Richard Floramo. Present at the ritual were the boss of the family, Raymond Patriarca Jr.; the *consigliere*, Joseph Russo; and five *capiregime*. The new recruits were asked to wait in another room until they were called in. As each recruit was called, Russo and Patriarca proceeded to take his oath. Each inductee swore that he would abide by *omertà*, the code of silence, and promised to kill without hesitation any police informant posing a threat to the Patriarca family, even if the informant were his son or brother. Each inductee was required to identify the finger with which he pulls "the trigger," which we can assume was then cut to draw blood for use in the ritual. The inductee was then asked to repeat after Russo the following:

Io, Vincenzo [I, Vincenzo]
Vòglio entrare [Want to enter]
In questa organizzaziòne [Into this organization]
Per protèggere [To protect]
La mia famiglia [My family]
E per protèggere [And to protect]
Tutti i miei amici [All my friends]
Io le giuro [I swear]
Di non svelare [Not to divulge]
Questo segrèto [This secret]
E di ubbidire [And to obey]
Di amore [With love]
E omertà [And silence]
Questo è il santo della nostra famiglia [This is the holy image of
    our family]
Come si brucia [As burns]
Questa santo [This saint]
Cosi si brucerà [So will burn]
La mia anima [My soul]
Giuro [I swear]
Di entrare vivo [To enter alive]
In questa organizzazione [In this organization]
E di uscire mòrto [And get out dead][49]

After the oath, the inductees were told the other rules of Cosa Nostra.[50]

In an unprecedented case, an initiation ceremony was invalidated after it was discovered to have been taped by one of the inductees, George Fresolone. Fresolone, a long-time associate of the Philadelphia Scarfo family's faction operating in northern New Jersey, decided to work as an agent for the New Jersey State Police Organized Crime Strike Force after he became disillusioned with the mob. For two years he wore a tiny microphone strapped to his body, thus recording incriminating conversations of members of the Philadelphia Cosa Nostra. In July 1990 Fresolone was told that he was to be inducted into the family.

The ceremony, which was performed by Anthony Piccolo, then acting boss for the Scarfo family, took place in the Bronx on July 29, 1990. Four new recruits, including Fresolone, were to be made on that day. One of them was Nicholas Olivieri, an associate of the Gambino family who lived in New Jersey and reported to a Gambino *caporegime* there. By agreement with the Gambino family, Olivieri was "loaned out" to his close friend and mentor, Pasquale Martirano, a *caporegime* in the Scarfo family who died of cancer a week after the initiation ceremony.

The validity of the initiation ceremony was quickly questioned by some members of the Scarfo and Gambino families who felt they had not been properly informed about Fresolone's and Olivieri's initiations. The Gambino family, for instance, objected that Olivieri had not been officially "released" to the Philadelphia family. The family pointed out that a list of names of the recruits had not been circulated among the five New York families. They felt that the list should have been circulated as a courtesy to the New York families since some of the inductees had been working with the Gambino family in northern New Jersey. On the other hand, some argued that since the Scarfo family did not operate in New York, it was not obliged to circulate the names.

The situation worsened when, at the wake of Pasquale Martirano, John Riggi, the boss of the DeCavalcante family, refused to be introduced as *amico nos* to the recent made members as they made their entrance into the funeral parlour. Word was passed to others not to recognize the new members.[51]

Olivieri remained with the Scarfo family after being officially discharged by the Gambino family. He was put "on the shelf," and was not recognized as a made member. As for Fresolone, sensing his life was in danger, he went into hiding as a government witness.

The validity of other initiations was questioned when the Commission learned that, decades earlier, Sam DeCavalcante had decreed that the use of a gun and a knife were not essential to the initiation ceremony. This fact was confirmed by revelations that Vincent Palermo made to the FBI with respect to his induction ceremony, held in 1976, during which he was told by DeCavalcante himself that these accessories were not required.[52] When DeCavalcante stepped down in 1982, John Riggi maintained the practice for some years, until a DeCavalcante soldier reported the variance to a member of the Mafia in New York. The Commission ordered the entire membership of the New Jersey family to be re-inducted according to the original procedure and practice of Cosa Nostra.

In statements made to the FBI, Vincent Palermo confirmed that the New Jersey–based DeCavalcante family was subservient to the five New York families. According to Palermo, when the DeCavalcante family wished to induct a new member, it had to submit the candidate's name for approval by the New York families. Should one of the five oppose, the proposed membership would be rejected. Indeed, a rule made by the New York families prohibits the DeCavalcante family from initiating members who reside outside of New Jersey. The New Jersey family transgressed that rule when it took into its ranks two Manhattan residents who were operating a social club in Little Italy.[53] In the early 1990s, John Gotti allegedly decreed that the Gambino family would not recognize any New Yorkers who, after being refused membership in any of the five New York families, sought admission into the DeCavalcante family. New York–born Joseph Sclafani, for example, was refused membership in the Gambino family. He crossed the Hudson River to be made into the DeCavalcante family. The Gambino family did not recognize Sclafani as a made member. Since then, the four other New York families have also enforced the rule.

Sometimes, initiations are carried out in odd places. In January 1993 Michael Spinelli was inducted into the Lucchese family while being detained at the Metropolitan Correctional Center in Manhattan. The initiation took place in the bathroom, in the presence of Anthony Casso and Anthony Baratta, underboss of the Lucchese family. Instead of the usual accessories, Casso used toilet paper, which he set afire in Spinelli's hands. Spinelli's initiation came as a reward for attempting to kill Patricia Capozzalo, the sister of Peter Chiodo, a former *caporegime* in the Lucchese family, who became a government witness. Although Spinelli was officially recognized as a made member by the Lucchese family, members of other Cosa Nostra families who were being held at the detention centre allegedly refused to recognize him for a while because Spinelli's sponsor, *caporegime* Richard Pagliarulo, was not present at the initiation ceremony, as he was jailed in another wing of the detention centre.[54]

Antonino Calderone pointed out that in cases of emergency—where an initiation has to be held inside a penitentiary, for instance—the ceremony can be performed without the presence of a member of the family the novice is joining. But in any circumstance, the initiation should occur in the presence of three men of honour, even if they come from different families.[55]

In Chicago there are no formal induction ceremonies because Sicilian traditions are less prevalent there. When an Italian is made in the Chicago Outfit, he is simply given an handshake, and everyone goes to celebrate in a restaurant.[56]

The only Canadian initiation ceremony on record came to light with the discovery of a document found in August 1971 in the residence of Frank Caccamo, a ranking member of the 'Ndrangheta in Toronto. Police were searching Caccamo's residence for restricted guns, for which Caccamo had no registration. While police were carrying out the search, they found notepapers contained in a plastic slip in a kitchen cupboard. A forensic examination of the papers' contents revealed a recital of the rules, regulations and procedures of the 'Ndrangheta. The document, written in an ancient Italian dialect, explained how members are inducted into the *Onorata Societa* (Honored Society), what they must swear to, what rituals they must follow and what phrases they must answer with when asked specific questions.[57] It is assumed that members of the Sicilian Mafia operating in Canada, such as the Rizzuto and Caruana-Cuntrera crime families, are subject to similar initiation rites. However, no evidence has been found to confirm that these ceremonies are practised in Canada.

EFFECTS OF THE INITIATION ON A MADE MEMBER

"Getting made is the greatest thing that could ever happen to me. I been looking forward to this day ever since I was a kid," said Jilly Greca, an ecstatic new member of the Colombo family, after his initiation.[58] The moment the new member is initiated, his world changes. People around him treat him with deference. Nothing is done without his permission. When he arrives in public places, such as restaurants or bars, people will stand up, give him a chair, come up to him. A made member, whether he is liked or hated, gets respect, especially in his own neighbourhood, where he is seen as being above the ordinary person.[59] A made man sees himself as different from the citizens, those who are in no way connected with the underworld.[60]

Moreover, being made confers special status on the new member. It means formal acceptance by his peers—he has proven himself by his faithfulness to a code of "honourable" behaviour.[61] The new member is perceived by his confederates as someone who is "safe" to deal with, since he has been vouched for by his family. Indeed, the new soldier has nothing to fear from other criminals, as they will not try to steal from him or compete against him. He enjoys and relies on the protection of his crime family, which can through violence enforce and protect his criminal activities.[62] The neighbourhoods in which Cosa Nostra members reside or operate become free of crime. In return, the residents, whether by instinct or self-protection or fear of reprobation, report any stranger or suspicious car patrolling the streets.[63]

Induction into Cosa Nostra means a lifetime membership for the new inductee. Angelo De Carlo compared Cosa Nostra to the Free Mason organization: "Once a Mason, always a Mason. Same as this thing—Cosa Nostra. Once you're in this thing, you're always in it."[64] A member cannot leave the organization by simply submitting his resignation. When Frank Sindone, a Cosa Nostra soldier in the Bruno family, felt he had made enough money and wanted to quit the family, he was not allowed to start a new life.[65] Even if a member retires due to illness or other reasons, he is indebted to Cosa Nostra and is expected "to perform any action derived from his capacity as a 'man of honour,'" according to Tommaso Buscetta.[66] A long jail term does not cause a member to lose his status. Members can only be expelled from Cosa Nostra, either temporarily or permanently, if they violate the rules. But even someone who has been banned from Cosa Nostra is bound to observe the rules of the organization.[67]

As a trusted member of the organization, the made member has access to a great deal of privileged information shared by a network of people operating inside labour unions, political offices, businesses and, of course, the underworld.[68] His status draws new criminal partners who want to take advantage of his immense network of connections. The soldier is able to consolidate his position as a criminal entrepreneur, and hence is able to become a big earner for the family.[69] Everything is made easy for the Cosa Nostra member. He is able to borrow money at low interest rates, and is protected from police, violence and the intimidation of competitors.[70] Making money will often become his sole objective.[71] An "earner" is someone who has the skill to generate cash in different ways and from different sources. Earners are always welcome and admired. (Some associates are good earners too. Patrick Kelly, a successful businessman who worked with many organized-crime figures in New Jersey, would certainly have been made a member if he were of Italian descent. He had the respect of many Cosa Nostra members, and particularly of Dominick DiNorscio, a soldier in the Bruno family.[72])

There are considerable differences between the status and privileges enjoyed by a member and those of a family associate. The associate, although subject to all of the rules and obligations, has none of the privileges. Being formally inducted gives the soldier considerable influence and prestige. He has a rank, a status. He is respected. His words carry weight because he can rely on the use of violence to back them up. He has immediate access to the power base of his family and knows its intimate structure and operations. If a dispute arises between a made member and an associate, the member has a clear and overwhelming advantage. He can present and defend himself before the family, while an associate must be represented by an another member called a "rabbi." Even if the associate is a good earner and enjoys respect from others, he has no formal recognition because he has not taken the oath. He is not regarded as equal. He cannot go against a made member without the intervention of another family member.[73,74]

THE OPENING AND CLOSING OF
MEMBERSHIP IN COSA NOSTRA

When the Castellammarese Wars ended in 1931, with the Luciano-Genovese group emerging victorious, the families agreed to stabilize the number of their members. A family could not increase its membership at the expense of the other families without their consent and that of the Commission. This rule has been applied mostly to the New York area, as the five Cosa Nostra families located there must share a relatively small territory. Each family was allocated a territory and a number of soldiers.

From 1931 to 1954 the "books," as they are called, were closed. No new members could be admitted to Cosa Nostra. They were opened again from 1954 to 1957, apparently because it was feared that membership in Cosa Nostra might decline to such a point that it could come under threat from other, non-Italian organized groups. During this period, the Commission authorized the admission of several hundred new members, and Cosa Nostra began an active recruiting campaign.

Amazingly, Frank Scalice, the underboss of the Anastasia family, sold memberships into Cosa Nostra for $50,000. According to Valachi's testimony before the Senate Committee, it caused a great scandal when it was discovered that the proceeds of these sales were shared by boss Albert Anastasia.[75] The selling of memberships upset older members because it lowered the standards of admission in Cosa Nostra. It was also a violation of the rule concerning the period of probation a candidate must go through before being admitted into Cosa Nostra. At the Apalachin meeting, the leaders of the families decided to nullify the memberships of all who, according to Valachi, were declared "useless and unfit."[76]

The admission of a large number of new members unquestionably posed a security risk to Cosa Nostra. The books were closed once again in 1957 due to fears that informers working for police agencies could infiltrate the families, particularly when Attorney General Robert Kennedy declared war against union leaders and Cosa Nostra in the mid-1960s.[77] They were reopened in New York in June 1977, when the Commission allowed each of the five New York families to initiate ten new members.[78] Between 1957 and 1977 admissions to Cosa Nostra occurred only to fill a vacancy left by a death or retirement. Between 1977 and 2001 admissions were again allowed only to fill a vacancy.

In 2001 the FBI reported that the New York families, particularly the Genovese and the Lucchese families, were calling for new blood within their ranks. Plagued by a series of defections and successful police undercover operations, their memberships had declined over the years. According to police sources, the memberships of the five families dropped from 634 to 570 members in 2000 alone. An FBI agent who infiltrated the Genovese family has stated that the New York families agreed to reopen the books.[79]

THE TRANSFER OF MEMBERS
FROM ONE FAMILY TO ANOTHER

As a matter of loyalty, a Cosa Nostra member remains tied for his entire life to the family that admitted and initiated him. While he can easily switch to another *regime* within the family, transferring to another family is more difficult, as it requires the approval of both families.[80] However, a member may be authorized to operate within another family while his membership stays with his mother family. As Joseph Valachi explained, a member is entitled to move to another city where there is a Cosa Nostra family. But he needs a "letter of reference" from the family he belongs to.[81] When a transfer is approved, the member must submit himself to a period of probation with the new family.[82]

While transfers are not encouraged, because they make the resolution of conflicts or disputes more complicated, they are not uncommon. Joseph Valachi changed allegiance three times during his criminal career. He started with the Gaetano Reina family (which later became the Lucchese family), switched to the Maranzano family, and ended up with the Luciano-Genovese family until his defection in 1963. Aladena Fratianno and John Rosselli asked to be transferred from the Chicago family to the Los Angeles family. Rosselli later moved back to Chicago, as did Fratianno, but the latter apparently did so without telling the Los Angeles boss, Jack Dragna. It did not seem important to Fratianno since the Los Angeles family was under Chicago's jurisdiction.[83] When Joseph Colombo was appointed boss of the Profaci family in 1964, he asked permission from the Chicago family to take Joseph Campagna back to New York. Campagna had previously worked for the Colombos before working for the Chicago family for a number of years.[84]

Not all family bosses are open-minded about transfers. John Gotti, for example, was firmly opposed. Under Gotti's rules, a member of his crew could not even think of asking to be transferred to another regime. "You don't get released from my crew. You have lived with John Gotti and you will die with John Gotti," he once told an underling.[85]

An interesting case occurred in Sicily in the summer of 1962. A soldier in the Porta Nuova family had fallen in love with the daughter of a Mafia member from the Noce family. Her father, Calcedonio di Pisa, opposed the marriage. The young soldier, Rosario Anselmo, came to see Tommaso Buscetta, a member of that family, for advice. Buscetta told him to go ahead with his plans. Anselmo, now married, was entitled to be reassigned to the Noce family, which di Pisa opposed. Buscetta's interference had infuriated di Pisa, and he went to the Cupola to propose that relatives should always remain members of the same Mafia family and not be allowed to switch from one family to another. The Cupola ruled that di Pisa's proposal would be impractical and impossible to enforce.[86]

For family associates, transferring from one family to another always requires an authorization from the family with whom they are registered. Associates must be tied to a Cosa Nostra member if they want to do business. If an opportunity arises for an associate to do business with another member, he must be "released" by the first member before doing so. Salvatore Gravano was assigned to Frank Spero, a Colombo *caporegime*, for four years, and was "on the record" with the Colombos, meaning that he belonged to them. Following a dispute between Gravano and Spero's brother, a sit-down was held between representatives of the Colombo and Gambino families. Gravano asked for permission to transfer to Salvatore Aurello, a Gambino *caporegime*. His request was granted, and Gravano was released to the Gambinos.[87]

Chapter 4

The Code of Conduct

Criminologists and experts on organized crime believe that the American Cosa Nostra is merely a transplant from its Sicilian roots that has evolved in America. The first generation of Cosa Nostra members brought with them their cultural values, along with a mistrust of public authorities and strangers. These core values, which are the foundation of Cosa Nostra's code of conduct, have never changed. The code of conduct is based on three irrevocable values: secrecy, discipline and respect.

SECRECY

The rule of secrecy is a basic and essential requirement of all members of Cosa Nostra. Members are required not only to conceal their activities, but also to deny the very existence of Cosa Nostra, even to their relatives.[1] "This Thing [Cosa Nostra] cannot be exposed. [Not even to our] sons, or the wife, or the daughter, whoever, we gonna keep it to ourself. Never admit to it." This warning was repeated several times to a new inductee during the course of an initiation ceremony performed on October 29, 1989, by Raymond Patriarca Jr. and *consigliere* Joseph Russo.[2] Knowledge of Cosa Nostra makes members' families vulnerable and, in turn, makes the member himself vulnerable. By not telling his wife about Cosa Nostra, a member protects himself should his wife become estranged. Crime boss Vito Genovese and Michael Coppola, a *caporegime* who served under Genovese, both became embarrassed when their wives revealed their husbands' hidden interests in rackets during divorce proceedings.

Tommaso Buscetta, a former Sicilian Mafia member who defected in 1984, believed that secrecy, rather than violence, was the real power of Cosa Nostra. No one knows everything inside Cosa Nostra. Information is purposely fragmented. A boss can order a murder, but will never know who carries out the execution or how it was done unless it becomes public knowledge.[3] Knowledge is shared on a need-to-know basis. Members mind their own business. A man of honour talks only about things that concern him and will answer questions only if asked personally and specifically.[4] This is especially important when a member holds a position of command, since he could be connected to a large criminal network.

Like terrorist organizations, a Cosa Nostra family is broken down into cells, known as *regime* or crews. Members of a crew work together and rarely deal with members from other crews. FBI agent Joseph Pistone observed that, during his six years of work as an undercover agent, he knew people only by their nicknames.[5] The circulation of news is restricted to the essential facts, and there is certainty that the reported news is true: made members are obliged to tell the truth when speaking about Cosa Nostra.[6] Tommaso Buscetta stated that failure to tell the truth may carry the death penalty.[7] For the protection of members, Buscetta advises that when a member discusses Cosa Nostra with another member, he should do it in the presence of a third person who can confirm the facts. Should a member ask a question out of simple curiosity, he is looked upon with suspicion. Suspicion is the norm in the world of Cosa Nostra. Trust is the exception.

Secrecy should not be confused with omertà, the obligation of silence, which strictly prohibits members from any form of collaboration with the authorities or from seeking the assistance of police when they are the victims of a crime.[8] Tommaso Buscetta mentions an exception to the rule: if the car of a mafioso is stolen, he may report the theft to police— not necessarily to find the thieves, but only to prevent situations in which the police could link the owner of the car to a crime in which his vehicle was used.[9]

If a Cosa Nostra member is arrested by police, the entire family examines the possibility of an informant.[10] To avoid being considered an informant, a member intending to register a plea of guilty to a felony or racketeering charge must seek the authorization of his crime family. In 1989 Peter Chiodo, a former *caporegime* in the Lucchese family, pleaded guilty to racketeering charges without first getting permission from boss Vittorio Amuso, who came to suspect that Chiodo was co-operating with the government. After Chiodo survived a murder attempt, he became a government witness.[11]

Also in 1989, Thomas Spinelli, a soldier in the Gambino family, appeared before a grand jury that was investigating the killing of Paul Castellano. Spinelli was scheduled to testify again, and informed members of his *regime* that he was going to tell the truth because he did not want to face a perjury charge. Spinelli refused to meet with his *caporegime*, James Failla, who had no choice but to inform John Gotti about Spinelli's intentions. Not long after, Spinelli disappeared, and his body was never found.[12]

A true man of honour does not talk to authorities. In 1985 during the "Pizza Connection" trial, held in New York, one of the defendants, Gaetano Badalamenti, a former Sicilian Cosa Nostra member, was cross-examined by the prosecution on whether he was a member of the Sicilian Mafia. The old mafioso replied: "I have never said it, and if I were, I would not say it. I would respect my oath."[13] On his death bed, Joseph Ferraro, critically injured by gunshots after Antonio Lombardo, president of the *Unione Siciliana*, had been shot and killed in September 1928 in an ambush, refused to name his assailants when an Assistant State's Attorney questioned him at the hospital.[14]

Since the 1990s, however, many American and even Sicilian members of Cosa Nostra have admitted to their membership in the organization. This constitutes a serious breach of the rules that, surprisingly, has gone unpunished. (One reason for this is the efficiency of the Witness Security Program, which shelters adherents to the program from reprisals.) The first case was that of Salvatore Avellino, a former *caporegime* and chauffeur of Anthony Corallo, boss of the Lucchese family. In 1993 Avellino was brought up on racketeering charges involving the garbage business in Long Island. While testifying, he told a Federal Court that he had retired from Cosa Nostra. He admitted that he had been inducted into the organization in the 1970s. Avellino allegedly made this unusual admission in an effort to avoid a long imprisonment. He told the court he had been free to quit Cosa Nostra at any time.[15]

On September 24, 2001, Giuseppe "Pippo" Calò, a high-ranking member of the Sicilian Mafia, admitted the existence of Cosa Nostra and confessed his membership in the Cupola from 1979 to 1981. Calò made this stunning statement while he and other Mafia bosses were appealing, before an Italian court, a sixteen-year sentence for the killing of judge Paolo Borsellino in July 1992.[16]

In another case, Alphonse "Little Allie Boy" Persico, the son of Carmine Persico, boss of the Colombo family, pleaded guilty in December 2001 to a series of racketeering charges, and was sentenced to eighteen months in jail. The plea agreement included a statement of facts, in which Persico acknowledged that he was the "acting boss of the Colombo family." Previously, Anthony Trentacosta, a soldier in the Gambino family, had admitted at his racketeering trial in fall 2001 that he was a made member of the Gambino family. The admission was required by the prosecution to satisfy the conditions for a plea agreement. Trentacosta, who supervised criminal activities in southern Florida for the Gambino family, was charged in September 2000 with nine others in the murder of a stripper. Trentacosta's admission of membership became part of the evidence introduced by the prosecution.[17]

In August 2002 Vincent Gigante, the boss of the Genovese family, who was facing a trial for extortion and obstruction of justice by simulating mental illness, instructed his lawyers not to fight the government's contentions that the Genovese family is a criminal enterprise—but he would deny any role in criminal charges laid against him. The tactic was allegedly a move to prevent the government from providing evidence that proved the existence and criminal activities of the Genovese family over the last fifty years and to avoid conviction based on guilt by association.[18]

An unprecedented number of members, from soldiers to bosses, in almost every Cosa Nostra family have violated the code of secrecy in return for lighter sentences: Aladena Fratianno, the former acting boss of the Los Angeles family (1978); Angelo Lonardo, the former underboss of the Cleveland family (1983); Vincent Cafaro, a soldier in the Genovese family (1987); Alphonse D'Arco, the acting boss of the Lucchese family (1991); Salvatore Gravano, the former underboss of the Gambino family (1991); Ralph Natale, the former boss of the Philadelphia family (2001); Joseph Defede, the acting boss of the Lucchese family (2002); Salvatore Vitale, the underboss of the Bonanno family and brother-in-law of boss Joseph Massino (2003).

Many prominent American mafiosi have broken the rule of secrecy by writing their memoirs—although most did so once they became government informants or were retired. Among them were Vincent Teresa, a soldier in the Patriarca family, with My Life in the Mafia; Salvatore Luciano with The Last Testament of Lucky Luciano; Aladena Fratianno with The Last Mafioso; and Michael Franzese with Quitting the Mob.

However, the most prolific Mafia authors of all were certainly the members of the Joseph Bonanno family. In 1971 New York Times investigative reporter Gay Talese released Honor Thy Father, an account of the history of the Bonanno family based on interviews with former boss Joseph Bonanno's son, Salvatore. Not to be outdone, in 1983 Joseph Bonanno wrote his memoirs while in exile in Tucson, Arizona. A Man of Honor related the history of the American Cosa Nostra and, in particular, Bonanno's status as a member of the Commission. (Not long after the publication of the book, Rudolph Giuliani, then a United States Attorney in Manhattan, issued a subpoena for Joseph Bonanno to testify before a court in a racketeering case against reputed members of the Commission. Bonanno refused to appear and was charged with civil contempt. He was sentenced to, and served, fourteen months in jail.) In 1990 Rosalie Profaci, the wife of Salvatore Bonanno, released Mafia Marriage, an account of her difficult daily life as a wife and daughter-in-law in the Bonanno family. Finally, in 1999, Bound by Honor was published, a personal account of Salvatore's life and career in the Bonanno crime family.

DISCIPLINE

A Cosa Nostra member obeys orders given to him and does not ask questions. When taking the oath of allegiance to Cosa Nostra, new members are asked if they would be ready to kill their own sons or brothers should it be learned that they have become informants. "Would you do that without hesitation?" asked Joseph Russo of Richard Floramo and Carmen Tortora as they were inducted in the Patriarca family. Both replied that they would.[19]

Cosa Nostra's code of discipline is so strict that the rule of a boss could be equated with the rule of a dictator in any modern civilization. Members accept and accede to discipline and see it as crucial for the security of the organization.[20] As explained by sociologist Donald R. Cressey, totalitarian governments are supported and enforced through fear and harsh discipline. The rule of law in Cosa Nostra is applied, it can be argued, in a despotic way. In other words, the code of organized criminals, while protecting the members, is ultimately intended and enforced for the protection of the boss.[21] When a Cosa Nostra member infringes a rule, explained Tommaso Buscetta, he puts himself outside the established order. The rule is his only safeguard. Once outside it, he loses the protection it confers.[22]

Loyalty is paramount to the survival of an underground organization. Members put the interests of the organization before their own interests and those of their family. A true man of honour lives by the rules and, if necessary, will die for them. He is a "stand-up" man. He does not talk to police. He respects the families of others members. He has guts, he is true to the code.[23] Traditionally a Cosa Nostra member gains stature and respect by proving his loyalty to crime leaders. He will not hesitate, when ordered, to kill or intimidate people. The higher a member reaches in the upper echelons of the family, the greater his loyalty to the family.

Orders must be obeyed, of course. And they must be executed properly. But Cosa Nostra orders are given in vague terms so that the family boss, whatever happens, will always be right. A refusal to obey an order is regarded as an act of rebellion against the authority of the boss. The culprit is killed right away.[24]

However, for the last two decades, well-applied discipline has deteriorated in Cosa Nostra.[25] The breakdown may be explained by differences in perception and mentality between the older and the younger generations of Cosa Nostra members. This inevitably brings conflict and tensions. It is difficult to keep both older and younger generations at peace and on good terms. The youngsters are eager to take risks and act aggressively, while the elders are more inclined to adopt a conservative approach in dealing with crime business. Often, elders will perceive the young generation as defiant and less loyal. Such conflict led to violent clashes inside the Bruno-Scarfo family for several years after the murder of Angelo Bruno in March 1980.

As some crime families have declined and aged, new blood has been added in the form of younger members, some of whom may have been initiated too hurriedly. Francis Salemme, a former member of the Boston family, now a government witness, observed that the "admission standards for Cosa Nostra have dropped considerably since 1988."[26] Boss John Stanfa of the Philadelphia family believed that Cosa Nostra was deteriorating because too many "unqualified" men were admitted into the family.[27] The new generation of mafiosi has grown up with a different set of values from those of their elders, who, for the most part, were born in Sicily. They are attracted to easy and quick money and are more prone to violence. Honour and loyalty to the organization come second. They are also more inclined to run to law enforcement authorities when they get in trouble with their crime family for what may be a minor transgression of the code of conduct.[28]

The new generation of members—sometimes labelled the "Me" or the "Yuppie" generation—possessed a mentality that was in complete opposition to the moral values and qualities expected of a Mafia member: humility, obedience, respect and discipline. The youngsters adopted a high-profile lifestyle, displaying wealth and power and bragging about their performance in crimes. Many young members of Cosa Nostra ignored the decree to avoid dealing in narcotics such as heroin and cocaine, despite having sworn to the "no drug deal" when taking the oath of allegiance. And because these young entrepreneurs had access to huge amounts of drugs at wholesale prices, some of them became drug users themselves. Drug use has been another cause of the erosion of discipline in Cosa Nostra.[29]

The ascension of these young mafiosi to the top echelons caused friction and dissension in the family. They lacked the talent and ingenuity to run criminal activities or to oversee large-scale criminal operations without resorting to violence on an ongoing basis.[30] To a certain extent, it was an application of "The Peter Principle": Individuals moved too quickly into commanding positions for which they were not qualified.[31] Their inexperience made them more visible, and hence more vulnerable. One example is John Gotti Jr., who was appointed *caporegime* by his father when he was in his late twenties. He became acting boss after the imprisonment of his father in 1992. His quick rise caused a lot of discontentment among the elder *capiregime*, many of whom had been serving the Gambino family for decades. And he paid for his inexperience: on September 3, 1999, after pleading guilty to charges of racketeering and extortion, young Gotti, at age thirty-five, was sentenced to six years and five months.

Today's Cosa Nostra members are inclined to abide by rules only when it suits them. According to Joseph Armone, an eminent *caporegime* in the Gambino family, members are not true to any one philosophy: "They pick and choose among all different ones. They choose loyalty when it suits them. They choose independence when it suits them. They choose tradition when it suits them." Members change the rules when circumstances do not play in their favour.[32]

RESPECT

Respect and deference are important traits in Cosa Nostra members, especially towards older and ranking members. Respect is shown by gestures and attitude. Tone of voice changes when one is in the presence of a ranking member. Everyone stands up when a boss comes into the room. A seat is proffered. People open doors for and hold an umbrella over the boss, as Salvatore Gravano used to do for John Gotti when walking on New York sidewalks. Respect is, of course, not based solely on one's position within the family but also on seniority. Older soldiers are treated with consideration and are often consulted for their wisdom and experience. Respect and reverence are also extended to retired members.

Respect can be extended to several generations of a Cosa Nostra member's family. Respect will be given to a member's grandchildren, even if they have committed a serious blunder. Help will be provided to them.

However, Cosa Nostra members are responsible for their relatives' conduct and are encouraged to stay away from those who exhibit unpredictable behaviour.[33]

Paolo Violi, the underboss of the Montreal family, once stressed the importance of the aura of respect from low-ranking members. "If you are good, they will respect you. If you are bad, they will not respect you anymore," he said to Giuseppe Settecasi, a *capomafia* from the Agrigento province of Sicily, who was visiting members of the Montreal Cotroni-Violi organization in 1972.[34] The worst thing that can happen to a family boss or to a ranking member is to lose respect. It constitutes a threat to both his honour and his authority. If an insult or sign of disrespect is not immediately dealt with, the member will be perceived as weak by his peers, and his authority will diminish. Respect is generated by fear. When a member no longer inspires fear, not only has he lost authority, but his days may be numbered as well.

Outsiders who have connections to Cosa Nostra are also expected to show respect towards family bosses. Mike Coiro, a New York criminal lawyer who was having dinner with Jimmy Burke, a Lucchese family associate, apparently failed to stop at John Gotti's table. Gotti vehemently reproached Coiro for his lack of respect by threatening him. Coiro apologized.[35]

The new generation of recruits in Cosa Nostra seems to lack this notion of respect towards elders. A new recruit in the Lucchese family happened to venture into a gambling operation belonging to the Gambino family. A sit-down was called between the two families, and the matter was resolved smoothly. Anthony Corallo, then boss of the Lucchese family, summoned the young recruit to lecture him on the importance of protocols in Cosa Nostra. When Corallo had finished, the young recruit said to an appalled Corallo, "Yeah, whatever."[36]

There have been numerous incidents in which Cosa Nostra members have been disrespectful to a senior or ranking member. The most notorious is certainly that of Carmine Scialo, a soldier in the Colombo family who managed large gambling and loansharking operations on Coney Island. When under the influence of alcohol, Scialo would become very arrogant. One day in October 1974, Scialo was at a popular Italian eatery and spotted Carlo Gambino. Scialo started harassing Gambino, insulting him in front of the others. Gambino said nothing and stayed calm. Scialo's body was found not long after at Otto's Social Club in South Brooklyn, encased in the cement floor.[37] Gambino's quick response to this outrageous behaviour not only preserved his honour, but his credibility as well.

Respect of rank is strictly observed at the wedding receptions and funerals of Cosa Nostra members. When Salvatore Bonanno married Rosalie Profaci in August 1956, representatives of all twenty-four families of the American Cosa Nostra attended. The seating arrangement required a lot of tact and diplomacy so no one would be offended. Men close to the Bonanno family were seated near the dais, while others were seated according to their rank in the hierarchy of the Bonanno family.[38] Police often cover Mafia weddings or funerals to observe the respect given to ranking Cosa Nostra members by their underlings. These "marks of attention" sometimes allow police to assess how far a Cosa Nostra member has recently risen within the family's hierarchy.[39] At the funeral of Carlo Gambino, all the *capiregime* of the Gambino family paid their respects to Paul Castellano, Gambino's successor.

In December 1985 Paul Castellano offended many of his peers by choosing not to attend the funeral of his underboss, Aniello Dellacroce, who had died of cancer. Castellano's absence was perceived as a gross violation of protocol, as Dellacroce enjoyed a great deal of respect among the New York Cosa Nostra families. Castellano defended his absence on the grounds that he feared his presence at the funeral could bring him negative publicity prior to his upcoming racketeering trial for his alleged involvement in an auto theft ring.

THE FUNCTION OF THE CODE

Several studies by Sicilian sociologists and police officers have discussed the function of the Mafia's code of conduct. One description, provided by Giuseppe Alongi, says the code ensures:

1. Absolute obedience to the chief.
2. Reciprocal aid in case of any need whatever.

3. An offence received by one of the members will be considered an offence against all and avenged at any cost.
4. No appeal to the state's authorities for justice.
5. No revelation of the names of members or any secrets of the association.[40]

Antonino Cutrera breaks down the code's functions as:

1. To help one another and avenge every injury of a fellow member.
2. To work with all means for the defence and freeing of any fellow member who has fallen into the hands of the judiciary.
3. To divide the proceeds of thievery, robbery and extortion with certain consideration for the needy as determined by the *capo*.
4. To keep the oath and maintain secrecy on pain of death within twenty-four hours.[41]

Both descriptions stress the necessity of protecting the identity of members, providing assistance to members who are imprisoned or in difficulty, and never appealing for help to authorities. In addition, Cutrera states that the proceeds of crime must be shared among members. These essential characteristics can be found in both the Sicilian and the American Cosa Nostra.

As explained by sociologist Francis Ianni, who studied the function of the code of conduct within the Luppolo family (a fictional name), criminal organizations, like legitimate organizations, require a code of rules that regulates relationships between the network and the outside world. The code keeps the network functioning, defines relationships within it and establishes who is inside and who is outside the network. The code sets out what is "good" and what is "bad," what behaviours are appropriate, or not.[42] In his study, Ianni uncovered three basic rules: a) primary loyalty is vested in the family rather than in the individual; b) each member of the family must act like a man and do nothing to bring disgrace on the family; and c) family business is a privileged matter and must not be reported or discussed outside the group. Ianni compared these rules with those of prison gangs, which place more importance on individual qualities: an individual must not act cowardly, nor be disloyal to his gang, nor be a "creep." The prison gangs' rules stress that the criminal activities of the group must be kept secret, a member must never cheat another member and, finally, a member must exhibit a certain competence in his criminal speciality, whatever it may be.[43]

THE CODE OF CONDUCT IN PRISON

When members of criminal organizations are incarcerated, they adhere to a set of rules that regulate interaction with fellow inmates. In general, members of Cosa Nostra serving time are regarded as model prisoners by prison authorities. They comply with prison regulations and do their time without causing any problems. As inmates, Cosa Nostra members conform to five cardinal rules: display manhood by being tough; do not interfere with inmate interests; do not engage in arguments with fellow prisoners; do not exploit inmates by selling favours or stealing; do not collaborate or show complacence with prison authorities. These rules were set up by prisoners for the group. They were made for the purpose of showing prison authorities that their conduct is regulated by their own set of rules, not the prison's.[44]

In many regards, Cosa Nostra members serving prison terms have a lot of prestige and influence over the other inmates. They also enjoy privileges that other prisoners cannot afford. For instance, Salvatore Luciano, while serving a long prison sentence in the late 1930s at New York State's Dannemora penitentiary, had absolute authority because of his high status in Cosa Nostra. He was also given preferential treatment by the prison staff. He was given the privilege of having a small electric stove in his cell. He even had a canary as a pet. Luciano would hold court in his cell or in the courtyard surrounded by inmates serving as bodyguards.

Other Mafia inmates, such as Carmine Galante and Sam Giancana, imposed strict discipline and order in the wings where they were assigned. Their fellow inmates were told to keep their cells clean and to lower noise at night. The Lewisburg Penitentiary was even known as the "Mafia school," where influential Cosa Nostra inmates taught future Cosa Nostra members. A large section of the penitentiary was unofficially ruled by Mafia inmates, who had made arrangements with prison officials to keep the institution free from disorder.[45]

THE USE OF VIOLENCE
TO ENFORCE THE CODE OF CONDUCT

Legitimate and democratically elected governments hold power through the consent of the governed. In return, these governments have the duty to preserve peace and social order through the use of sanctions such as the death penalty or imprisonment. Since Cosa Nostra functions in the underworld, it cannot use legitimate means to enforce its code of conduct. Cosa Nostra has its own system of sanctions used against members who walk outside the line.[46] Its continuity and cohesion are guaranteed by "enforcers," who maintain social order among the members and ensure that rules are obeyed.[47]

Cosa Nostra is not only a criminal organization, but a violent organization whose members are willing to use violence to reach their goals. Its members operate on the basis of fear and terror. Fear is the primary tool. Murder, or threat of bodily harm, are accessories. A crime leader must not only assert his authority over the group, but must make sure his authority is accepted by everyone. In many cases, violence is not necessary; the boss's ability to instil fear, combined with his willingness to order acts of violence, is much more effective than the enforcer's muscles.

The Rational Use of Violence

Violence is not the raison d'être of organized-crime groups; it is a by-product.[48] It is exercised to reach precise objectives: to sanction a violation of a rule and, at the same time, to convey a clear message to everyone concerned that rules must be obeyed. Violence, or the threat thereof, is used to preserve the organization's security, to maintain discipline over members, to eliminate growing competitive criminal enterprises and to protect the boss from plots to overthrow him.

Violence is applied according to strict rules. For instance, violence against a family member or associate must first be authorized by the family boss. When it is planned against a Cosa Nostra member belonging to another family, permission from the boss of that family is required as well; otherwise, the violence would be considered an act of war.

In theory, the use of violence within a structured and a disciplined criminal organization is never spontaneous. It is always planned for a specific reason. The late Sicilian judge Giovanni Falcone explained that Cosa Nostra uses violence as the ultimate solution only after all other means—warnings, intimidation, threats—have failed. The manner in which the violence is applied has no importance. Cosa Nostra will choose the easiest and fastest way to reach its goal.[49] But violence must be rational and carefully applied. When violence becomes systematic, non-functional and random, it creates a state of instability and will not accomplish its ends.

Mobsters sometimes exhibit inexplicable, irrational behaviour. Frank Manzo, a *caporegime* in the Lucchese family, was having lunch with Leonard Orena, son of Colombo boss Victor Orena. Manzo felt compelled to tell Leonard that his father was "a piece of shit." Enraged, the young Orena broke a bottle of ketchup over Manzo's head and quickly left the premises. Manzo called on a friend to help him track down Orena. They finally spotted him driving on a highway. When their car reached Orena's, Manzo fired several shots at him but missed. This incident, which could have triggered a war between the Colombo and Lucchese families, was finally resolved after several heated sit-downs between the two families. Meanwhile, Manzo fled New York and remained in hiding in Europe for two years. He was later ordered to pay a substantial compensation to Orena.[50]

In June 1963 Nicodemo Scarfo got into an argument with an Irish longshoreman over a table in a restaurant that both men wanted. Scarfo, at the time a soldier in the Philadelphia family, stabbed the man to death. He was, of course, arrested and was charged with involuntary manslaughter.[51] Angelo Bruno, who was very annoyed by this incident, ordered Scarfo, after his release from jail, to leave the city forever. Scarfo was forced into exile in Atlantic City, known at that time as the "Siberia of the underworld."[52] After Bruno's death in March 1980, Scarfo took command of the Philadelphia family. Scarfo's reign was an unstable one, and very short. He spent half his time in jail and the other half defending himself against indictments. He used violence to compensate for his lack of respect and prestige. Scarfo's decisions were irrational and paranoid. He surrounded himself with young and inexperienced members whom he promoted for their loyalty rather than their skills. He ordered the murders of several members whom he believed posed a threat to his leadership.[53]

The indiscriminate use of violence can be a double-edged sword. Violence is used not only by the leaders but also by subordinates, especially when a crime boss becomes a despot. Several notorious crime leaders have been overthrown and executed for their tyranny. Think of Giuseppe Masseria and Salvatore Maranzano, both executed in 1931.[54]

The Use of Violence Towards Outsiders

On occasion, psychotic individuals put the organization's security at risk. The history of the underworld is rife with psychopathic killers who lost control. Psychopaths are the most dangerous individuals, as they have no fear of death or physical violence against themselves.

Vincent "Mad Dog" Coll was one such psychopath. Of Irish descent, Coll was born in 1909 in the Hell's Kitchen district of New York City. He was proud of his nickname because it reflected his disregard for human life. In 1931, in the midst of the Castellammarese Wars, Salvatore Maranzano gave Coll a $25,000 contract to kill Salvatore Luciano at Maranzano's office, where Maranzano had called Luciano for a meeting. Luciano got a tip that the meeting was a set-up and moved quickly to have Maranzano killed by gunmen posing as police officers. Because of his unpredictable behaviour, Coll was seen as a danger to the underworld and was murdered in February 1932 by the New York syndicate.[55]

Like Coll, Dutch Schultz became a danger to the underworld. Born in 1902 in the Bronx, Schultz built a crime empire in Harlem. In 1935 Thomas Dewey, the District Attorney of New York City, began a war on vice and racketeers. One of his targets was Schultz, who got pinched for undeclared income taxes. Schultz tried to persuade the national crime syndicate board to murder Dewey. His proposition was rejected right away because the members of the syndicate were concerned about repercussions and the public uproar Dewey's killing would generate. But Schultz adamantly persisted in his desire to kill Dewey. As he was not receiving any support from his peers, he announced that he would do it himself. Before he could go any further with his plan, Schultz was murdered, in October 1935.[56]

The threat or the use of violence is limited only to individuals who have interactions with the underworld. In principle, it should not be directed to ordinary citizens. However, in 2002, Louis Daidone, the acting boss of the Lucchese family, disregarded the rule when he instructed a *caporegime* to send a soldier to request that the landlord of a Brooklyn apartment stop a tenant from playing loud music that was annoying a neighbour who was a close friend of Daidone. Despite several warnings from the Lucchese soldier, the noise persisted. The landlord was finally assaulted and severely struck in the face. Daidone and other members of the Lucchese family were charged accordingly. In this case, Daidone, in his capacity as the leader of a Cosa Nostra family, should not have used his influence and power to inflict bodily harm on someone who had nothing to do with organized crime.[57]

Chapter 5

Rules of Conduct

More than any other criminal organization, Cosa Nostra functions under a formal set of strict rules that regulate not only the conduct of its criminal operations but, more importantly, the conduct of its members among themselves, with their associates and with "outsiders." As Cosa Nostra families operate within a structure with members holding ranking position, the rules become imperative to enforce discipline, respect and loyalty among members. The rules are intended to maintain peace, stability and economic order among families. In that regard, breaking the security of the organization, seducing the wife of a member or cheating on the sharing of proceeds of crime are serious breaches that are inexorably punished by death.

RULES FOR MEMBERS OF COSA NOSTRA

Rules of Introduction

It is imperative for Cosa Nostra to protect itself against any intrusion from or infiltration by gang rivals or police. Rules of introduction are meant to prevent such infiltration. One of the most important rules explained to new members when they join Cosa Nostra deals with how introductions are carried out between made members, and between made members and outsiders.

It is strictly forbidden for a Cosa Nostra member to introduce himself to another member. The introduction must be done through a third party who is also a made member. Joseph Russo, the *consigliere* in the

Patriarca family, explained to a new inductee during an initiation cere-mony: "You never, never introduce yourself, under no conditions. The only way you can meet another friend of ours is through another friend. This is a basic rule, it should never be broken. If it is broken, it is punish-able by death."[1] Even two Cosa Nostra members who know by reputation that they are both made cannot introduce themselves. They have to be introduced as "friends of ours" by a third party.[2]

For example, Joe, who is a made member, wants to be introduced to Carlo, another Cosa Nostra member. Joe cannot present himself directly to Carlo. The introduction must be done through another made mem-ber, say Alfonso, who already knows Joe and/or Carlo. Alfonso will say, "Joe, this is Carlo, a friend of ours" or "*amico nos*." By saying "friend of ours," Alfonso is indicating that Carlo is a Cosa Nostra member, that he is "one of us," that he can be trusted when talking about Cosa Nostra business. If Carlo had not been a member of Cosa Nostra, Alfonso would have said, "I introduce to you Carlo, a friend of mine." In that context, Joe would have understood that Carlo is not a Cosa Nostra member, but a personal friend to Alfonso. Consequently, Joe and Alfonso cannot—and will never—talk about Cosa Nostra business in Carlo's presence.

The same rule applies within the Sicilian Mafia, as Tommaso Buscetta explained when he testified in New York City at the "Pizza Connection" trial in October 1985. "If I were to meet some of their members—in Palermo—I needed an introduction by somebody else. I could not intro-duce myself by myself to these people."[3]

The rule of introduction is strictly applied. Say two members who do not know each other are in a heated discussion about a racketeering activity. One of them, to intimidate the other, tells him that he is a mem-ber of Cosa Nostra. By saying this, he has transgressed the rule of secrecy. Both members should have reported to their respective *capiregime* to resolve the problem. Under no circumstances can they reveal their membership in Cosa Nostra if they have not been properly introduced.[4] If a member is determined to have caused a security risk by breaking this rule, he can be killed.

The Rule of Summoning

The second rule a Cosa Nostra member must abide by is the obligation to come forward, at any time of the day or night, when summoned by a hierarchical superior. The member is expected to put the organization ahead of himself and his family. The rule is explained at length to new inductees before the initiation ceremony starts. The prospective candidate is asked if he would leave his dying mother to meet his superior in a matter of emergency. Of course, the inductee replies that he would.[5]

The rule of summoning can be very constraining to Cosa Nostra members, especially when the order comes from the family boss or from the Commission. Joseph Zicarelli, a soldier in the Bonanno family operating in New Jersey, once told Sam DeCavalcante, alluding to Joseph Bonanno's refusal to comply with the Commission's order to appear, "You're my boss. You say, 'Come in.' Where is my right? I don't have no rights!" Zicarelli was saying that, whatever the rank a member holds in Cosa Nostra, he has no excuse for refusing his boss when he is summoned.[6] Larry Zannino, a *caporegime* in the Patriarca family in the 1960s, was at his daughter's funeral when he responded to a call from his boss, Gennaro Anguilo, to settle a dispute between Boston and Somerville mobsters over a question of gambling and loansharking territory. Zannino put "The Thing" first, ahead of his personal family's affairs.[7]

The failure to obey a summons carries the death penalty. In 1957, after an attempted assassination of Frank Costello failed, Vito Genovese, fearing retaliation, took refuge in his home in Atlantic Highlands, New Jersey, and summoned all his *capiregime* for a show of loyalty. Only one failed to show up—Anthony Carfano. He was found shot dead in his car in September 1959. On December 12, 1989, John Gotti lamented to his underboss, Frank Locascio, "He's gonna die because he refused to come in when I called." He made this comment about Louie DiBono, a family soldier who refused to obey Gotti's order to meet to resolve a dispute between DiBono and Salvatore Gravano.[8] DiBono's body was found in October 1990.

It is a breach of protocol for a *caporegime* to send for another *caporegime* through a non–Cosa Nostra member. The order must be carried out by a member. Mike Sabella, a *caporegime* in the Bonanno family, violated this rule by sending an associate to set up an appointment with Frank Majuri, a *caporegime* in the Sam DeCavalcante family. DeCavalcante instructed Majuri to advise the messenger that he was not competent to deliver the message.[9] In another rule of protocol, when a soldier is summoned directly by the family boss, he is exempted from checking in with his *caporegime*; the summons may mean that the *caporegime* is slated to be killed.[10]

In several instances, obeying the rule of summoning has been costly for Cosa Nostra members who were called for a meeting but instead were set up to be killed. Anthony Strollo, a *caporegime* in the Genovese family, told his wife in April 1962 that he was going out to buy cigarettes. He was never seen again.[11] Dominick Napolitano, a prominent *caporegime* in the Bonanno family, was summoned to a meeting in August 1981. His body was found a few weeks later. Strollo and Napolitano may have known why they were being summoned. They probably knew that their fate was sealed; despite that, they felt they had to abide by the rule: they came forward when asked by their superior.

In September 1986 several members of the DeCavalcante family were charged and convicted on a 117-count federal indictment and sent to jail. One of them, Gaetano Vastola, a soldier in the family, remained free on the street for over a year despite being sentenced on two counts for twenty years each. This lenient treatment led members of the DeCavalcante family to believe that Vastola may have been co-operating with police. Vastola was ordered by his *caporegime* to come in, but he refused to comply. The same order was given to Danny Annunziata, a family soldier and the brother-in-law of Vastola, who also refused to come forward. It was then decided that Vastola had to be killed. The murder contract was given to the John Gotti family. Vastola was warned by the FBI of the plot to kill him. In 1992 Gotti was charged with conspiring to murder Vastola and was found guilty.

An interesting case occurred in Montreal in the early 1970s within the *decina* led by Vincenzo Cotroni, a member of the Calabrese Mafia, whose family answered to the Bonanno family. Nicolo Rizzuto was born in 1924 in the province of Agrigento, Sicily, arrived in Canada in 1954 and joined the Cotroni crime family. Over the years, Rizzuto greatly annoyed Cotroni and his underboss, Paolo Violi, by not bothering to inform them of his whereabouts. Rizzuto often travelled to Sicily and to Caracas, Venezuela, where he met with members of the Caruana and Cuntrera crime family, who had settled there.[12] The Caruana and Cuntrera was a powerful Sicilian Mafia group that originated in Agrigento. Cotroni and Violi tried many times, with no success, to get in touch with Rizzuto so that he could tell them what he was doing. Both complained to the administration of the Bonanno family and requested that Rizzuto be expelled from the Montreal faction. Rizzuto was of the opinion that, as a Sicilian, he did not have to report to Cotroni when doing business in Sicily. But by refusing to come forward, Rizzuto had deeply embarrassed Cotroni and had put him in a difficult situation. Emissaries from the Sicilian Mafia and the Bonanno family were sent to Montreal to resolve the conflict. Following a sit-down, the Bonanno family decreed that Rizzuto would not be expelled from the Montreal family.

Doing Business

In his autobiography, former Cosa Nostra boss Joseph Bonanno explained that a soldier must get permission from his *caporegime* or his boss to do business, whether legal or illegal, with a member of another Cosa Nostra family.[13] On the other hand, a soldier does not need approval to conduct business with a non-member, although the *caporegime* must still be informed. *Capiregime* themselves are subject to the rule: they must seek permission from the boss for all business deals. It was probably for breaking this rule that Robert DiBernardo, a *caporegime* in the Gambino family, was killed when it came to the ears of his boss, John Gotti, that he had allegedly made secret partnerships with members of the Genovese faction in New Jersey.[14]

When a Cosa Nostra member dies or is imprisoned for a long time, the family divides his business interests. Whether a business is a racket or legitimate, ownership generally remains with the partners. If there are no partners, the family redistributes the ownership. In the case of legitimate businesses, ownership is retained by the member's relatives. When a member is released from jail, the crime family is expected to return the business interests to the member, as the family has the duty to take care of the member's relatives.[15]

Sharing the Proceeds of Crime

The practice of sharing the proceeds of crime is not new. The idea was prevalent in secret societies active in Sicily at the end of the nineteenth century. The *Stoppaglieri* of Monreale, an organization with 150 members, was committed to distributing among its members the proceeds of ransoms, extortions, robberies and other crimes and to helping members who had been arrested by securing witnesses for their defence. Members in especially difficult circumstances would receive special care.[16] The same policies prevailed with the *Fratellanza* (Brotherhood) of Agrigento, whose members pledged to help each other and to co-operate in criminal activities.[17]

In the Hells Angels, each member of a chapter works for himself and can engage in any type of criminal activity on his own without asking permission. Cosa Nostra members and their associates, by contrast, are required to share the proceeds of crime with the upper echelons of the family. By sharing his criminal gains, the soldier is paying a "tribute" to his *caporegime* for the privilege of "full protection." Soldiers must pay a tribute not only when a criminal deed is done on his own family's territory, but also when the action occurs in another family territory, paying tributes to both families.[18]

At the initiation ceremony, the rule is explained at length to future members. Raymond Patriarca Jr. told a newcomer, "Actually, all business deals, legal or illegal, should be brought to the table." Patriarca further stressed the importance of bringing mutual aid and assistance to members when doing business: "If I'm in the garbage business and you own a dump, before you go to BFI [Browning Ferris Industry—a legitimate business] and go do business with them, if you know anybody at this table can aid you in a business, legitimate or illegitimate, your obligation is to come to us first."[19]

In the early 1980s, four of the five Cosa Nostra families of New York City reached an agreement on the sharing of the proceeds of high-level criminal operations. During a construction boom in the city, the Italian crime groups took control of the Concrete Workers Union, allowing Cosa Nostra families to create a "club of six"—the six major concrete contracting firms were the only ones who could bid on major projects. From that point on, the families exacted a "tax" of one percent of the total contract, plus two dollars for every cubic yard of concrete poured. This tax brought enormous profits to the New York families.[20] Only the Bonanno family was not invited to share in the profit, as it was temporarily expelled from the Commission for dealing in narcotics.

Cosa Nostra members are only human. They do not always declare all of their income to their *caporegime*, just as some citizens do not report all of their income to the Internal Revenue Service (IRS). However, the practice of skimming monies has proven fatal to many Cosa Nostra members, even for insignificant amounts. Such treachery is without exception punished by violent death as a clear message to anyone who might be tempted to do the same.[21] Underworld history furnishes many examples of Mafia members who have been killed because they kept for themselves the proceeds of crime or gave false figures on their earnings.

The case of Sicilian brothers Salvatore and Matteo Sollena is an example. The Sollenas had been smuggled into the United States by the Gambino family, and operated pizza parlours in Atlantic City for Rosario and Giuseppe Gambino. The Sollenas had a direct connection with drug laboratories in Palermo and Milan and controlled shipments of heroin to Philadelphia and southern New Jersey. Atlantic City was, at that time, under Scarfo's control, but the Gambino brothers were authorized to sell drugs there.[22] According to police, the Sollena brothers ran afoul of the Scarfo family over dealing drugs and holding onto the proceeds. They were found brutally murdered in November 1983.

Another example is that of Michael Pappadio, a *caporegime* in the Lucchese family. When his boss, Vittorio Amuso, found out that Pappadio was hiding the proceeds from about fifty businesses related to the garment industry, he summoned Pappadio to a sit-down and stripped him of the garment industry business. Refusing to comply,

Pappadio carried on his activities. A few weeks later, on May 13, 1989, Pappadio was lured to a meeting in a bakery in Queens, where he was shot several times and killed.[23]

In June 1989, Vincent Craparotta, a New Jersey contractor, was bludgeoned to death with golf clubs. Craparotta was in charge of the expansion of gambling activities in southern New Jersey for Michael Taccetta, a powerful New Jersey–based *caporegime* in the Lucchese family. In 1993, at Taccetta's trial for his role in Craparotta's murder, it was confirmed that the motive for Craparotta's execution was that he failed to share with the Lucchese family his earnings from lucrative videogame operations and other businesses.

Competition Against Other Members

A Cosa Nostra member is prohibited from interfering with the business of another member and must refrain from engaging in unfair competition. This is to prevent territorial disputes or, worse, deadly clashes. Cosa Nostra members are allowed to start or expand an illegal business, but not by stealing the agents or customers of a Cosa Nostra member or associate.[24] Vincent Amarante, a soldier in the Bonanno family, was forced to close down two "numbers banks" (illegal lotteries) in the early 1990s, following a sit-down with the Gambino family. The gambling centres were too close to an existing gambling operation run by Bartholomew Borriello, a soldier in the Gambino family.[25] Members from several families operating in the same area are expected to observe protocols to avoid disruptive competitive activities. They are encouraged to carry out mutual favours or form partnerships.[26] Such agreements or arbitration among Cosa Nostra families are ratified by the Commission.

Soldiers can have an interest in more than one business, legitimate or illegitimate—whether it be clubs, restaurants, dice games, usury operations or lottery or bet-taking establishments.[27] As is often the case in the legitimate business world, patronage and support are expected from friends and members of a family. Bonanno stated that, when doing business, the main objective for a crime family is to achieve monopolies. If a member of a family owns a bakery, everyone is expected to encourage him. If two members of the same family own bakeries within the same block, one of them will have to move to avoid competing against the other.[28]

If a Cosa Nostra soldier catches wind of a "big score"—say he hears of an opportunity to perform a jewellery heist in a warehouse—before going any further he must get permission from his *caporegime*. The *caporegime* will make sure that no other Cosa Nostra member—from that family or another one—is on the same job.[29] From the moment a Cosa Nostra member receives the green light from his *caporegime* to start a crime venture, no other members can muscle in. Doing so would be considered stealing the member's earnings. A Cosa Nostra member has an advantage that independent criminals do not: the protection of his family ensures that no member or outsider will interfere with his business.

Competition may be harsh and an activity difficult to sustain, particularly when the competition comes from rival crime groups. Underworld members all know that it is not "honourable" to report the criminal activities of a competing crime group or enemy to the police. Still, tipping the police on an enemy's criminal activities can reduce the "heat" from police, especially if they are focusing on a single crime group or activity. But it can also backfire, as in the case of the late Richard Wiseman of Montreal, an independent criminal whose operations were protected by Paolo Violi, at the time the boss of the Montreal Mafia. The owner of seventeen prostitution/massage parlours, Wiseman wanted to control all the parlours in Montreal, a multi-million-dollar business. Wiseman had been the target of a series of police raids when, in 1976, he decided to offer a police officer of the Montreal Urban Community Police Department $2,000 a week to "close his eyes" to Wiseman's prostitution ring. With the authorization of his superiors, the police officer played the game and accepted payments. Wiseman also gave the officer a list of nine competing studios that he wished the police to raid. Wiseman was subsequently arrested for bribery.[30]

Stealing from or Cheating Other Members

Another cardinal rule, which carries the death penalty if violated, states that a Cosa Nostra member is forbidden from stealing or cheating another Cosa Nostra member. The same rule prevails in Sicily.[31]

Kidnappings

United States

Cosa Nostra rules forbid its members to kidnap other members for extortion purposes. The rule, which originated in Sicily, was instituted to prevent bloody wars between families. However, Cosa Nostra members have often been kidnapped by rival gangs. During the mid-1960s, a series of kidnappings of Cosa Nostra members was carried out by a New York–based gang called Kidnap Inc. The gang, made up of Black Muslims and Puerto Rican racketeers, had first kidnapped street drug dealers. Stimulated by their repeated success, they decided to go after bigger fish—members of Cosa Nostra. The victims were chosen from the Gambino and Lucchese families. Several *capiregime* were kidnapped and released after they paid a ransom. The victims kept their misadventure secret. They were afraid to tell their bosses how much money they had paid for their release, lest the bosses learn they were hiding undeclared money. Moreover, most of the kidnapped *capiregime* were involved in drug trafficking, a secret sideline they did not want their bosses to learn about.[32]

The reason behind these kidnappings was allegedly to force Cosa Nostra to give black gangsters a larger share in the numbers rackets and allow them to start and run their own operations.[33] They also wanted to share profits from the sale of narcotics. The kidnappers seemed to be well informed about when Cosa Nostra members were involved in an important drug deal. Enraged by these kidnappings, the New York Cosa Nostra families posted a $50,000 reward to anyone who could lead them to those responsible. In 1968 two black drug dealers associated with Cosa Nostra were found murdered.[34]

Mickey Spillane [no relation to the famous author of the same name], a member of the Hell's Kitchen gang in West Manhattan, always thought that the extortion of choice was kidnapping wealthy businessmen, especially underworld members.[35] Probably inspired by the Kidnap Inc. gang, Spillane began to kidnap members of Cosa Nostra. One of them was Eli Zicardi, a soldier in the Genovese family who ran bookmaking operations for Anthony Salerno, a *caporegime* in the Genovese family. A ransom of $100,000 was paid for his release, but Zicardi was never seen alive afterwards.[36]

James McBratney, a large and ruddy Irishman, was also fond of kidnapping. He successfully kidnapped a Staten Island loan shark and got a $21,000 ransom for his release. In the early 1970s, he kidnapped the nephew of Cosa Nostra boss Carlo Gambino. McBratney had no idea that the abduction of Emmanuel Gambino would seal his fate. Negotiations went on for several months, and a $100,000 ransom was agreed on for the nephew's release. It is not clear whether the ransom was ever paid. But in January 1973 the family recovered the body of Emmanuel. McBratney did not live long afterwards. The prime suspect in his murder was John Gotti. For his work, Gotti was invited to join the Gambino family as a soldier. In 1975 Gotti was sentenced to four years for the McBratney murder. When Gotti become boss of the Gambino family several years later, he is alleged to have said that he did not want anyone to hang around with kidnappers. "I already killed a kidnapper," Gotti said, "and I don't want you around them."[37]

The most sensational kidnappings ever staged by Cosa Nostra occurred in the mid-1960s, when a faction rebelled against boss Joseph Profaci. Profaci was an old, conservative Mafia boss who ruled his family with ironclad discipline. Moreover, he failed to give rewards and incentives to his soldiers. This, among other resentments, was the cause of the insurrection led by the Gallo brothers—Larry, Joseph and Albert. It all started in November 1959, when Profaci ordered the murder of Frank Abbatemarco, who had failed to pay a "street tax" levied by Profaci. The contract was passed to the Gallo crew on the agreement that Profaci would turn over Abbatemarco's rackets to them. After the killing, the Gallos expected their due, but Profaci reneged on his promise. Anger and resentment grew within the Gallo faction. On February 27, 1961, in a well-planned scheme, four high-ranking members of the Profaci family were kidnapped. Profaci was himself a target, but managed to escape at the last minute. The hostages were underboss Joseph Magliocco; *capo-regime* Salvatore Mussachio; Frank Profaci, the boss's brother; and John Scimone, a chauffeur and bodyguard.

Caught by surprise and unable to reach a peaceful solution, Profaci requested the Commission's intervention. Although he sat on the Commission, Profaci was not allowed to voice his opinion other than as an injured party. The Commission ordered Joey Gallo to free the hostages. In return, the Commission would hear the Gallos' demands. After hearing both sides, the Commission ordered the parties to enter into negotiations. The Patriarca family was mandated to act as mediator and appointed the family underboss, Henry Tameleo, to that role. Ultimately, the Commission ordered the Gallo crew dismantled. The books were opened to allow the Genovese family to admit members from that crew.[38]

Sicily

Kidnapping has long been practised in Sicily. Cosa Nostra viewed this activity as less repugnant than prostitution. Kidnappings were practised for a sole purpose—to raise money for cigarette smuggling and drug trafficking, as the logistics of these activities were costly.[39] However, in 1974 the Cupola banned the kidnapping of wealthy persons in Sicily because it brought too much attention from the police and raised public disdain. Kidnappings were still permitted elsewhere in Italy, particularly in the north. The Cupola's edict was aimed at the Corleonesi clan, whose kidnappings had put Cosa Nostra's security at stake. The rule carried the death penalty for transgressors.[40]

Antonino Calderone, a former member of the Catania Mafia, said that in 1976 he heard that Michele Greco, a high-ranking Mafia member, had ordered the deaths of the people responsible for the abduction of a woman, even though she was released. Greco wanted to send a clear message to everyone concerned that the no-kidnapping rule would be enforced in Sicily.[41]

However, the rule has often been violated by high-ranking members of Cosa Nostra, especially by the Corleonesi clan, headed by Luciano Liggio (also spelled Leggio). In one particular instance, Liggio kidnapped and murdered the father-in-law of a powerful financier who was under the protection of Stefano Bontate, a Liggio rival. Salvatore "Toto" Riina, another former boss of the Corleonesi, ordered the kidnappings of several Palermitan businessmen. According to Antonino Calderone, these kidnappings were done solely for monetary purposes.[42]

Conduct

Hitting Another Member

When Salvatore Maranzano gained control of the New York Mafia in 1930, he clearly stated that under no circumstances was a Cosa Nostra member justified in hitting another member. Maranzano insisted that when a conflict arose between two members, they should seek advice from their *capiregime*. The purpose of this rule is to avoid endless vendettas among members of the same family or different families.[43]

Members are required to stay cool and behave properly under any circumstances, even when under pressure. A man of honour who slaps another member displays a loss of self-control.[44] Hitting a member is an issue that must not stay unresolved. According to Ralph Salerno, a former police officer in the New York City Police Department, when a made member is hit or slapped, he is put in a situation in which he has a moral obligation to restore his honour. He may ask for and obtain permission to kill the person who dared to raise a hand to him. If he leaves the matter as it is, he will lose the respect of his peers, and no one will want to take orders from him.[45] Gene Gotti, brother of the infamous John Gotti, is reported to have been involved in a dispute in a Manhattan bar in which he slapped a relative of a Gambino family *caporegime*. The *caporegime* was in a position to ask for revenge, and Gene's life was in peril. Gotti intervened to avoid a vendetta, and managed to restore everyone's dignity.[46]

When the son of Frank Cocchiaro, a member of the DeCavalcante family, was beaten by a Black Muslim, Sam DeCavalcante became very upset. He sought the advice of the elder New York boss, Carlo Gambino. Gambino allegedly replied that, while Cocchiaro was entitled to demand satisfaction, there was a danger that such action could destroy the *borgata* (family). If the DeCavalcante family were involved in a long confrontation with Black Muslim groups, the latter might emerge victorious. Gambino recommended that any retaliatory measure be delayed for two to three months. In this case, loyalty to the organization was put ahead of personal honour.[47]

A Cosa Nostra member is also prohibited from making any form of threat towards another member. Salvatore Gravano, the former *consigliere* of the Gambino family, found himself in an argument about money with soldier Louis DiBono in the presence of other Cosa Nostra members. Gravano told DiBono that if he had stolen the money, he would not have time to enjoy it, because Gravano would "wind up killing him." As a result of this threat, DiBono filed a complaint with his *caporegime*, Pasquale Conte. The matter was put before the family administration, and a sitdown was held so that each party could tell his side of the story. Several high-ranking family members finally intervened to resolve the issue. Gravano and DiBono were asked to shake hands and forget the matter.[48]

Roy DeMeo, another soldier in the Gambino family, was punched in the eye by Joseph Brocchini, a soldier in the Colombo family who was actively involved in pornography film stores in Manhattan's Times Square. DeMeo is alleged to have said that he would not file a complaint with his *caporegime* but, instead, would have Brocchini killed without asking permission. A few weeks later, Brocchini's body was found at his used-car dealership. The murder scene had been made to look as if Brocchini had been the victim of a robbery: his employees were blindfolded and handcuffed and the office ransacked.[49] DeMeo was later killed on the orders of Paul Castellano, who believed DeMeo to be out of control.

Conduct Towards Law Enforcement Agents and Government Officials

Cosa Nostra members are expected to be professional in their relations with law enforcement agents and government officials. High-ranking Cosa Nostra members are, of course, responsible for their soldiers' actions, and must set the standard. For example, an underboss and a soldier of a New York family once crossed paths with a police officer on the street. The soldier showed his disdain towards the police officer by spitting at him. The underboss then apologized to the police officer. It is likely that punitive action was taken against the soldier.[50]

In another instance, Thomas Lucchese was at a meeting in a restaurant when several detectives investigating a Mafia-related shooting stormed in. One of the detectives approached the table where Lucchese was sitting, greeted him and asked to be excused for the interruption. One of the men sitting with Lucchese stood up and started to insult the detective. Lucchese slapped the member in the face and ordered that he immediately apologize to the detective, which the man did right away.[51]

In April 1970 Joseph Colombo Jr., son of boss Joseph Colombo Sr., was arrested for melting coins into silver ingots. While on trial (he was acquitted), two Colombo family men followed Denis Eugene Dillion, the federal prosecutor in the case, and started to intimidate him. When Colombo Sr. was told about the incident, he approached Dillion in the courtroom and apologized to him, then slapped the henchmen.[52]

Experienced Cosa Nostra members always adopt a neutral attitude when approached by law enforcement officials. Joseph Armone, a *caporegime* in the Gambino family, was always polite when speaking with police, and "comported himself as an amiable enemy, totally devoid of personal malice."[53] Paul Castellano, too, was always very polite in his gestures and speech.[54]

Anthony Caponigro, a member of Angelo Bruno's family in Philadelphia, was not known for his tact when dealing with law enforcement officers. In a taped conversation in 1962, Angelo De Carlo, a *caporegime* in the Genovese New Jersey faction, told an associate that the sheriff of Orange County had complained that he had been receiving persistent calls at his home from Caponigro. Apparently, Caponigro had propositioned the sheriff about arranging protection for a gambling joint. The sheriff told De Carlo that Caponigro had dared to show up at the sheriff's home without being invited. "He outfoxed himself," said De Carlo, who told the sheriff not to bother with Caponigro's problem.[55]

If arrested, Cosa Nostra members are expected to show no resistance and to make things easy for law enforcement officers when being processed for booking. Cosa Nostra learned long ago that using violence against law enforcement officials is counterproductive. It only brings unnecessary police scrutiny and pressure upon the organization.[56]

There have, of course, been times when high-ranking Cosa Nostra members have lost their tempers when confronted by law enforcement officials. One of the best-known examples is that of Carmine Lombardozzi, a veteran member and *caporegime* of the Carlo Gambino family. On August 27, 1965, two New York City detectives arrested Lombardozzi for extortion. Lombardozzi violently resisted his arrest by punching one of the two officers. He was subsequently charged with felonious assault.[57] Following this incident, Lombardozzi was demoted from *caporegime* to soldier for a time. This was the second instance of violence against officials that Lombardozzi had been involved in. In April 1963, at Lombardozzi's father's funeral, an FBI agent taking photographs was attacked by four men, who smashed his camera and fractured his skull with the butt of a gun. Two brothers and two nephews of Lombardozzi were arrested. Carlo Gambino reprimanded his *caporegime* for his inability to control his relatives and prevent the attack.[58] As a result of this incident, the FBI decided to put pressure on the Gambino family. Federal agents interviewed several ranking members, including Carlo Gambino, and informed them that the FBI was keeping close watch on the Gambino family's activities.[59]

New Orleans boss Carlos Marcello lost his temper after being provoked by an FBI agent, who suggested that Marcello had had sexual intercourse with his brother's wife. Marcello hit him, and was arrested for assaulting an FBI agent, a federal offence. At the trial, the charge was dismissed after a petition for a change of venue because of the publicity the brawl had caused in New Orleans.[60] In Boston, Gennaro Anguilo, a high-ranking member of the Patriarca family, assaulted government officials on two occasions: an IRS agent in 1966, and a coastguard officer who had boarded Anguilo's yacht to investigate a minor boating violation in 1973.[61]

Sam Giancana was not easy on law enforcement authorities. If police officers wanted to serve him a subpoena or were tailing him too closely,

Giancana uttered obscenities at them. In one particular instance in 1961, he and his girlfriend, Phyllis McGuire, were met at Chicago's O'Hare International Airport by FBI agents, who served a subpoena on McGuire ordering her to appear before a grand jury investigating Giancana's activities. Giancana burst into a rage at the agent.[62]

The Use of Firearms

A Cosa Nostra member is prohibited from carrying a gun unless it is required for a specific purpose. He is also forbidden to attend a meeting or a sit-down with a gun, as this could be interpreted as a lack of trust of the other attendees.[63] (Some Cosa Nostra members, such as Anthony Mirra, a soldier in the Bonanno family, have circumvented this rule by carrying folding knives with long blades.[64]) The rule against carrying guns goes back to the 1930s, and is meant to prevent Cosa Nostra members from being caught by police without lawful gun licences. Most members have a criminal record; their applications for gun permits would be denied. When a member walks on the streets with an unregistered gun, he is highly vulnerable. If he is put under arrest for unlawful possession of a firearm, he may not get the support of his crime family. Moreover, he may be admonished for his negligence.

In January 1998 John Gotti, while incarcerated at the Marion penitentiary, showed his anger and astonishment at his son's carelessness when he learned that police had seized guns that were linked to his son, Junior. A week earlier, in the course of an investigation into John Gotti Jr., federal authorities had seized three guns, a two-shot derringer, a .32-calibre handgun with a silencer and an AR-15 assault rifle. The firearms were discovered within the wall of a social club in Queens. A sum of $358,000 in wedding gifts was also found on the premises, as was a list of members recently inducted into the five New York families. "He is an imbecile," said Gotti to his brother, Peter, and daughter Vittoria, who were visiting him.[65]

The Use of Drugs

Members of Cosa Nostra, and particularly those of the older generation, do not use drugs. Drug use is perceived as a potential breach of security for the organization. Made members who use hard drugs are a liability to the crime family, particularly if they are caught by police. Using drugs can induce a highly paranoid state or panic, which might lead a member to become a police informant.

There have been some high-profile cases of members using drugs. Anthony Bruno Indelicato, son of the murdered Bonanno *caporegime* Anthony Indelicato, was a heavy user of cocaine whose habit made him violent. Armond Dellacroce, son of Aniello, disappeared in 1985 after being indicted with several others on drug charges. He was found dead three years later of a cocaine overdose. According to a source close to the Gotti family, Vincent Gotti, the youngest of the Gotti brothers, was also a drug user. He was indicted for cocaine peddling. His brother, John, banned him from the Bergin Club, the Gotti headquarters in Queens, because his numerous felonies and misdemeanours had attracted attention from police. Anthony Rampino, a close associate of John Gotti, was a heroin dealer who became a heroin addict. He was denied membership in Cosa Nostra because of his addiction and a previous drug conviction.

Nicholas Mormando, a soldier in the Gambino family, and a member of the Salvatore Gravano regime, developed a severe crack/cocaine habit. By 1986 Mormando's addiction had made him uncontrollable. Following a sit-down on his case, it was decided that Mormando had to be killed, as the Gambino administration feared he would become a police informant.[66] Michael De Batt, also a heavy cocaine and crack user, was murdered because he was a bad example to members of his crew. In Canada, the only documented case of a Mafia member killed for drug usage is that of Domenic Racco, murdered in December 1983 by the Musitano crime family of Hamilton, Ontario. Racco was the son of the late Michael Racco, an influential leader of the 'Ndrangheta in Toronto.

The Treatment of Women

Protection of and respect for women is strongly emphasized. Joseph Russo, the Patriarca's family *consigliere*, was overheard saying to a future member that courting and marrying a woman is encouraged, provided "your intentions are honourable."[67] A Cosa Nostra member is prohibited from making seductive approaches to other members' daughters or sisters unless his intentions are "honourable," and he is always prohibited from seducing another member's wife. The rule has been set up, naturally, to protect the organization from bloodbaths resulting from "matters of honour."[68]

When the rule is transgressed, an offended husband or fiancé does not need to seek permission to kill the offender; he is considered justified in killing him. Indeed, the failure to do so puts his honour at stake. Martin Light, a former New York lawyer for the Colombo family, testified before the President's Commission on Organized Crime that "for that—seducing a woman—you don't need the okay or a sit-down; you could just kill that person."[69]

Some cases can be very difficult to solve to everyone's satisfaction. In 1964 Sabato Muro, a soldier in the Gambino family, went to see Carlo Gambino to complain that his *caporegime*, Carmine Lombardozzi, had seduced his daughter. Muro demanded that Lombardozzi marry his daughter, as a matter of honour, otherwise he would handle the matter in his own way. Gambino ordered Lombardozzi to divorce his wife of twenty-seven years and marry Muro's daughter. He further ruled that Lombardozzi would continue to provide his wife and children with the same standard of living they were used to.[70] Lombardozzi lost considerable prestige in the eyes of his peers and was later demoted to the rank of soldier.

During a tense meeting of the Commission, Vincent Gigante, boss of the Genovese family, confronted John Gotti, accusing him of having an affair with the daughter of Aniello Dellacroce, the underboss of the Gambino family, who was married to a soldier of that family. Gotti allegedly replied that the woman was in the process of divorcing her husband. Moreover, Gotti argued, the woman was not the "real" daughter of Dellacroce, since she was the product of a relationship between Dellacroce and his mistress.[71]

In Cosa Nostra the institution of marriage is sacred, and a marriage cannot be broken up because of strain between husband and wife. Cosa Nostra bosses have often intervened to help members facing matrimonial difficulties. When Frank Perrone, a member of the DeCavalcante family, left his wife for another woman, Sam DeCavalcante was upset because Perrone had promised he would make a success of his marriage. DeCavalcante approached Perrone's eldest brother-in-law, who was not a member of Cosa Nostra, to ask him to persuade Perrone to "do the right thing."[72] Carlo Gambino had the same respect for marriage. He forbade his nephew, Emmanuel, from engaging in divorce proceedings against his wife. Emmanuel wished to marry his girlfriend, a scintillating blonde model. Gambino strongly opposed that union because it would expose the family to criticism. In the end, Emmanuel did not divorce his wife, and was allowed to keep his girlfriend as his mistress.[73]

Divorce is strictly prohibited for members of the Sicilian Cosa Nostra. Tommaso Buscetta stated that while American mafiosi were more flexible on this issue, the choice of a wife was for life for the older generation of Sicilian mafiosi. Buscetta was himself suspended from Cosa Nostra for six months for having extramarital affairs.[74]

But for many men of honour today, having a mistress is the norm rather than the exception. Cosa Nostra accepts this way of life, provided that its members are discreet and that the wife is never exposed to public scorn or derision.[75] Mafia etiquette requires that members not take their mistresses to the same restaurants or nightclubs where they would take their wives. Many Cosa Nostra members do not bother to follow this social protocol and parade themselves in public with women, some known prostitutes. This type of behaviour infuriated conservative family boss Carlo Gambino, who was known to be a faithful husband. Gambino was particularly upset when his underboss, Joseph Biondo, left his wife for a young prostitute. Gambino expected Biondo to exhibit better behaviour, considering his rank in the family hierarchy. Biondo was subsequently demoted and put "on the shelf."[76]

When Paul Castellano's daughter discovered that her husband was unfaithful, it hurt her so deeply that she had a miscarriage. Castellano ordered his son-in-law, Frank Amato, murdered. His daughter lost her husband, but the family's reputation and honour were maintained.[77]

It is a well-known rule that no one—whether a Cosa Nostra member or an outsider—is to visit the wife of an imprisoned Cosa Nostra member. "You would never be safe if you stopped and spoke to my wife while I was locked up," John Gotti once warned, alluding to members of another Cosa Nostra family who had stopped at the home of a member's wife. "You tell your skipper [caporegime] I said, 'You ever go to a guy's house while he is in jail, I'll kill you.'"[78] In October 1971 Felix Alderisio, a debt collector and hit man for the Chicago family, ordered from his jail cell the killing of member Sambo Cesario, who had had an affair with Alderisio's mistress. The contract was carried out after Alderisio died while still in prison.[79]

When Cosa Nostra members are in jail or on the run from the law, the protection of their relatives is important, and those who have been designated to look after them are held responsible should anything happen to them. In 1937 Vito Genovese had to flee the United States to escape being prosecuted for a murder. While he was exiled in Italy, his wife, Anna Petillo, operated a nightclub with her brother and another member.[80] Anna allegedly fell in love with a woman. Steve Franze, the person who was supposed to "look after" Genovese's wife, was subsequently murdered. He had failed to protect the family boss from disgrace and humiliation.[81]

Women's Roles in Cosa Nostra

Daughters of Cosa Nostra members usually marry sons of Cosa Nostra members. These marriages cement alliances between Cosa Nostra families. In 1958, during the hearings of the United States Senate Select Committee, which was conducting an inquiry into the Apalachin meeting of November 1957, a study of linkage by blood and marriage was presented before the Committee. The study showed the family interrelationships of the attendees from the New York–New Jersey area, the Rochester-Auburn-Syracuse area, the Utica area, the Buffalo–Niagara

Falls–Youngstown area and the Detroit–Cleveland area. All of those present were related by blood and/or marriage to the daughters or sisters of the other attendees.[82]

Members of the Caruana crime family, a prominent Sicilian Mafia family in Montreal and Toronto, have married their daughters and sons to the children of the Cuntrera crime family, another prominent Sicilian group in Canada. Vito Rizzuto, the leader of another Sicilian Mafia group in Montreal, married his two sons and a daughter to the children of key lieutenants of his organization. But today, Mafia daughters also marry outside of Cosa Nostra circles.

Being married to a Cosa Nostra member is not always easy. Rosalie Bonanno, née Profaci, was married to Salvatore Bonanno in August 1956.[83] In her memoirs, written in 1990, she described how important the family values were in providing strength, protection and security. She also explained how difficult it is to be the spouse of a mafioso. In her childhood, she lived in a cloistered world, protected by a strong father. She could not go outside unless escorted by a male of her own blood. She was educated by nuns, who prepared her for her future role of wife and mother. As a wife, she was very submissive and respectful towards her husband and to her father-in-law. She learned quickly that she must keep her mouth shut and never ask questions about her husband's activities. Under no circumstances could she ask her husband his whereabouts or, above all, where the money came from. Her husband was the sole provider to the family, and he would not let her ask her own family for any kind of financial assistance.[84] Like other Mafia wives, Rosalie Bonanno accepted the fact that her husband would leave home for days and she would not know when he would return. On the other hand, she knew that he would bring in enough money to pay for life's necessities and care for the children.

Vittoria Gotti, the wife of John Gotti, was from a different generation than Rosalie Bonanno. Although she went along with the Mafia protocol and etiquette, she did not fear her husband. Whatever her husband's rank in the Cosa Nostra, she expected him to be the provider. At the beginning of his career, Gotti was in prison for an attempted burglary. He was unable to secure a decent income for his family. His wife sued him before the Domestic Relations Court for non-support. It was quite embarrassing for her husband, who was hoping to become a made member in the Gambino family.[85]

While most of the older generation of wives of Cosa Nostra members are traditional—they stay at home, cook, clean the house and look after the kids—some have been eager to follow their husbands' career paths. Constance Rastelli was one such exception. The wife of Philip Rastelli, who, in the early 1960s, was a soldier in the Bonanno family, she did not hesitate to get involved in her husband's criminal activities, driving the getaway car during robberies, for example. Later, in the midst of the confrontation between the Bonanno family and the Commission, Philip Rastelli sought refuge in Montreal under the protection of Vincenzo Cotroni, then leader of the Montreal Bonanno faction. Constance suspected her husband of having an affair with another woman while in Montreal. She crossed the border and found her husband and the woman, whom she beat severely. She threatened to kill her husband if he continued to have affairs. Rastelli did not take the warning seriously, and continued his liaison. When he returned to New York, he was confronted by his wife, who fired several gunshots at him but did not wound him. Not only was he greatly humiliated, but Constance threatened to talk to police (which she did) about her husband's activities. She was later found shot to death.[86]

Today, the role of women in the Mafia has changed considerably, especially within the Sicilian Mafia. While women are still excluded from initiation ceremonies, Cosa Nostra uses women to relay messages to Mafia members incarcerated in high-security prisons or to help their husbands escape police searches. Carmela Santapaola, wife of Benedetto, the boss of Cosa Nostra in the province of Catania, took care of her husband's business after he was arrested by Italian police in 1993. Carmella's involvement in Mafia affairs led to her violent death in September 1995, when she was shot to death in front of her daughter by two individuals posing as police officers.[87]

The "Godmother" phenomenon emerged for the first time within the Neapolitan Camorra in the late 1970s, when Rosetta Cutolo took over the criminal activities of her brother, Raffaele, a leader of the Camorra who had been arrested and sentenced to life imprisonment for several murders. Rosetta ran the organization for thirteen years, until her arrest in 1993.

Customs

Kissing on the Cheeks

Kissing close friends on both cheeks is a form of greeting practised in several Europeans countries. In the world of Cosa Nostra, kissing on the cheeks is widespread among members in New York City.[88] It shows respect and solidarity among members. Ralph Salerno, a former New York City police officer, reports, "It is customary for members and associates to kiss a don (a boss or other respected ranking member) when entering or leaving his presence. When bosses meet they mutually embrace and kiss each other; this is repeated upon departing."[89]

In Sicily, according to Antonino Calderone, a former member of the Catania Mafia, kissing on the cheeks is done among men of honour only.[90] In the United States, kissing can also indicate a high level of acceptance for an associate. Tino Fiumara, a soldier in the Genovese family, showed his respect for Patrick Kelly, an Irishman working for Fiumara, by customarily kissing him on the cheek.[91]

The practice of kissing among made members has caught the attention of those outside Cosa Nostra, thanks in part to movies such as The Godfather. Because of this, it has been strongly recommended to new inductees in Boston that when greeting each other in public they shake hands instead of kissing.[92]

The custom of kissing on the cheeks proved costly to Robert Lino, a caporegime in the Bonanno family. In March 2001 he was seen greeting Richard Cantarella, the Bonanno acting consigliere, following a lunch at Umberto's Clam House, in Manhattan's Little Italy. Lino had pleaded guilty to having masterminded a $50-million Wall Street stock scam and had been ordered to home confinement, with an electronic monitoring device on his ankle, pending sentencing. He was ordered to avoid any contact with known criminals. When FBI agents observed Lino kissing Cantarella on the cheeks, they immediately arrested him for violating his bail conditions.

Dress Code

Dress code has been a subject of particular attention in Cosa Nostra. For a long time Hollywood portrayed gangsters wearing wide-brimmed fedoras, black suits, shirts with white ties and white alligator shoes, and carrying a violin case. Indeed, this was the typical dress code of the American mafioso between the First and Second World Wars. When Salvatore Luciano took over Cosa Nostra in the 1930s, he radically changed that. His suits and shirts were expensive, but tailored conservatively, without ostentation. He expected the men around him to adopt the same style. The idea was to look "legit," like businessmen.[93]

Cosa Nostra members are expected to look tidy. Vito Genovese was once alleged to have said to an enforcer working for Anthony Strollo that next time he met him he would like to see him "with some teeth"(meaning he should pay a visit to a dentist).[94] When Joseph Valachi became a government informant, he did not like to be interviewed by the District Attorney when unshaved because he felt it showed a lack of respect.[95] Benjamin "Lefty" Ruggiero, a soldier in the Bonanno family, often lectured FBI undercover agent Joseph Pistone on how to look neat. He told Pistone to shave his moustache: "No real wiseguys wear mustaches except some of the old mustache Petes. You gotta look neat, dress right, which means at night you throw on a sport jacket and slacks."[96] Some Cosa Nostra leaders even dictate to their members how to dress and what jewellery to wear. Nicodemo Scarfo, the former boss of the Philadelpia family, regarded the use of cologne by men as effeminate and prohibited his men from using it in his presence.[97]

By the end of the 1970s, the standard dress code was a grey Armani jacket, black turtleneck and gold chain. This became so obvious and so distinctive to the eyes of law enforcement that Vincent Gigante allegedly prohibited members of his family from wearing the "Mafia uniform."[98] Today, dress is mostly casual and not distinctive.

The Use of Nicknames

The use of nicknames is common not only in Italian organized crime but is widely in use in other criminal organizations, such as the outlaw motorcycle gangs.[99] Nicknames are used to conceal the real identity of their members to make it difficult for law enforcement officers to identify who is being talked about. Criminals generally refer to each other by their nicknames. Members of Cosa Nostra may go their entire lives without ever knowing the real identity of their confederates. During introductions, nicknames are commonly used. It is considered improper to ask for someone's real name; a member is supposed to ask questions only about matters that pertain to him.[100]

Some famous underworld nicknames have been:

- "Joe Bandy"—Joseph Biondo, former underboss in the Gambino family
- "The Fish"—Vincent Cafaro, soldier in the Genovese family
- "Tony Bananas"—Anthony Caponigro, former *consigliere* in the Bruno family
- "Big Paul"—Paul Castellano, former boss of the Gambino family
- Sam "the Plumber"—Sam DeCavalcante, former New Jersey boss
- "Charlie Wagons"—Carmine Fatico, *caporegime* in the Gambino family
- "Sammy the Bull"—Salvatore Gravano, former underboss under John Gotti
- "Big Joey"—Joseph Massino, current Bonanno family boss
- "Johnny Pops"—John Papalia, former *caporegime* in the Todaro family
- "Sonny Black"—Dominick Napolitano, former *caporegime* in the Bonanno family
- "The Snake"—Carmine Persico, former boss of the Colombo family

A nickname can be attributed to someone for many reasons. It can derive from someone's past history (Paul "the Waiter" Ricca was once a waiter in a restaurant) or from a particular incident (Thomas Lucchese was known as "Three-Finger Brown" because he lost a finger on one hand). It may relate to a physical characteristic (Jimmy Alo was known as "Jimmy Blue Eyes") or it may convey status (Giuseppe Masseria was known as "Joe the Boss").[101]

The use of nicknames has become so entrenched in the underworld that real names sometimes no longer have significance. In 1987 Anthony Salerno, at the time boss of the Genovese family, was presented with a list of the names of prospective members to be initiated by the Bonanno family. He did not recognize any of them because there were no nicknames on the list. "I don't know none of them," complained Salerno to Mathiew Ianniello, a *caporegime*, in an FBI-taped conversation, "They don't put the nicknames down there." Phil Rastelli, boss of the Bonanno family, had used the real names of candidates to make sure no Cosa Nostra members would say anything against the candidates he was proposing for membership.[102]

RULES BETWEEN MEMBERS AND ASSOCIATES

The level of acceptance of an associate is displayed in how he is greeted. A handshake or hand on a shoulder shows that he is fairly close to an organized-crime figure. A kiss on the cheek while a handshake is taking place demonstrates that the person is an accepted member or an associate of a crime group. These were the greetings practised within the John DiGilio crew, as related by a former associate of that group during his testimony before a United States Senate committee.[103]

A soldier must get permission from his *caporegime* to do business with an associate. Nicholas Caramandi, a soldier in the Scarfo family in Philadelphia who turned government informant in June 1986, had known a Philadelphia contractor for fifteen years. The contractor boasted to Caramandi that "although he was not a soldier in Cosa Nostra," he was "with" Cosa Nostra and had received Scarfo's approval to do business with members of the Philadelphia family. Caramandi had to get consent from his *caporegime*, Thomas Del Giorno, before going any further.[104]

The *caporegime* is held liable for his crew members' actions as well as those of the associates. Once an associate is "put on the record," a made member becomes responsible for his actions.[105] When Benjamin Ruggiero told FBI undercover agent Joseph Pistone that he had put "a claim" on him before the family administration, he meant he had officially vouched for Pistone's trustworthiness. "I'm responsible for you. You're responsible to me. I hope everything you say about yourself is true. Because if you fuck up, we're both gonna go bye-bye," warned Ruggiero. From the moment Ruggiero endorsed Pistone, Ruggiero was personally responsible for his conduct should Pistone prove unreliable.[106] A few years later, a dispute arose when Anthony Mirra, a soldier in the Bonanno family, claimed that Pistone "belonged" to him, because he had worked for him at a discotheque. On the other hand, Ruggiero alleged that he had introduced Pistone to Mirra. Several sit-downs with upper-level Bonanno family members were required before Pistone was officially put "on the record" with Ruggiero.[107]

Former Gambino family *consigliere* Salvatore Gravano explained that when somebody is "on the record" he is connected to a made member or to a family. He enjoys protection from that family. If the associate operates a gambling joint or a club, no one else can move in on it.[108] Henry Hill, a long-time associate of the Lucchese family, felt that being associated with an organized-crime family was like buying insurance protection against rivals.[109] Once they are "registered" with a Cosa Nostra family, associates are bound by the same rules of conduct as made members. Associates, however, do not enjoy the same privileges that made members do.[110]

In dealing with organized-crime members, associates are expected to participate and collaborate by giving a portion of their earnings to the member to whom they are connected. An associate to Harry Riccobene, a high-ranking Cosa Nostra member in Philadelphia, was admonished for not giving a fair part of his proceeds to Riccobene.[111] The associate must also inform the soldier of his whereabouts any time he goes out of town.[112] Sam DeCavalcante, the Cosa Nostra boss in New Jersey, would often remind his underlings that he wanted to know everything they were doing. He called it "registering." All family members' activities, including those of the associates, had to be cleared by the boss.[113]

Sometimes an associate might be loaned to another Cosa Nostra family. In such cases, the loan must be approved by the family for which the associate works, and the soldier or the *caporegime* responsible for that associate will, of course, get a percentage of any earnings for the duration of the loan. Some associates command a great deal of respect from family members for their talent at making money. Jimmy Burke, an Irish criminal who belonged primarily to the Lucchese family, commanded such respect. The Colombo family entered into negotiations with the Lucchese family so they could benefit from Burke's talent.[114]

If an associate, after committing crimes with or for Cosa Nostra members, feels he has been in some way betrayed or cheated, his only recourse is to get protection from the soldier he "belongs" to. The associate is also subject to punishment by those he is associated with.[115] When a dispute arises, an associate must always take the side of a Cosa Nostra member, even if he is wrong. On the other hand, a Cosa Nostra member will never side with an associate against a Cosa Nostra member. When there is dissension between an associate and a made member, the associate cannot defend himself, but must be represented by an *avvocato*.

An associate must show respect to a Cosa Nostra member. "The worst thing you can do is embarrass a wiseguy," Benjamin Ruggiero told Joseph Pistone, an undercover agent for the FBI. An associate does not participate in a conversation with a *caporegime* or a boss unless he is asked to. Mafia protocol also prevents associates from seeking a meeting with the family boss, unless they are very close to him. They must go through the member to whom they are linked.

Associates are expected to adopt a low profile when in public and avoid displaying wealth. Carmen Zagaria, an associate of the Cleveland family, was fond of wearing expensive jewellery, which gave him high visibility. Zagaria was cautioned in August 1981 by former Cleveland underboss Angelo Lonardo, now a defector, not to be "flashy" in public.[116]

In April 1963 Harold Konigsberg, a money collector and loan shark associated with Joseph Zicarelli, a Bonanno soldier in New Jersey, caused a commotion when he entered a gambling joint owned and operated by Puddy Hinkus, an associate registered to Anthony Caponigro, a member of the Bruno family in Philadelphia. Konigsberg allegedly assaulted Meyer Rosenberg, a Jewish organized-crime figure from Atlantic City, who owed money to Konigsberg. Following that incident, Rosenberg made a charge against Konigsberg to the police. The incident was reported to Angelo De Carlo, a *caporegime* for the Genovese family in New Jersey. De Carlo said: "That guy, Konigsberg, should get an okay for every move he makes. He should find out if people are connected—to a Cosa Nostra family. That could have been anybody's joint. What the hell, he can't walk in any joint and hit people. He doesn't know who's connected."[117]

In September 1964 Sam DeCavalcante was called on to settle the case of a man named "Johnny" who owed about $20,000 to a certain "Harry" from Tampa, Florida, who was associated with the Profaci family. DeCavalcante strongly advised Johnny to make a settlement. Apparently, the Profaci family had complained to DeCavalcante about Johnny and warned that he was liable to be hurt physically and financially if he did not pay Harry. DeCavalcante knew that Harry, while not a soldier, was under the Profaci family's protection, and he did not want to get involved in a dispute with Joseph Profaci, who had a seat on the Commission. DeCavalcante implied to Johnny that, even though he was the friend of Robert Occhipinti, a close associate and cousin of Sam DeCavalcante, he should not rely on that should he choose to overlook Sam's advice. Johnny agreed to comply with DeCavalcante's proposal.[118]

RULES REGARDING OUTSIDERS

Outsiders are freelance criminals who gravitate around made members and their associates. They may also be businessmen, lawyers or accountants working on the fringe of the law. As a matter of protocol, but mostly for security reasons, an outsider must be formally introduced to a Cosa Nostra member by a third party. Security can sometimes be a matter of concern when Cosa Nostra members do business with legitimate businessmen. Robert Occhipinti cautioned Sam DeCavalcante not to call a trucker who owed him some money. "I can handle him for you. Save yourself for the big ones," advised Occhipinti, who did not want DeCavalcante exposed.[119]

Former national Teamsters president Jackie Presser, who was from Cleveland, was very well connected with the families of Cleveland and Chicago. When it was learned after his death in August 1988 that Presser had been an FBI informant for several decades, it put Anthony Salerno, then the boss of the Genovese family, in a difficult situation, because he had sponsored and promoted Presser's candidacy for president of the Teamsters before the members of the Commission.[120]

Cosa Nostra matters are not to be discussed in front of outsiders. In the spring of 1981 three important members of the Cleveland family met in a restaurant with Chicago Cosa Nostra boss Joey Aiuppa and his underboss, Jack Cerone. Milton Rockman, a Jewish lawyer and close friend to Aiuppa, was with him. After a while, Rockman was asked to leave the table as Cosa Nostra business was about to be discussed.[121]

A Cosa Nostra member will always back another Cosa Nostra member, whether the latter is right or wrong, in a dispute with an outsider. Frank Zannino, a *caporegime* in the Boston Patriarca family, made this clear to two of his soldiers who were not sure what position to adopt: "I'm a *caporegime* and I'm talking to you as a soldier. Don't you ever dare, in your fucking life, ever tell me that you're neutral with an outsider, whether he's right or wrong. If you have to give the edge, it's the soldier that's right."[122]

Outsiders can secure the right to stay in business under the Mafia's protection by paying a tribute for the privilege of operating on Cosa Nostra territory.[123] They must obtain permission for their activities with the local crime family. An outsider who is connected to a Cosa Nostra member must be introduced properly before he can do business in an area already under the jurisdiction of a Cosa Nostra family. For example, a Jewish bookmaker was operating a large-scale bookmaking operation in Toledo, Ohio. The man was a friend of Aladena Fratianno, the former acting boss in Los Angeles. Fratianno arranged to introduce his friend to the *caporegime* of Detroit, responsible for Toledo, so that the Detroit family would be made aware of the bookmaking operation on their territory.[124] In return for letting Fratianno's friend operate, the Detroit family would benefit from payoffs.

The protection of the Mafia can come in handy. Mickey Cohen, a West Coast freelance gangster in the 1940s, held up a bookmaking shop run by individuals that had links to Jack Dragna, at that time the Cosa Nostra boss on the West Coast. Cohen and his gang took more than $30,000 in cash and all the jewellery worn by the bookmakers. Although Cohen learned through underworld informants that he had robbed a Cosa Nostra bookmaking operation, he refused to return the loot. Meetings were arranged between Dragna's associates and Cohen in a lawyer's office. They told him that the amount of money he had stolen was not as important as a valuable stickpin that belonged to one of the bookmakers, who wanted it back at any cost. Cohen gave back the stickpin and the matter was over.[125]

Organized crime is to some extent similar to a legal government. It provides work and protection to its citizens, and the latter must pay taxes in return. This is the analogy that Carmine Persico, leader of the Colombo family and now imprisoned for life, used to an independent criminal who had swindled half a million dollars from a large retail store in Brooklyn, a Colombo territory. The man wanted to know why he had to pay a share of the money he had stolen. Persico told him that since he had done the job on Persico's territory, he had to pay a tax. "Now, you have to pay your taxes on it just like in the straight world. Why? Because we let you do it. We're the government."[126]

Outlaw Motorcycle Gangs

In the social order of the underworld, outlaw motorcycle gang members are considered the lowest class by Cosa Nostra. Bikers are perceived as unpredictable, undisciplined and brainless. If there is a need to talk to them, they will not be directly addressed by ranking Cosa Nostra members but dealt with by someone else.

However, bikers have often been used to perform dirty jobs for Cosa Nostra. These requests for assistance are sporadic, rather than common practice. According to the testimony of a former Pagans member in Philadelphia, Pagan outlaw motorcycle members were in contact with associates and members of a New York Cosa Nostra family and participated in extortion, counterfeiting, auto theft, drug trafficking, false identification and the beating of a union member. They were sometimes required to serve as bodyguards for members during meetings involving heroin deals.[127] In 1985 the Patriarca family used the Hells Angels to collect loansharking debts.

On several occasions, outlaw motorcycle gangs in Canada, particularly the Hells Angels, have formed partnerships with the Sicilian Mafia in importing large quantities of drugs. The Toronto-based Commisso crime family, run by brothers Rocco Remo and Cosimo Elia Commisso, often resorted to the services of Cecil Kirby, a former ranking member of Satan's Choice, an Ontario motorcycle gang.[128] Kirby was an enforcer, involved in arson, extortion and murder for the Commissos. In May 1981 the Commisso brothers were charged with conspiracy to murder two prominent Sicilian crime figures in Toronto, Paul Volpe and Pietro Scarcella.[129] The murder plots had been unveiled when Kirby became an informant.

Chapter 6

Territories and Areas of Jurisdiction

Leaders such as John LaRocca, boss of the Pittsburgh family, ingrained in his members a strong adherence to the concept of territories. Members were assigned to geographical areas that were regarded as their specific territory. After LaRocca's death in 1984, Michael Genovese (a cousin of Vito Genovese) was less rigid in applying the rule. The notion of "territory" still exists, but it is not strictly defined and families' territories often overlap.[1] Today it is acknowledged that the concept of territory relates more to the domination of a particular criminal activity than the domination of a geographical area.

For an organized-crime group to survive, it must maintain strict control over its territory, since that territory represents its sources of revenue. It must be able to keep away any rival groups that may attempt to take over lucrative rackets. The family boss must be informed at all times about all activities, legal and illegal, members of his family are involved in within the family's territory. Controlling a territory means controlling gains, whether they are illegal or not. A crime group achieves and maintains the domination of a territory through the threat of violence. For instance, John Gotti strongly warned Michael Franzese, a former member of the Colombo family, that he was not welcome to open a flea market in Long Island, near one already operated by a Gotti associate. Franzese abandoned the idea after he was threatened.[2]

There may be several other criminal organizations operating in a given area where one or more Cosa Nostra families are established. Most of the time Cosa Nostra exercises control over other criminal groups by exacting from them a percentage of their illicit revenues for the privilege of operating in the area. In areas where Cosa Nostra has a strong influence, they can forbid other groups from engaging in certain criminal activities.

CRIMINAL ACTIVITIES IN
ANOTHER FAMILY'S TERRITORY

Rules and protocol demand that crime groups—Cosa Nostra or otherwise—that wish to operate in a particular territory must first seek permission from the family in control of that area. It is a fundamental rule of law in Cosa Nostra.[3] Also, a member must have the approval of his own family before he makes plans to set up a criminal activity in another family's territory. Getting Cosa Nostra families to do business together is a delicate process, sometimes involving long negotiations.

An example of the intricate requirements for approval involves Frank Balistrieri, the boss in Milwaukee, who answered to the Chicago family. His control over the vending machine business was so solid that it was almost impossible for anybody else to place and operate a machine in the city. Balistrieri had achieved this control by using hidden ownership, intimidation and violence. In the late 1970s the FBI initiated an investigation by using an undercover agent to pose as an independent vending machine businessman trying to start a business in Milwaukee. The purpose of the operation was to find out if the Balistrieri family would try to muscle the "independent operator" and put him out of business. As expected, the undercover agent met with some difficulty in putting machines into offices in the city. He called upon another undercover FBI agent, Joseph Pistone, who had successfully penetrated the Bonanno family in New York, to see if he could gain the influence of a Cosa Nostra member. Pistone approached Benjamin Ruggiero, a soldier in the Bonanno family, and told him about the problem in Milwaukee. Ruggiero had to get permission from his *caporegime*, Mike Sabella, who then had to get permission from boss Carmine Galante for Ruggiero to go to Milwaukee to see Balistrieri. The Balistrieri family accepted New York's proposal to let an independent operator install vending machines in Milwaukee, but the deal was not recognized by the Chicago family, as it had not been consulted.[4]

Tony Plate was a soldier in the Gambino family from 1931 until his disappearance in 1979. He ran a large loansharking operation for the family. Plate was also known for his talent at handling legal situations for the Gambino and other families.[5] Because of his influence and power, Plate reported directly to the family's underboss. However, the Jack Dragna family of Los Angeles became so upset with Plate that a sit-down was needed between the two families. Paul Castellano, boss of the Gambino family, and Aladena Fratianno, the representative for the Dragna family, met in New York City. The West Coast family complained that Plate was, through a certain John G. Monica whom he protected, getting involved in criminal activities in California. "Me and Dragna are going to stick by the rules. I can't come into New York and do something illegal unless I get permission, am I right?" Fratianno said. "What we do in California is our own business. We don't come to New York to protect New York guys from other New York guys, that's against the rules. And we don't expect New York guys to do it in California. That's strictly out of bounds."[6] Plate was ordered to conform, and he withdrew from California.

In small states such as New Jersey, where several Cosa Nostra crews operate in the same area, ignoring protocol can be particularly serious. That was the case for Anthony Russo, a long-time Genovese family member. On June 12, 1978, Russo was summoned before his *caporegime*, Ruggiero Boiardo, who was responsible for the Genovese family's interests in New Jersey. Boiardo criticized Russo for not having followed proper channels when doing business with other crews in New Jersey, as well as in Florida and Las Vegas, Nevada. Boiardo wanted to make sure that Russo understood that, before he got involved in legal or illegal business with outsiders in another city, Russo should have made thorough checks on the people he wished to associate with, and especially on whether these people were connected to other made members.[7]

When John Gotti became boss of the Gambino family in December 1985, he violated the rule concerning territory. Gotti saw an opportunity to make unauthorized incursions into the lucrative rackets controlled by the Genovese family. He relied heavily on the alliance he had made with the Scarfo family in Philadelphia, and moved into areas of northern New Jersey where the Genovese family was already established. Gotti's men even began to persuade Genovese members and associates to join in Gotti's ventures.[8]

One of the most important sources of income for Cosa Nostra is illegal gambling. These activities often present complex territory problems, especially in New York City where several Cosa Nostra crews do business in a relatively small area. Cosa Nostra families take measures to make sure that boundary lines are respected by everyone. In 1963 Angelo Bruno, the boss of the Philadelphia family, was asked by Gerardo Catena, the Genovese family's representative in New Jersey, to tell two of his *capiregime* to remove their new gambling joint from Newark, New Jersey, because the Genovese men resented the Bruno members' presence.[9] The necessary approvals had not been obtained.

But the rule is often ignored by small-time gambling operators. Around 1978 John Gotti, at the time a soldier in the Carmine Fatico *regime* in Queens, ordered the tenant of a bookmaking operation to stop his activities, as another bookmaker was already paying a tribute to Fatico for permission to operate in the area. "You can't operate here," said Gotti.[10] The new bookmaker was forced to move.

THE FAMILIES OF NEW YORK CITY AND NEW JERSEY

After the Castellammarese Wars in 1931, the Italian crime families in New York agreed to share the city among the five existing families. Criminal activities were much more extensive in New York City than in such places as Buffalo, Boston, Detroit, Chicago and Philadelphia. Furthermore, the distance between these smaller cities kept the families within them from forming associations. As a result, there has traditionally been only one Cosa Nostra family in each city other than New York.[11] The peace treaty in 1931 favoured the Luciano-Costello-Genovese alliance, enabling this family to secure itself a powerful seat on the Commission from the very beginning.[12] Since then, all five New York families, always the largest contingent of Cosa Nostra members, have been represented on the national commission and have kept New York divided amongst themselves.

After the murder of Giuseppe Masseria in 1931, New York City was divided as follows: the Gambino family was given Queens and Brooklyn; the Genovese family, Manhattan and the waterfronts; the Lucchese family, the Bronx; and the Profaci and Bonanno families shared Brooklyn. Although Manhattan remains a Genovese territory, the other four families have several interests in Manhattan as well.

At first, the New York families confined their activities to their place of origin. Over the decades they have extended their criminal operations outside New York and established themselves in areas of New Jersey. The Gambino family, for example, has claimed control over all numbers and gambling operations in Newark, New Jersey, just across the Hudson River from New York City. The family's interests are overseen by a Gambino *caporegime*, who makes sure that the family's interests are protected and it gets its share of profits.[13] A faction in southern New Jersey deals in narcotics and alien smuggling and is closely aligned with Sicilian Mafia families. The southern New Jersey faction reports directly to New York.[14] The Gambino family also operates in the states of Pennsylvania, Connecticut, Maryland, Florida and California.

The Genovese family, one of the most influential Cosa Nostra families in the United States, has maintained its influence not only in Manhattan and other New York boroughs, but also in New Jersey, Massachusetts, Connecticut and Miami, Florida. The Genovese family is involved in a fairly large range of criminal activity, including narcotics, gambling, loansharking, prostitution, labour racketeering, extortion, collusive theft, money laundering and the infiltration of legitimate enterprises.[15] According to Alphonse D'Arco, a former *caporegime* and acting boss for the Lucchese family who became a co-operating witness in 1991, the Genovese family has always maintained a close relationship with the Chicago family. In fact, the Genovese family appoints one of its members *il messaggero* (messenger) between themselves and the Chicago family.[16]

The Lucchese family, the smallest family in New York City, has its base of operations in the Bronx and Brooklyn. As the family became involved in drug trafficking, it expanded its influence in several northern counties of New Jersey as well as in other states, such as Pennsylvania and Maryland, and in the District of Columbia. The New Jersey–based factions run by Anthony Accetturo and Michael Taccetta were very powerful until the arrest of Accetturo and Taccetta in the mid-1980s. The Lucchese family's criminal activities include illegal gambling, loansharking, narcotics trafficking, takeovers of legitimate businesses, fraud, cigarette smuggling, extortion and, to a lesser extent, race fixing, arson, pornography and stolen property.[17]

The Bonanno family has maintained its influence in New York City by its continuing involvement in narcotics, gambling, labour racketeering, extortion and loansharking. It exerts its influence over the criminal activities of the Montreal family, mainly the smuggling of illegal aliens and narcotics into the United States. The family, through the strong leadership of soldier Joseph Zicarelli, was in control of gambling activities in the northern counties of New Jersey during the 1960s. In certain areas of New Jersey, members of the Bonanno organization interacted closely with members of the Profaci-Colombo family. Their common bond was Roma Foods, which was the exclusive distributor for Grande Cheese Co., a Wisconsin-based firm controlled by Joseph Bonanno.[18] The Bonanno family also has interests in Florida, Arizona and California.

The Colombo family has developed its criminal activities in New Jersey through a network of criminals led by Salvatore Profaci, son of Joseph Profaci. He conducts its operation from Roma Foods Enterprises, Inc. The group maintains relationships with members of the Bruno, Bonanno and Genovese families. Roma Foods has businesses in twenty-seven other states.[19]

The DeCavalcante family, now led by John Riggi,[20] has the distinction of being the only Cosa Nostra group based in the state of New Jersey. Its members are primarily involved in gambling, narcotics distribution, loansharking, production and distribution of pornography, illicit transport and dumping of toxic waste, labour extortion and political corruption. It controls most of the illicit activities in Union County and, to a smaller extent, in the Port Elizabeth area. It uses the city of Elizabeth as its headquarters. The family is a relatively small crime group, with about thirty made members.[21] Although most of its members operate in the southern part of New Jersey, some are active in southwest Connecticut. The DeCavalcante family has always maintained a good relationship with the New York families, particularly the Gambino family.

Territorial lines are often blurred when two or more crime groups form a partnership in search of higher profits from legal or illegal activities.[22] Family territories are not always contiguous in a given area, as Joseph Valachi explained during his testimony before a United States Senate Committee in 1963: "You see, Senator, you take Harlem, for instance. We have about four families all mixed up there. There isn't any territory. You find Brooklyn guys in New York and New York guys in Brooklyn. They all get along very well. If anything, you have in Brooklyn, in fact they help protect it for you. I would not say there's territories."[23]

Harlem, by cultural and ethnic standards, has traditionally belonged to black crime groups. Leroy Barnes, a major Harlem heroin trafficker convicted in 1975, was asked by the members of the President's Commission on Organized Crime, why the New York Cosa Nostra families did not venture into Harlem to deal in heroin. "They probably concluded that the fox isn't worth the chase, and they decided to stay out," answered Barnes.[24] Although heroin trafficking in Harlem represented substantial revenues, Cosa Nostra families distanced themselves from this territory to avoid bloody confrontations. Barnes continued, "The Blacks felt that Harlem, in a sense, belonged to them, and I think that they were willing to fight for the territory."[25] In Chicago, the family was forced to leave black ghettos after the Blackstone Rangers, a street gang with a membership of 1,500, warned Cosa Nostra to leave the area or be killed.[26]

For other ethnic criminal groups such as the Yakuza—a Japanese organized-crime group—it can be very difficult to engage in business in New York City without the knowledge of Cosa Nostra. The Yakuza in New York had to deal with Cosa Nostra, especially in the bar and prostitution business. Cosa Nostra's strong influence made it impossible for the Yakuza to set up operations on its own. That is perhaps why the Yakuza is much more active in Los Angeles, where Cosa Nostra is less entrenched.[27]

THE PHILADELPHIA FAMILY

Due to its proximity to New York City, Philadelphia has for a long time been in the shadow of New York's underworld. After the murder of John Avena in August 1936, the Cosa Nostra's Commission appointed Joseph Bruno boss of the family in Philadelphia.[28] The move was an unprecedented instance of the Commission exercising its prerogative to appoint the boss of a family. At the time, the Philadelphia family also had jurisdiction in the southern part of New Jersey, placing Atlantic City under its control. The New York families did not object, as they regarded Atlantic City as a resort town without much opportunity for money-making.[29]

In the early 1960s, the Commission was forced to declare a moratorium on membership in the New York families of Cosa Nostra because it feared infiltration within its ranks. The Kennedy administration had declared open war on organized crime, particularly the Cosa Nostra infiltration into the Teamsters labour union. Since the Commission was very pleased with Angelo Bruno's leadership in Philadelphia, however, it decided to repay Bruno by allowing him to admit new members into his family. Furthermore, as a mark of respect to Bruno, the Commission ceded several lucrative gambling territories in North Jersey to Bruno's family.[30]

The Philadelphia family, along with the Commission, agreed on a protocol by which Philadelphia members could operate gambling joints in Trenton, New Jersey, in partnership with New York–based Cosa Nostra members. If a member of a family from another city wished to open a business in an area where Bruno family members operated, he had to consult the Bruno family first, and offer a fifty-percent share in the profits. Phil Testa, then the underboss of the Bruno family, explained the agreement to Nicodemo Scarfo as follows: "In other words, they have an agreement for card games and crap games. Say like you're from New York and I want to open up this game. I say, 'Look I want to open up. You've got fifty percent.'"[31]

OPEN TERRITORIES

The concept of "open territories" or "open cities" was introduced in the 1930s by the Cosa Nostra Commission when the state of Nevada legalized gambling and allowed casinos to operate in Las Vegas. Cosa Nostra was quick to jump at the tremendous revenue opportunities that casinos and gamblers would bring to the state. The Commission decreed that any Cosa Nostra families would be allowed to operate or have an interest in casinos in Las Vegas. No violence of any sort was to be tolerated. Any disputes regarding gambling or criminal activities would be settled by the Commission.

The "open territories" are Las Vegas, Nevada; Miami, Florida; and Atlantic City, New Jersey. Any Cosa Nostra member is free to operate in these areas; however, he has the obligation to report his activities to his family.[32]

Las Vegas, Nevada

In 1931 gambling was legalized in Nevada as a Depression-fighting measure. But it was only after the end of the Second World War that casinos began to flourish, as Italian and Jewish underworld figures from Chicago and New York made their way to the streets of Las Vegas. Famous casinos such as the Flamingo, the Desert Inn, the Dunes, the Thunderbird, the Sands, the Tropicana and the Stardust were all linked to members of the underworld, such as Benjamin Siegel, Meyer Lansky, Moe Dalitz (of Cleveland), Raymond Patriarca Sr. and Frank Costello.

As several Cosa Nostra families and Jewish crime groups had significant interests in Las Vegas casinos, it became essential for these groups to appoint representatives or "referees" in case of disputes. Moe Dalitz, who owned the Desert Inn, functioned as informal referee when territorial disputes arose between the various crews. Dalitz's job was to oversee Cosa Nostra's interest in Las Vegas by making sure that the money-skimming operations in the casinos proceeded smoothly.[33] Skimming money is the practice of stealing monies from the casino cash boxes, the cashier's cage, the slot machines and the sports race book set up in the hotel. The skimming of money has been a major source of revenue for Cosa Nostra families involved in casinos. It cannot be done without the participation of casino employees.[34] The Kansas City Cosa Nostra family, then led by Nick Civella, had the responsibility of overseeing the skimming of monies for the Chicago family, to which it answered.

With the establishment of casinos in Las Vegas, the Chicago family exercised a very strong influence, which it has maintained ever since the opening of the Flamingo Hotel, originally owned by Benjamin Siegel. Gambling activities in Las Vegas have to be cleared by the Chicago family. In the early days John Rosselli, a prominent member of the Chicago family, was the official representative for the family and was responsible for overseeing gambling operations.

Following Benjamin Siegel's murder in June 1947, authorities learned that several hotels were linked to members of organized crime. The Nevada Gaming Commission was created to "police and keep out" organized crime's infiltration of the casino industry. In 1963 the Gaming Commission revoked Frank Sinatra's licence to operate a casino when it discovered that Sam Giancana had an hidden interest through Sinatra.

In 1977, following a meeting of the Cosa Nostra Commission, it was ruled that the Chicago family would oversee all gambling operations in Las Vegas. The families of New York, Philadelphia and New England would oversee the Atlantic City gambling operations. Las Vegas was no longer an "open city" for the eastern Cosa Nostra families.[35]

Miami, Florida

For nearly a century, Miami and its surrounding area has been a vacation spot for mobsters. As early as the 1920s, South Florida was a place of refuge for the Capone gang. As years went by, Miami became an "open city" and several underworld figures live there permanently.

Any Cosa Nostra family can conduct activities such as gambling and loansharking in Miami, as long as it does not interfere with the business of the Tampa-based family, formerly led by the Trafficante family. The latter has always had a presence and criminal interest in Miami, but it is believed that the Tampa family never had sufficient manpower to control the whole state of Florida and, in particular, the Miami area.[36]

In 1978 law enforcement agencies identified more than seventeen Cosa Nostra families operating in Dade County. There were about 117 Cosa Nostra members living in Florida. The families were involved in a wide variety of criminal activities, ranging from financial fraud to book-making, lottery, prostitution, pornography and labour racketeering.[37] As Cosa Nostra contingents in southern Florida increased in number, the Commission decided to appoint Joseph Paterno, an influential *capo-regime* in the Gambino family, the "boss" of that area. Paterno's role was to arbitrate the disputes that would inevitably arise among family representatives from all over the country.

Dade County has also been a place of refuge for several Canadian organized-crime groups. During the 1970s the Quebec Crime Probe Commission held hearings on organized-crime groups in Montreal. Several key members, such as Jos Di Maulo, William O'Bront and Romeo Bucci, all linked to the Vincenzo Cotroni crime group, chose to flee to Florida to avoid appearing before the Crime Probe.

Atlantic City, New Jersey

In 1976 New Jersey authorities, following a referendum, authorized the development of casinos in Atlantic City. The first casino opened in 1978. Today there are twelve licensed casinos in operation, which draw millions of visitors from across North America and around the world, and there is a growing interest in the development of additional mega-resort casinos.

Until 1976 Atlantic City was under the jurisdiction of the Bruno family. In the spring of 1978 Paul Castellano, boss of the Gambino family, allegedly met with Angelo Bruno in Cherry Hill, New Jersey, to solicit Bruno's permission to let the Gambino family step into Atlantic City.[38] Bruno did not oppose the request, and Atlantic City became an "open city." With gambling in Atlantic City came an increase in drug trafficking on the part of Cosa Nostra; this soon brought the downfall of Angelo Bruno, who insisted that members of his family stay away from the narcotics trade there. On March 20, 1980, Bruno was brutally murdered by a dissenting faction within his own family.[39]

In January 1986 John Gotti, the newly self-appointed Gambino boss, met with Nicodemo Scarfo in New York to renegotiate the agreement concluded between Castellano and Bruno years before. This resulted in the creation of an alliance between the Lucchese, Gambino and Genovese families, primarily in legitimate business ventures such as junkets, limousine services and maintenance companies. These families also exerted control over labour racketeering, prostitution, loansharking and drug trafficking in Atlantic City.[40]

OTHER REGIONS

New Orleans

The New Orleans Mafia was one of the first Mafia families to settle in North America. Its origins date back to 1869. Because of its ancestry, the New Orleans family is respected by the other Mafia groups, and it was given the privilege to manage its own business without consulting the Commission. When Joseph Valachi was asked what he knew about the New Orleans family, he replied that he knew little, except that going to Louisiana always required permission: "They don't want visitors. It was an absolute rule."[41]

Regions Controlled by an Outside Family

In the western states, there seems to be no clear-cut Cosa Nostra hierarchy. After the Second World War, cities such as Los Angeles, San Francisco, San Diego and San Jose developed good economies. Small Cosa Nostra groups got permission to establish themselves in these cities. These groups are all under the supervision of the Chicago family. The Chicago family also oversees Cosa Nostra activities in Kansas City, Milwaukee, St. Louis and Denver.[42]

Nor does the Cleveland family act without supervision. Angelo

Lonardo, former underboss in the Cleveland family, stated that the Cleveland family is not an independent group. The family reports to the New York–based Genovese family, which represents Cleveland on the national Commission.[43]

CANADIAN TERRITORIES

Control and jurisdiction of territories outside the United States prompted clashes in 1965 and 1966 between the crime families of Joseph Bonanno and his cousin, Stefano Magaddino, in Buffalo. In 1965 Magaddino argued before the Commission that the "Montreal faction" should be under the control of the Buffalo organization, which already exerted its authority over the cities of Niagara Falls, Hamilton and Toronto, Ontario. Magaddino's firm convictions grew stronger when, in July 1965, Paolo Violi, who had settled in Montreal in 1963, married Grazia Luppino, the daughter of Giocomo Luppino, a prominent 'Ndrangheta leader in Hamilton and close ally of Magaddino. Intense negotiations followed among representatives of the Magaddino and Bonanno families. A first meeting was held in Hamilton on March 30, 1966, at the home of Giacomo Luppino. In attendance were Vincenzo Cotroni and Paolo Violi from Montreal, and Peter Magaddino, Stefano's cousin, from Buffalo.

In November of the same year, another meeting was held, this time in Montreal. A New York delegation led by Salvatore Bonanno met with Cotroni. This meeting caused a lot of trouble for Cotroni, who faced strong pressure from the Bonannos not to switch his allegiance to Magaddino. When Magaddino learned about the Montreal meeting, he accused Cotroni of collusion with Bonanno. Cotroni defended himself by saying that he felt compelled to meet the young Bonanno, who had a personal message to deliver on behalf of his father: Montreal must remain under the Bonanno's jurisdiction. Magaddino did not succeed in his quest to gain control of Montreal. The Bonanno family's strong influence over Montreal still remains today, as the operations and activities of organized crime in Montreal are dominated by the Sicilian-born

Vito Rizzuto, whose crime family is viewed as one of the most influential organized-crime groups in Canada.

SICILIAN MAFIA MEMBERS
OPERATING IN THE UNITED STATES AND CANADA

In 1984 Tommaso Buscetta, testifying for the prosecution at the "Pizza Connection" trial, revealed for the first time the existence of a "Sicilian Arm" of Cosa Nostra that had been in operation in the United States since the late 1950s. After the Second World War, many Sicilian Mafia members and associates immigrated to the United States and Canada. While many of these Mafia members established ties with the American Cosa Nostra, for instance with the Bonanno, Gambino and Lucchese families, they did not form new crime families. Their allegiance remained with Palermo, Sicily. One of the main reasons Sicilian Mafia members left their motherland for the United States and Canada was that Italian authorities implemented, as part of the Anti-Mafia Act provisions, the notion of *soggiorno obbligatorio* (mandatory residence), which enables an Italian court to order a member of the Sicilian Mafia to reside in an isolated area, such as on an island of Sicily, or under house arrest at his usual residence for a certain period of time so as to not have any criminal contact with other mafiosi.[44]

In 1957 several meetings took place between Sicilian and American Cosa Nostra leaders. The purpose of these meetings was to renew links between the organizations and to form an international heroin network. It was agreed that the Sicilian Cosa Nostra Commission would control criminal activities in the United States concerning policy or activities related to substantial investments in drug trafficking.

In 1965 Tommaso Buscetta visited New York City, where he met members of the Gambino family. He was given the rules regarding dual membership and operations in the United States. As a member of the Sicilian Mafia, Buscetta was not permitted to engage in criminal activities for the American Cosa Nostra, nor to speak on its behalf. Sicilian Mafia members were welcome in the United States and Canada to find a place of refuge from police or to visit family, relatives or friends. However, they needed permission from the American Cosa Nostra before engaging in criminal ventures of any kind. The American mafiosi were particularly touchy about that rule. They were concerned that the Sicilians would get involved in heroin smuggling without their knowledge, as some American crime families remained opposed to heroin trade.[45]

It is virtually impossible to state the number of members of the Sicilian Mafia in activity in the United States. They are said to be established mainly in New York City and in Cherry Hills, New Jersey. Others have settled in Boston, Buffalo, Chicago, Philadelphia and Dallas. It is not clear whether there is an agreement between the American Cosa Nostra and the Sicilian Mafia to let the Sicilians operate in certain defined locations.[46] However, law enforcement agencies in New York City have observed Paolo La Porta, a made member of the Palermo Cosa Nostra, travelling regularly between Palermo and Brooklyn, the traditional territory of the Bonanno family. La Porta is reported to have said to an informant that Brooklyn is a territory in which the Sicilian Cosa Nostra is allowed to operate, especially in heroin smuggling and trafficking. The Sicilian Mafia has agreed to pay a tribute to the American branch for the privilege of operating "franchises" for the importation and distribution of heroin in New York City. As author Claire Sterling put it, the Sicilians occupy Brooklyn as tenants, and the landlords, the New York families, collect the rent while closing an eye to what is going on. Although both groups display mutual respect, the Sicilians answer only to the Palermo Commission.[47]

The question of dual membership (for a Cosa Nostra member to belong to both the Sicilian and the American Cosa Nostra) has been an issue among the families for some time. In a conversation recorded in April 1974 by the Montreal Urban Community Police, Paolo Violi, the Calabrese boss of the Montreal crime family, explained to Carmelo Salemi, a high-ranking member of the Sicilian Agrigento family, that a made member—whatever the rank he holds in a family—has to submit to a probation period with the Montreal faction lasting five years before he will be officially recognized by New York. Salemi had come to Montreal to persuade Violi to recognize Giuseppe Cuffaro, a member of the Caruana crime family who had been living in Montreal for a few years, as a member of the Montreal *borgata*. Violi told Salemi that a member of the Sicilian Cosa Nostra could not automatically become a member of the American Cosa Nostra. "You can't talk about your family here—Montreal. You can't talk about anything," said Violi, meaning that Sicilian mafiosi can live in Montreal and maintain their contacts, but cannot participate in the family's criminal businesses.[48] The Sicilians took exception to that rule and claimed they had a right to participate in criminal activities in Montreal and get a share. On January 22, 1978, Paolo Violi was murdered by the Sicilian faction for having enforced the rule too strictly.

Chapter 7

Rules Regarding Criminal Activities

Cosa Nostra provides services and commodities to the public that are prohibited by law. "We serve needs," declared Nicholas Caramandi, a former Mafia member of Philadelphia, to another member. "People come to see us when they can't get justice, or to borrow money that they can't get from a bank. There are no favours we can't do. We are the best."[1] From that perspective, the essence of Cosa Nostra's criminal activity is not predatory, but rather centred strictly on profitable activities.

Cosa Nostra's structure and organization has enabled it to develop and control many large-scale criminal enterprises. For several decades it has remained entrenched for the most part in "traditional" crimes: gambling, sport betting, loansharking (shylocking), cargo hijacking, theft, fencing stolen goods, infiltration of legal businesses using frauds, scams, bankruptcy, arson, pornography and prostitution. In the New York City area in particular, through intimidation, extortion and corruption, Cosa Nostra has largely penetrated the construction industry by gaining control over construction unions and the supply of labour. It has also engaged in the corruption of public officials. Trafficking in drugs such as heroin is another very important source of income, although it has been the subject of contention within Cosa Nostra families by virtue of a ban imposed by the Commission.[2]

In the northeastern United States, labour racketeering and infiltration of the construction trades are among Cosa Nostra's primary activities, while firearms trafficking is common in the north-central region. The Philadelphia family has traditionally been involved in the trafficking of methamphetamine. Forgery and arson are prominent in the southern and western regions. In the Midwestern states, gambling activities are the main source of revenue, supervised by the Chicago family. Chicago is also one of the few cities where prostitution is controlled by Cosa Nostra. The New Orleans family's gains are mostly derived from the infiltration of legal businesses.[3]

In the early 1980s Nicodemo Scarfo allowed his soldiers to engage in "shakedown practices," which were no more than a violent form of extortion perpetrated on independent criminals involved in loansharking, sport betting, numbers banking and drug dealing. These criminals did not benefit from the protection of the Scarfo family. The victims had no choice but to pay a certain amount of money if they did not want to be attacked by other members of the family. Black criminals were not targeted by shakedown practices, as Scarfo knew they would not feel threatened by it. Criminals with political connections and the Pagans outlaw motorcycle gang were also not targeted.[4]

Modern technologies such as the Internet and e-mail have been attracting the attention of organized-crime families, as they provide anonymity for perpetrators who conduct massive securities manipulations and stock frauds. As early as the 1990s, several members of the New York families, as well as Russian organized-crime groups, became extensively involved in these new and very lucrative areas of criminal activities. They have also turned to insurance and health care fraud and computer scams.

APPROVAL FOR CRIMINAL ACTIVITIES

A boss or a *caporegime* can order a soldier to commit a crime or allow him to engage in a criminal activity. A soldier cannot engage in a criminal activity without the clearance of his superiors. This is a basic rule in Cosa Nostra. He might interfere with another member's interest or cause a breach of security in the family should the unauthorized activity draw attention from police. Checks to make sure another member is not involved in the same type of activities in that area are required. This is to prevent unfair competition among members. In taking these measures, a member ensures he will benefit from the protection his crime group will provide in case of a police investigation or arrest. Moreover, he will be able to survive heavy financial losses if the activities are not successful.[5]

A soldier or an associate who is engaged in an unauthorized criminal activity, such as selling drugs, will not receive the support of his family. This is what happened to Henry Hill, a close associate of the Lucchese family, who was warned not to sell drugs while he was serving a sentence in jail, but managed to do so anyway. Paul Vario, a Lucchese *caporegime*, refused to place bail for Hill because of his stubbornness.[6]

Although, in general, a member is obligated to inform his boss of his involvement in criminal activities, the strictness of the rule varies from one Cosa Nostra family to another. For instance, in the Philadelphia family, under the leadership of Angelo Bruno, every member had to ask permission of the boss before engaging in any gambling ventures, "numbers" businesses,[7] bookmaking or crap games. But activities such as selling stolen goods had to be cleared only at the *caporegime* level.[8] On the social ladder of crime, a soldier does not under any circumstances approach a high-ranking organized-crime family member directly. Ranking and hierarchy are strictly enforced as a matter of protection for the upper family's hierarchy.[9] John Gotti once lectured a cohort as to what he would say if one of his soldiers came to him and proposed a business deal: "I can't bring myself down. I'm a boss, you know what I mean? I gotta isolate myself a little bit." Gotti reminded the member of the rule that a soldier with a new business deal must first go through his *caporegime*.[10]

When Nicodemo Scarfo took command of the Bruno family in the early 1980s, control over members' criminal activities became more centralized. Scarfo asked for fifty percent of the illegal profits from the soldiers. He insisted on being informed of everyone's criminal activities. According to Nicholas Caramandi, who turned government witness, a soldier who did not keep his boss informed about his criminal activities was marked for death.[11] Scarfo further instructed *capiregime* of the family to start collecting extortion payments from all drug dealers, loan sharks, bookmakers and other racketeers operating on Scarfo's territory. One of these operators, Frank D'Alfonso, a small shop owner, refused to pay the so-called "street tax." D'Alfonso, who was not a made member, operated on the fringe of Philadelphia organized crime. D'Alfonso got a severe beating that put him in the hospital for several weeks. Despite this, he continued to defy Scarfo. Scarfo's credibility and authority were challenged. On July 23, 1985, D'Alfonso was shot and killed on the street.

CRIMINAL FRANCHISES

One of the purposes of criminal franchises is to reduce a crime family's risk by separating its members from direct involvement in illegal activities. By allowing independent criminal groups to operate in districts under Cosa Nostra control, a Cosa Nostra family maintains control and receives a share in the profits with very little risk. A family may also decide to franchise a criminal activity because its members have no expertise in that sphere of activity.[12]

A Cosa Nostra family must be able to police the activities of independent criminals operating on its territory. In Chicago during the reign of Anthony Accardo, the "street tax" rule was strictly enforced. Burglars, thieves or fencers could not operate in the city without paying a "tax" to the Chicago family. The family prohibited operations in the Forest Park section, where several prominent Mafia leaders resided. In 1978 a series of killings of independent burglars and fencers left the Chicago police puzzled until an informant told the FBI of the motives behind these murders, which bore the underworld trademark. It all started in December 1977, when five robbers broke into a vacant building on the North Side, and with acetylene torches broke through the wall of an adjacent jewellery store. The thieves stole more than $1 million worth of diamonds and other jewels. The owner of the store, who was vacationing in Florida when the burglary occurred, happened to be a close friend of Anthony Accardo. When Accardo learned about the theft, he ordered the burglars to return the goods, which was done, although reluctantly. It was suspected that Accardo was given some of the jewellery for his mediation. The burglars thought they had not been treated fairly by Accardo. Two of them foolishly decided to break into Accardo's home while he was in Florida. The burglars had signed their death warrants. They ignored a decree known to all freelance criminals that River Forest was "mob" territory and was strictly hands-off. Accardo did not file a complaint with police. In the following weeks, the bodies of the two were found atrociously mutilated. Later, two more burglars and two associates were also found murdered.[13]

The most common franchises—numbers operations and street sales of heroin—are frequently handled by other ethnic criminal groups, such as African Americans and Puerto Ricans. In New York City, for example, Cosa Nostra used to have exclusive control over illegal gambling operations. In the early 1970s Cuban organized crime, also known as the "Corporation," took a great interest in policy operations and thus increased its involvement in this racket. According to law enforcement authorities, an alliance was concluded between the Corporation and the Genovese family through the mediation of James Napoli, a Genovese *caporegime*. The Cubans pay a tribute to the New York City Cosa Nostra families to operate there by sending envelopes every week.[14] In the early 1980s the Puerto Rican numbers rackets fell under the control of the Cuban Corporation. The Cubans, under the leadership of Jose Battle, also took over the numbers operations once controlled by the Lucchese family on the Upper West Side, New York, and by the Gambinos in Staten Island.

In the 1960s the Zerilli family of Detroit also gave up active participation in the numbers business to local black crime groups, although the Zerillis keep control of these activities through the number wire service and receive a percentage of the proceeds that are generated.[15]

THE BAN ON DRUG TRAFFICKING

Cosa Nostra has a history of dealing in heroin trafficking in the United States. Cosa Nostra was one of the few criminal organizations, along with Asian criminals, that dealt in heroin in the early part of the twentieth century. After the Second World War, the American Cosa Nostra became more and more involved in heroin trafficking, as the United States became one of the most important drug markets in the world. The five New York families were responsible for bringing in ninety-five percent of all the heroin smuggled into the United States. New York City had, at that time, half of the country's heroin addicts.[16]

For a number of reasons, Cosa Nostra gradually became reluctant to continue to engage in smuggling and distributing drugs. The organization has always feared that its members or associates would become addicted. Those caught faced lengthy jail time, and enormous pressure would be put on them—making them more inclined to co-operate with authorities. As Cosa Nostra members did not sell drugs on the streets themselves, they would also have to deal with less-disciplined gangs, who might betray them to police.[17]

In 1948 Frank Costello, then acting boss for the Genovese family, ordered the soldiers of his family not to traffic in heroin anymore. Although his soldiers were attracted to the tremendous profits generated by heroin, several of them had been hit with arrests and convictions. Costello feared his family could collapse because of the arrests. The edict applied only to the Genovese family.

While heroin trafficking was an important source of income for Cosa Nostra, it also attracted the attention of law enforcement officials. The Federal Bureau of Narcotics and Dangerous Drugs, the forerunner of the Drug Enforcement Administration, led a vigorous fight against drug traffickers, and was the first federal law enforcement agency to recognize the existence of the Mafia in the United States.[18] The harsh sentences provided for in the Narcotic Control Act of 1956 caused Cosa Nostra to seek out and rely on European heroin suppliers, especially the Corsicans and the French "cooks," who transformed the morphine base into heroin of a high degree of purity. Under the Act, drug traffickers could be sentenced to forty years. Carmine Galante, then the underboss of the Bonanno family, was jailed for twenty years; Vito Genovese, the boss of the Genovese family, received a fifteen-year jail term; John Ormento and Natale Evola, two capiregime in the Lucchese family, got forty years.

Faced with strong public opposition and incessant law enforcement surveillance, Cosa Nostra was forced to alter its policy regarding drug trade activity in the United States. The organization sensed that the public was not concerned about people who bet on sports, borrowed money from a loan shark or were involved in prostitution and gambling. These

(top) Salvatore Luciano, founder of the American Cosa Nostra (circa 1951)
(bottom) Frank Costello, former boss of the Genovese family, at the Kefauver
Hearings in New York, 1951

(top) Albert Anastasia, New York boss, at the Kefauver Hearings in New York, 1951
(bottom) Vito Genovese, New York boss, after his conviction for drug trafficking, in 1959

(top left) Stefano Magaddino, boss of the Buffalo family (circa 1958)
(top right) Joseph Bonanno, New York boss (circa 1958)
(top bottom) Joseph Profaci, New York boss (circa 1958)

(top) Anthony Accardo, Chicago boss, at the Senate Hearing on Labour Racketeering, in 1958

(bottom) Joseph Valachi, a soldier in the Genovese family, the first Mafia member of the American Cosa Nostra to testify at the Senate Subcomittee Hearings, held in October 1963

(top) Mug shot of Carmine Galante of the Bonanno family (circa 1947)
(middle, left to right) Aniello Dellacroce, underboss of the Gambino family;
Joseph Colombo, boss; Carmine Tramunti, former boss of the Lucchese family
(bottom, left to right) Carlo Gambino, boss; Philip Rastelli, former boss of the
Bonanno family

(top left) New Jersey Cosa Nostra boss Sam DeCavalcante (circa 1970)
(top right) Paul Castellano, former boss of the Gambino family, leaving Federal Court in New York, in February 1985
(bottom) Tommaso Buscetta, making his appearance at the Maxi Trial held in Palermo, in early 1986. For the first time, a high-ranking Sicilian Mafia member would publicly discuss the inner workings and rules of the Sicilian Cosa Nostra.

(top) John Gotti, former boss of the Gambino family, surrendering to federal marshals to face racketeering charges, in March 1986
(bottom) Salvatore Gravano, former underboss and Mafia turncoat, during his hearings on charges of ecstasy trafficking in February 2000

(top left) Montreal crime boss Paolo Violi, testifying at the Quebec Probe on Organized Crime (circa 1975)

(top right) Montreal crime boss Vincenzo Cotroni (circa 1975)

(bottom) Hamilton Cosa Nostra boss John Papalia

crimes were viewed as "harmless." On the other hand, the public and authorities reacted strongly against drug peddlers. The American Cosa Nostra had to take a definite stand on drug importation and distribution. In that regard, two important meetings were held among high-level Cosa Nostra members to establish new rules.

The first meeting, held in Binghamton, New York, in October 1956, was convened to discuss post–Second World War domination of the United States heroin market by Cosa Nostra. The meeting, attended only by leaders of the American Cosa Nostra, formulated a strategy to be proposed to their Sicilian counterparts. Sicily would become a platform for the smuggling of heroin to the United States. It would replace Cuba, which had fallen into political turmoil by that time, as the point of transit for heroin en route to the United States.

A second meeting took place a year later at the Hotel des Palmes, in Palermo, during the week of October 12–16, 1957. Delegates from the United States were Joseph Bonanno, Carmine Galante, John Bonventre, brothers Antonio, Giuseppe and Gaspare Magaddino, John Priziola and Santo Sorge. The Sicilians were represented by Genco Russo and Salvatore Greco, among others.[19] The Sicilian Cosa Nostra was authorized to import and distribute heroin in the United States, while the American Cosa Nostra families, although they would not be directly involved in the business, would open the territory in exchange for a percentage of the profits.

After the spectacular murder of Albert Anastasia on October 25, 1957, the American Cosa Nostra decided to withdraw from the smuggling and sale of heroin. At the Apalachin meeting in November 1957, the Commission decreed a ban on the drug trade for all American Cosa Nostra families. While meeting in Palermo, the Commission had given the Sicilian Cosa Nostra permission to smuggle drugs into the United States, however, as an oraganization the Sicilian mob refused the opportunity. On the other hand, Sicilian members were allowed to be involved on an individual basis if they invested their personal funds.[20]

Joseph Valachi talked about the ban in October 1963, when he testified before a Senate Committee: "No narcotics. You are in serious trouble if you were arrested for narcotics. After Anastasia died in 1957, all families were notified—no narcotics." The ban was ignored by the Lucchese family. The Magaddino family of Buffalo went on smuggling heroin because of its proximity to the Canadian border. According to Valachi (who, at the time of his testimony, was himself serving a twenty-year prison term for conspiracy to traffic heroin), drug trafficking had become the main source of income for many Cosa Nostra soldiers. They could not resist the temptation to get rich quickly.[21] "They defied the rule," said Valachi, because the profits were so huge.[22] The defiance caused a serious breakdown in discipline.

If arrested on a drug charge, a soldier knew he would not receive any financial or legal assistance from the family. Valachi revealed that the Chicago family gave its soldiers $200 a week to motivate them to stay out of drug trafficking. Later the compensation was raised to $250 a week.[23] The Chicago policy angered the New York Cosa Nostra soldiers, who had simply been ordered to stop any involvement with drugs without being given any compensation in return. The Chicago family levied a street tax on certain businesses it owned to raise the funds to subsidize soldiers. "If they were caught after getting that kind of payment, there was no chance at all for them. They would pay with their lives," said Valachi. Two members of the Chicago family to whom weekly allocation payments had been made were murdered for breaking the rule. One of them was identified as Joe DeMaca.[24]

The so-called ban imposed on drugs has been in effect ever since. But it has never been observed to any great degree, although the number of arrests in Cosa Nostra dropped sharply in the early 1960s.[25] The ban is more of an elaborate campaign to convince the public that Cosa Nostra is involved only in so-called victimless crimes, such as gambling and bookmaking.[26] Still, even today, the rule is always stated during initiation ceremonies: "No drug dealings under pain of death." Because anyone arrested on a drug charge in New York State is liable to serve a life sentence (the same sentence applied to murder), the Cosa Nostra families perhaps fear that their members, if caught with heroin in their hands, will tell all they know to get a lenient jail term.[27]

Paul Castellano, the successor of his brother-in-law, Carlo Gambino, was a strong adherent to the "no drug dealing" rule. Castellano was from the old guard. Known as the "Pope," he was a successful businessman in the poultry industry. He viewed members of Cosa Nostra as "gentlemen doing smooth business." For him, drug activities were "street trash," a "nigger business."[28] He distinguished two types of criminal activities: "white-collar," which were labour racketeering and construction bid-rigging, and "blue collar," which were auto theft, hijacking and loan-sharking.[29] When he took over the Gambino family in 1976, he solemnly announced his opposition to drugs and warned all the family crews to stay away from them. He decreed that anyone caught dealing drugs after 1962 could never become an initiated member of the Gambino family.[30] Further, he pressured the Commission to sanction the death penalty against anyone caught in the drug racket who involved other family members.[31] As a Gambino *caporegime*, John Gotti passed the word that he would not back those members of his *regime* caught dealing in drugs.

Despite the ban, drug trafficking persisted in the Gambino family. Everyone knew that quick money made from the drug trade exceeded that made from traditional rackets such as hijacking and loansharking.[32] In April 1984 the United States Department of Justice charged thirty-one members and associates of the Bonanno and Gambino families with heroin trafficking. The traffickers had been operating a network through pizza parlours in New York City, Philadelphia, Detroit, Chicago and other cities. Nearly two metric tons of heroin and cocaine were smuggled between 1979 and April 1984. The heart of the distribution ring was in Brooklyn. It was operated by Salvatore Catalano, a Sicilian Mafia member, who held the rank of *caporegime* in the Bonanno family and who developed relationships with the Gambino family. When Anthony Corallo, then boss of the Lucchese family, heard the news of the heroin bust, he burst into rage. "Anybody f— with junk, they gotta be killed. That's all. We should kill them. We should have some example," he said to his chauffeur, soldier Salvatore Avellino. The conversation was picked up by a bug placed in Avellino's car by the FBI.[33] The case, which became known as the "Pizza Connection," revealed the role of the Sicilian Mafia in international drug trafficking. The Sicilians were allowed to operate in New York in return for the payment of a tribute. It was further proof of the link between the Sicilian Mafia and the American Cosa Nostra.

Two other cases of drug trafficking—the Peter Tambone case and the Angelo Ruggiero tapes—led to high drama in the Gambino family.

The Peter Tambone Case

In April 1982 two members of the Gambino family informed Aniello Dellacroce, the underboss, that Peter Tambone, a sixty-two-year-old soldier in John Gotti's *regime*, was a heroin dealer. The news made its way to Paul Castellano's ears, and he summoned Dellacroce and Gotti to hear what they had to say. Since Tambone was a made member, he deserved to be killed for having violated the rule, Castellano told them.

A fair hearing on a charge of such gravity was almost impossible to hold because the accusation was made by two Cosa Nostra members. There was a presumption of guilt. According to Cosa Nostra rules and ethics, a member, on his honour, must tell the truth when speaking to another Cosa Nostra member. He cannot accuse another member unless the allegations are fully substantiated. Should the accusation be revealed to be untrue or unsupported, the accused would be given the opportunity to restore his honour by killing his accusers immediately.

Gotti was caught in a catch-22 situation. As a soldier in Gotti's crew, Tambone was responsible to Gotti. Gotti had no choice but to protect his soldier. However, if Gotti defended Tambone too vigorously he would be implying that two made members were lying—always a dangerous move—and that Gotti had intimate knowledge of Tambone's actions. Gotti's position was further complicated by Castellano already suspecting that Gotti's crew was trafficking. If Gotti took full responsibility for Tambone, Gotti would be implicated in the drug trafficking. Gotti was forced to negotiate a very delicate situation in order to save his own neck.

As Gotti was hesitant to murder Tambone at Castellano's request, Castellano informed him that he was going to seek the Commission's approval to get rid of Tambone. Castellano wanted to teach a lesson to everyone in the family by getting the support of the other families to enforce the no-drug-trafficking rule. A Commission meeting was called. Castellano and Vincent Gigante, the head of the Genovese family, voted for Tambone's death, while the bosses of the Colombo and Lucchese families voted against a death sentence. The Bonanno family, at that time led by Phil Rastelli, had lost its voice on the Commission because of its involvement in drugs. With only four families represented, the Commission was deadlocked. The matter being unresolved, Castellano became determined to expel Tambone from the family.

The Angelo Ruggiero Tapes

Castellano and Dellacroce did not get along. After the death of Carlo Gambino in 1976, everyone expected that Dellacroce would become the next boss. But Gambino designated his cousin, Paul Castellano, boss. The ongoing tension between the Paul Castellano and the Aniello Dellacroce factions did not come to an end with Tambone's expulsion. In 1983 the United States District Attorney laid down an indictment against several members of the Gambino family. Charged with trafficking in heroin were Angelo Ruggiero, Gene Gotti and John Carneglia. The indictment was based on information from tapes originating from wiretaps the FBI had installed years before in Ruggiero's residence. (Ruggiero was dubbed "Quack, Quack" because of his propensity to spell out everything he knew over the phone.)[34]

When Paul Castellano learned about the indictment in 1983, and the existence of the incriminating tapes, he summoned John Gotti and Ruggiero. He ordered them to surrender to him a copy of the tape's transcripts, which had been released to Ruggiero's lawyer. Castellano warned Gotti that if he did not receive the transcripts, he would dissolve Gotti's crew, demote him to a soldier rank and assign him and his men to another *caporegime*.[35] Gotti and Ruggiero sought advice from Aniello Dellacroce, who was fighting cancer, in spring 1985. Dellacroce wisely cautioned his nephew, Ruggiero, to comply with Castellano's orders: "If the boss wants the tapes, he gets the tapes. You don't understand Cosa Nostra."[36]

Ruggiero was opposed to surrendering the tapes. Not only would Castellano discover his involvement in heroin trafficking, but he would also learn that Ruggiero had broken another rule, which forbids a member to talk about Cosa Nostra Commission business with a non-member.

Ruggiero had disclosed to an associate, Eddy Lino, the Commission discussions regarding Peter Tambone.[37]

On December 2, 1985, Dellacroce died of natural causes. Two weeks later, Castellano and his newly appointed underboss, Thomas Bilotti, were murdered by Gotti in Manhattan. Ruggiero was eventually indicted on a federal charge of drug trafficking, but in 1989 he died of cancer before facing his trial.

On June 4, 2002, less than a week before the death of John Gotti, his brother Peter, a former New York City sanitation employee who, until his brother's death, was the acting boss of the family, was arrested and charged for racketeering activities.[38] Peter Gotti went on trial in January 2003. On March 17 a jury found him guilty of extortion, bid-rigging and other crimes aimed at controlling businesses on New York's waterfront. It will be interesting to see if Peter Gotti is able to run the family from behind bars, as his brother did. It appears the Gambino family will select Nick Corozzo, a well-respected *caporegime*, as the next boss of the family. The acting underboss is Arnold Squitieri, an obscure *caporegime* from New Jersey and close ally of John Gotti. Squitieri was convicted in 1988 by New Jersey authorities for conspiracy to distribute heroin. After serving eleven years in prison, he was released in March 1999 and was promoted to the rank of *caporegime*. In 2003 he was appointed acting underboss. The appointment of a former drug convict to the position of underboss is an indication that the current Gambino family does not shun drug trafficking activities.[39]

According to Italian authorities, it seems the Sicilian Mafia no longer purchases huge quantities of drugs from source countries to distribute at international levels. The family of Bagheria, near Palermo, who used to play a major role in the supply of heroin to the United States, is now reduced to supplying the low-level distribution networks in Palermo.[40]

OTHER FORBIDDEN ACTIVITIES

There are other types of criminal activities that Cosa Nostra may not authorize. When Carlo Gambino was in command of his family, he ordered his soldiers to avoid criminal activities such as counterfeiting, stock and bond frauds, and kidnappings. All these crimes were within the realm of federal jurisdiction. Gambino was well aware that federal agencies had sweeping powers to prosecute these types of offences, and he wanted to avoid exposure to high-risk crimes.[41] Gambino family members were forbidden to kill with bombs.[42]

In the Angelo Bruno family, drugs and violence were outlawed, as well as kidnappings, prostitution and counterfeiting. Bruno wanted to maintain order around him and to avoid heavy fines, especially in regard to counterfeiting. He had a disdain for those who were involved in prostitution. He saw living off the avails of prostitution as dishonourable.[43] His views were shared by several other Cosa Nostra families. In the Patriarca family, for example, a soldier was warned to stop his pimping activities.[44] The same rule prevailed in the Cleveland family.[45]

In Sicily, men of honour regard themselves as above common criminals. They perceive themselves as the elite of the underworld. Therefore, criminal activities such as prostitution and pornography are considered dishonourable. Those involved are highly scorned by others.[46] Today, members of the Sicilian Mafia perceive themselves as different from their American counterparts, who are more inclined to be involved in prostitution and pornography.

In Cosa Nostra, some types of crime are considered "weak" or "low." Luigi Ronsisvalle, a former Sicilian member, explained before the President's Commission on Organized Crime that a member of the Mafia does not rob a woman. This is seen as losing face. "Even can't face my wife. This was the worst a man can do is rob a lady. This is the lowest in society," said Ronsisvalle, after admitting to having robbed a woman.[47] In the ritual of admission to the Sicilian Mafia, a member pledges to never rob people.

In the American Cosa Nostra, thefts and armed robberies are considered "petty crimes" and are not allowed. "You are on your own [not protected by the family if caught by police]," stated Joseph Valachi, at his testimony before the Senate Committee.[48] In a taped conversation recorded by the FBI on May 24, 1965, Sam DeCavalcante complained to

Anthony Russo about one of his soldiers, Frank Cocchiaro: "Frank is a rough guy. I have to watch. Frank would do heist jobs—armed robberies—if I'd let him." Russo replied, "They have no other way of making a living, so what can they do?" referring to soldiers who were unable to make a living from gambling or legitimate activities.[49]

Chapter 8

The Judicial System
of Cosa Nostra

Not surprisingly, there are seminal differences between the judicial system of a democracy and that of the underworld. In a democratic system, citizens have the power to keep political leaders in place. In Cosa Nostra, strict obedience to a code of conduct and absolute loyalty to a family boss are expected from every member.[1] Leaders hold onto their positions of power only because they are able to instil fear in their peers. A change in the leadership of a crime family will occur only if the boss dies or consents to step down. Therefore, a change desired by members of the family is most often obtained through violence.

Citizens who commit a felony demonstrate that they no longer accept the rules and laws legislated by government and acknowledged by the community. They have become deviant. If caught, they must submit to a judicial process and accept a punishment that has been commonly agreed upon by society as a whole. The severity of the sanction will be in proportion to the gravity of the offence. The danger of breeding a society of criminals is greatly reduced when citizens are given advance notice that deviant behaviour will result in a fine or imprisonment.[2] Citizens must understand why a sanction is imposed to have a clear understanding of what conduct is expected from them.

In the world of organized crime, the notion of acceptable conduct is not so clearly defined. Leaders establish codes of conduct for the members of their families, but the rules are nowhere written down.[3] The absence of written offences with corresponding repercussions causes difficulty when there is conflict. Potential sources of conflict are numerous, but the most common ones are cheating and stealing: a drug purchaser refuses to pay his supplier; a drug supplier misleads a customer on the purity of the drug; someone refuses to pay a hired killer after he has fulfilled a murder contract.[4] To ensure respect in criminal transactions, the threat of reprisal must be explicit. Thus, conflict is likely to lead to murder unless the matter is quickly arbitrated. Cosa Nostra, therefore, has a judicial system that deals with disputes before they get out of hand.

ARBITRATION AND SETTLEMENT OF DISPUTES

Cosa Nostra settles disputes both within itself and with other crime groups and outsiders. These disputes may concern business practices or jurisdiction over territory or criminal operations. Its monopoly has come about because of the durability and stability of its criminal organization, but also because of its reputation of enforcing underworld rules by resorting to violence.[5] Cosa Nostra limits the scope of its jurisdiction to activities in which it is itself involved. It will not arbitrate disputes in the marijuana trade, for instance.

Rules of Procedure

Conflicts that arise in a given area are arbitrated by the Cosa Nostra family that controls that territory. For example, a conflict involving members of the Genovese family in a territory controlled by the Colombo family will be arbitrated by the Colombos. In principle, each Cosa Nostra family recognizes the legitimacy and hierarchy of the other Cosa Nostra families.

Dispute arbitration is not a specialized function; any ranking member may be called to be an arbitrator. The highest-ranking member present at a sit-down will hear the case and judge it on its merits. He has full authority to hear the case, to deliver a decision and to fix the terms of the settlement. All parties involved in a dispute are represented by a ranking member.

Non–Cosa Nostra members, whatever influence or power they may have within their criminal circles, cannot act as mediators but only as intermediaries. Independent criminals can access the arbitration services, but only if they have an established business relationship with Cosa Nostra, legal or otherwise.[6]

There is no substantive set of rules to govern dispute settlements, even within each family. Arbitrators and participants regard the decisions as self-enforcing, respected and obeyed by both parties. Disputes, also called "beefs," can occur between members of the same *regime*, between members of different *regimes* in the same family, between members of different families, or between members and associates or outsiders. Each scenario, as described below, follows certain rules of procedure.

Disputes Between Members of the Same Regime

If two or more Cosa Nostra members belonging to the same *regime* enter into conflict, they will first try to find a solution themselves. Quite often, minor disputes can be resolved peacefully. If the members cannot reach an agreement, or if one of them feels unjustly treated, they must take the problem to their assigned *caporegime* for a solution. If the *caporegime* does not succeed in satisfying both parties, then the matter is "put on the carpet" before the underboss or *consigliere*. In rare instances, the boss may be called on to intervene.

Disputes Between Members of Different Regimes in the Same Family

In this situation, if the parties involved cannot succeed in reaching an agreement, the *capiregime* are expected to act as mediators. The *capiregime* will convene a sit-down. If an agreement is reached, the *capiregime* will issue a notice regarding subsequent arrangements for each party, and the losing party must comply. If the issue of the dispute remains unresolved at this level of authority, the matter will be referred to the family boss, who will hear the case. (The boss may delegate his underboss or *consigliere* to take his place.) The boss's decision is final.

Disputes Between Members of Different Families

If a conflict arises between two or more members of different Cosa Nostra families, it must be directed to their *capiregime*, who will bring the case to their respective bosses.[7] Even if a solution has been already reached, each of the family bosses must be notified of the existence of the dispute. They will convene a meeting. If an agreement is reached, a notice will be issued to all parties. If they cannot reach an agreement, the matter is referred to the Commission. Following a hearing, the Commission will issue a notice to each party. The Commission's decision is final.[8] The notice may ask for a compromise between the parties, or a payment of damages on the part of one of the parties. Failure to comply with the notice gives the Commission the right to order punishment. Punishments are carried out by the *caporegime* or boss of the member who is at fault.[9]

Disputes Between Members and Associates or Outsiders

Independent criminals or crime family associates must have a *rappresentante*, usually a made member, who has introduced them to the family. The *rappresentante* is responsible for the associate's or outsider's actions.[10] Should the associate or outsider be found guilty of any violation, the sponsoring member will be held liable as well. During the sit-down, the independent criminal or the associate is requested to wait in another room. He is not allowed to present a defence himself, but must go through his *rappresentante*. The family will hear the made member first, regardless of whether he is the accuser or the accused. Then the *rappresentante* speaks on behalf of the associate or outsider.

The Sit-Down

The meeting where parties are brought together to solve a problem is called a "sit-down." If one of the parties is charged with improper conduct, for example stealing from or competing against another soldier, the member is allowed to present a defence. As in ordinary criminal courts, hearsay evidence is not admitted in the courtrooms of Cosa Nostra. Only hard evidence is accepted.[11] Sometimes, depending on the nature of the charge and the conclusiveness of the evidence, the accused may not be allowed to defend himself but must "answer" the charges. Once rendered, a judgement becomes "law," and serves as a warning for all parties involved. If one of the parties fails to comply with the judgement, he is either punished or killed.[12]

A "rabbi" is an individual who acts as a representative for a member involved in a dispute. He may act also as a family representative when a dispute involves two or more families. In 1962, after Joseph Magliocco died, Joseph Colombo took over the Profaci family. At that time, there was a Brooklyn faction, led by Joey Gallo, that sought a fairer share of criminal activities. A sit-down was called to resolve the issue. Raymond Patriarca Sr., the New England crime boss, was asked to act as mediator, while the Gallo faction was represented by Nick Bianco, who acted as rabbi.[13]

When a Cosa Nostra member has a grievance against another member, the matter must be "put on the carpet" as soon as possible. This is what Joseph Valachi, a soldier in the Genovese family, was told by his *caporegime*, Anthony Strollo, in 1946, when Valachi was accused of punching Frank Luciano, a member of the Vincent Mangano family (today known as the Gambino family). Valachi and Luciano owned a restaurant together. According to Valachi, Luciano had stolen money from the restaurant to pay his gambling debts.[14] Valachi got angry and hit Luciano. He had broken the rule that prohibits members from hitting a fellow member. A charge was laid against him, and a date was set for a sit-down to hear the case.

Disputes between members, and particularly between members of different families, must be resolved at the upper echelons of Cosa Nostra. The hearing is always called by the family from whom the complaint originates. In this case, it was the Mangano family. Albert Anastasia, at the time a *caporegime*, presided over the hearing. Both Luciano and Valachi were accompanied by their *capiregime*. Each party presented their arguments. Anastasia blamed Valachi for having hit

Luciano: "After all, you've been in this life of ours for twenty years. There is no excuse for you. You know you can't take the law in your own hands."[15] Anastasia ordered Luciano to end his business relationship with Valachi, and Valachi was permitted to keep the restaurant.

Ralph Salerno, a former New York City police officer and an expert on organized crime, related an incident that occurred in the early 1960s, when a group within the Profaci family decided to expand their gambling operations into a territory where gambling operations were already in place under the control of the Sam DeCavalcante family in New Jersey. Confronted with this unwanted competition, members of the DeCavalcante family immediately alerted their boss. The bosses met in a hunting lodge owned by Profaci in New Jersey. It was a way for Profaci to enter into New Jersey without losing face. It was then agreed that the Gowanus Canal, which bisected the area, would be the demarcation line between the two families for their gambling operations.[16]

Judgements delivered at "kangaroo courts" are carried out right away, with no right of appeal. Gregory Scarpa, a Colombo *caporegime*, told Martin Light, a New York lawyer for the Colombo family, that once a sit-down is over, decisions or sentences are executed right on the premises. Scarpa told Light about a sit-down he had attended in a Manhattan bar. Each of the parties was called separately to tell its side of the story. After deliberations, both parties came back into the bar to hear the decision. Then some were told to leave. Scarpa went out first. Soon after, he heard shots fired. The parties against whom the decision was rendered had been executed on the spot.[17]

Arbitration of Legitimate Business Activities

Cosa Nostra's influence also reaches areas of legitimate business activities controlled by organized crime. For a long time the Genovese family regulated personnel and solved disputes for the toxic waste industry. It infiltrated legitimate sanitation businesses by taking over the union. In 1976 Tino Fiumara, a *caporegime* in the Genovese family, was called in to arbitrate a dispute between Gabriel San Felice, a secretary-agent of a garbage company operating in several New Jersey cities, and Chris

Roselle, also a garbage contractor. San Felice complained that Roselle was stealing contracts from toxic landfills. Both men had extensive links with Genovese and Gambino family members. After two sit-downs, Fiumara ordered San Felice to hand over to Roselle some of his contracts.[18] He further told San Felice to report to Carmine Franco, a New Jersey garbage contractor and a close associate of Fiumara, should he have any problems in the future.[19]

Business executives of large corporations eager to expand their operations will sometimes call upon Cosa Nostra to mediate. In 1964 Mid-City Development Company, a Detroit-based corporation, had cash flow difficulties. It contacted Dominick Corrado, a *caporegime* in the Zerilli family, to get a mortgage loan from the Teamsters Central States Southeast and Southwest Areas Funds. The company later sought Cosa Nostra's help again for an additional loan of $200,000, but this time through James Plumeri, a *caporegime* in the Lucchese family. It was alleged that the Detroit family had not agreed with the terms of the loan. A dispute arose between the two families, and the matter was referred to the Commission. It was decided that the question would be heard and arbitrated by the Pittsburgh family, who appointed Frank Amato Sr., a high-ranking family member. After hearing the case, Amato ruled that the Detroit family had priority on the deal and was therefore entitled to handle the matter. But once the loan was received by Mid-City Development, the Lucchese family got a cut of the deal.[20]

SANCTIONS

A wide range of sanctions can be taken against a Cosa Nostra member, depending on the gravity of the fault. Disciplinary sanctions for a ranking member will usually be a demotion, a fine, a suspension or an expulsion. A soldier cannot be demoted, since this rank is the lowest one in a Cosa Nostra family. He is either disciplined or killed. He can also be deprived of the proceeds of his crime activities for a while, following a suspension for a certain period of time. Death sentences are imposed for serious offences such as breaching security or hitting or falsely accusing another made member.

Only a family boss can sanction an execution. However, an underboss or a *caporegime* is allowed to execute punishments such as a slap in the face, a reprimand or a suspension. Reprimands or corporal punishments are given in the presence of the other party to humiliate the offender and show his weakness.[21]

Demotions

The demotion of Joe Sferra from the position of *caporegime* was a well-publicized event. Sferra was removed not only as *caporegime* but also as business agent for a New Jersey union because of his repeated failure to follow instructions from his boss, Sam DeCavalcante. By removing Sferra from his union position, DeCavalcante undoubtedly saved Sferra's life. Sferra was defying crime boss Carlo Gambino, who wanted his men to work in unions that Sferra controlled. Sferra was officially told of his demotion by DeCavalcante, who justified his decision by saying he was "doing the right thing for our people, and that while he liked Joe Sferra, he liked the family more."[22]

The demotion of Joseph Biondo, an underboss in the Gambino family, is another well-known case. Biondo had, among other things, caused an outrage when he left his wife to live with a prostitute. Carlo Gambino could not tolerate his underboss's conduct, as an underboss must always be an example of good behaviour. When summoned by Gambino, Biondo refused to meet him. His refusal was an insult to Gambino, and it could have been fatal for Biondo. Gambino, however, chose to adopt a soft approach. A committee was appointed to meet with Biondo to examine his conduct. The committee recommended that Biondo be demoted to the rank of soldier.[23]

When a new boss takes over command of a family, ranking members will sometimes lose their positions. After Albert Anastasia, boss of the Gambino family, was executed in October 1957, his brother Tony, president of the 14,000-strong Local 1814 of the International Longshoremen's Association and *caporegime* in the Gambino family, was demoted to soldier and lost his union position.[24] When Nicodemo Scarfo took over the leadership of the Bruno family in March 1981, he promoted and demoted people at will. Among his notable demotions were Salvatore Merlino, from underboss to soldier, and Thomas Del Giorno, Lawrence Merlino and Ralph Napoli, from *capiregime* to soldiers.[25] Aladena Fratianno and Frank Bompensiero, of the Jack Dragna family of Los Angeles, were demoted from *capiregime* to soldiers after Dragna's death in 1957. Both men were apparently feared by new leaders Frank DeSimone, Nick Licata and Dominick Brooklier.

Although it happens rarely, there have been cases where a ranking member has asked to be demoted. John C. Montana, a *caporegime* in the Magaddino family of Buffalo, was a well-known and respected business-man. He owned a large taxicab company and served as city councilman from 1927 to 1931. He was named "Man of the Year" in 1956. He had suc-ceeded in hiding his ties to the underworld until his presence at the Apalachin conference was publicized. Senate hearings were held to investigate the purpose of this Mafia summit, and Montana was subpoe-naed to explain his attendance at the meeting. Montana told the commit-tee he had happened to stop at Barbara's home because he'd had mechanical problems with his car while en route to Philadelphia. Of course, the committee did not believe him. Following this unwanted publicity, Montana asked the Magaddino family to demote him to sol-dier so as not to compromise the security of other members of the fam-ily. Montana's action is a good example of someone putting the organization ahead of the individual. He kept the reduced rank until his death in 1964.[26] Joseph Barbara, the host of the conference, was also demoted to the rank of soldier.

Fines

Carmine Lombardozzi, a Gambino *caporegime*, was demoted to soldier for a whole series of transgressions: he failed to prevent his brother from assaulting an FBI man at his father's funeral; he seduced the daughter of a Gambino soldier; he punched a policeman; his name appeared too often in the newspapers. In November 1957 Lombardozzi was summoned to the infamous Apalachin meeting to account for his activities in the jukebox field. Vito Genovese, the self-appointed boss, wanted Lombardozzi killed to set an example. But Lombardozzi's boss, Carlo Gambino, pleaded for his life, saying that Lombardozzi had developed great expertise in financial manipulations on Wall Street that included stock thefts and swindles. In other words, Lombardozzi was too valuable to be killed for his violation of the rules. He was fined $10,000 and deprived of illicit income.[27]

Expulsion

One of the most publicized cases of banishment from the family was that of Joseph Bonanno, who, in 1966, was deposed as boss of his family for his repeated refusals to appear before the members of the Commission. Bonanno was challenging the legality of the membership of the Commission on the grounds that, according to Cosa Nostra rules, it had to be renewed and voted upon every five years. Bonanno was accused by the Commission of plotting the murders of three members of the Commission: Carlo Gambino, Thomas Lucchese and Stefano Magaddino, his cousin, who was, at that time, chairman of the Commission.

In October 1964 Bonanno staged his own kidnapping and went into hiding for two years. When his kidnapping was revealed to be a ploy to avoid having to testify before grand juries, he finally surrendered to the Commission. Bonanno's confrontation with the Commission ended when the Commission agreed to spare his life on the condition that Bonanno surrender control of his New York organization. Bonanno was also ordered to live outside New York City. He settled in Tucson, Arizona, in 1968, where he lived until his death in May 2002.[28]

When a Cosa Nostra member is banned, whether temporarily or permanently, he cannot try to contact any other member nor can anyone contact him, under pain of death.[29] The banned member also loses all privileges derived from his membership in Cosa Nostra. However, despite his expulsion, he will always be regarded as a Cosa Nostra member. Frank Bompensiero, the *consigliere* of the Los Angeles family, violated the rule by having a close relationship with Joseph Bonanno. Bompensiero allegedly approached the New York families to request that Bonanno be reinstated. As it turned out, Bompensiero was an informant for the FBI. He was shot to death in February 1977.[30]

The same rule prevails for Sicilian Cosa Nostra members who have been *posato*, or deposed. Some may be expelled from Italy entirely, as was Francesco Di Carlo, who, after his conviction in 1985 in London for heroin trafficking, became a government informant.[31] In an amusing twist, however, Di Carlo has since been incarcerated in Italy.

Chapter 9

The Code of Murder

In the world of organized crime, murder is not regarded as a criminal activity but as a tool. Unlike "non-professional killings" where motives are attributed to jealousy, passion or hate, underworld killings are business decisions based only on rational and calculated motives. Is it worth a loan shark's trouble to kill a person who is heavily indebted to him if there is little hope he will ever be repaid? Paul Castellano and Joseph Armone, an influential Gambino *caporegime*, once discussed the issue of whether murder is an effective way to resolve conflict. Armone believed murder is not always the solution. If someone is behind in his payments, nothing is accomplished by killing him. "The idea is to collect," Armone explained to Castellano. "You're making a living with him," agreed Castellano.[1] Yet, the purpose of murder is to dissuade others from making the same mistakes. And, sometimes, murder is the only option.

A murder contract successfully executed in a cold-blooded manner is perceived as an act of prestige by fellow members of Cosa Nostra. The killer's status will rise. It is without a doubt the foremost message of reliability and loyalty a member can send to his boss. Murder is the tool for upward mobility within a criminal organization. The murderer is known as someone who shows no fear and is never reluctant when asked to kill.

DEATH: THE ULTIMATE SANCTION

The death of a Cosa Nostra member may be ordered for several reasons. He may have been found to be an informant or he may have stolen money from another member, broken a promise or attempted to overthrow the family boss. He might have displayed improper conduct towards the wife or girlfriend of a member, been dealing in drugs or refused to see his boss when summoned. These violations all carry the penalty of death.

Underworld killings are intended to be a deterrent. They must convey a message that will be understood only by the underworld confederation: that a rule has been transgressed. Not only must everyone know the reason a victim has been killed, but everyone must know for whom the death sentence was carried out.[2]

In general, executions are done on the street. Occasionally, the body of the victim will bear marks of mutilation. These signs or marks are intended to tell members the nature of the victim's violation.[3] In Chicago, one mobster took pictures of a mutilated body and would show them to deter anyone inclined to disregard underworld rules. Murder becomes an effective deterrent when it is accompanied by an atmosphere of terror, a strong message to those close to the victim.[4]

Once a murder has been approved by a crime group, it becomes "legitimate"; no one can interfere, or oppose it, even relatives of the intended victim. The order to kill must be carried out at any cost, even if its accomplishment may take years. If the intended victim is the subject of an "open contract," it means that any made member can fulfil the contract, and indeed has a duty to kill that person when he is found.[5]

THE PLANNING AND EXECUTION OF A MURDER

An underworld murder is known as a "contract," an "assignment" or a "hit." Some use the expression "do a piece of work" or "whack somebody." Other use the phrase "clip a guy."[6]

The execution of a sanctioned murder involves various steps, and must be carried out according to strict rules. Underworld death sentences are normally executed by those at the lowest level of hierarchy in a criminal organization. Killing for Cosa Nostra is something that any member or associate may be called upon to do at any time.[7] A soldier who is given a murder contract is responsible for its fulfilment, and he cannot expect any remuneration or reward; the killing is part of his duty and responsibility as a member of Cosa Nostra. A Cosa Nostra associate has no obligation to fulfil a murder contract when asked, since he is not a made member, and his refusal will not be held against him. However, his chance to get made may be impaired forever.

In all American Cosa Nostra families, the underboss, the *consigliere* and the *capiregime*, who are part of the family administration, are not supposed to participate in a murder hit or even know the details of it. The rule was set up for security reasons, mainly for the protection of the family boss. However, John Gotti overlooked the rule; he always required Salvatore Gravano, a high-ranking member, to participate in murders for which that Gravano had personally requested permission.[8]

During the sometimes elaborate preparation for a murder hit, Cosa Nostra members do not talk about it. Everything is kept secret. Underworld killings are very difficult to investigate because they have been carefully planned over a very long period of time, they are carried out by professional killers and they are wrapped in *omertà*, the rule of silence that binds every participant to a murder. Numerous individuals take part in the planning stages, and each ignores or is unaware of what the others are doing. For example, one person will steal a car, while another will steal or adulterate licence plates from a different car. One person will provide a gun, another will make arrangements for the disposal of the body. The coordination of these steps can take several weeks to accomplish.

The person who has been tasked with executing the murder contract is generally brought in from outside the city where the marked person lives. If the killer is a hired gunman, he will not know the name of the victim or the reasons the victim is going to be killed. The hired gunman will usually be shown a photograph that will enable him to "case" the victim. The killer will want to learn the victim's regular habits and daily schedule so he can choose the most convenient moment to hit.[9] On occasion, the killer will be assisted by a "finger man," who will lead him right to the victim. This is done to prevent the murder of the wrong person, which has been known to happen.[10]

The intended victim may sometimes be summoned to a meeting where the killing will take place. If the person is suspicious, a close friend or relative he trusts will be used to make the approach. The trusted person tells the victim to go to a prearranged place, such as a bar or an office. Once the target arrives, he will be killed right away. The body may be left on the street, or taken away to be buried or dismembered in such a way that his identity will never be discovered.[11]

A botched murder contract can lead to the death of those who failed to accomplish the assignment properly. John Gattuso, a deputy sheriff in Greater Chicago, and Jay Campise, a member of the Chicago Outfit, were directed to kill Ken Eto, an associate linked to the Chicago family. Eto, who survived three bullets to the head, was able to identify his assailants. They were subsequently arrested and charged with attempted murder. In July 1983 the Chicago family arranged for the two suspects to be released on bail pending trial. Both disappeared soon after. A few months later their badly mutilated bodies were found in the trunk of a car.[12] Not only had they failed to accomplish their mission, but they had placed the top echelon of the family in danger.

It may happen that during the execution of the contract the gun fails to fire. In that case, the hired killer must retain both the gun and the shells to prove that the handgun did not fire because the mechanism failed.[13] This action will save his life.

THE LICENSING OF UNDERWORLD KILLINGS

According to Tommaso Buscetta, the rules regarding killings within the Sicilian Mafia are elaborate and strict. Killings are authorized only by the *capo* of the territory involved. In principle, every man of honour has to kill at least once before becoming a made member.[14] In general, members are forbidden to kill a woman, someone who is not a member of Cosa Nostra, or anyone for advancement or profit. However, Antonino Calderone, a former Sicilian Mafia member of Catania, Sicily, now a repentant, said that Cosa Nostra will not hesitate to kill a woman who talks to police about men of honour or a woman who is likely to threaten the security of Cosa Nostra. But in no case would Cosa Nostra kill the wife or girlfriend of a member who is in disgrace with the organization.[15]

It is also against the rules to kill a member who is in prison, as the odds of the killer being caught are very high. A prison is regarded as neutral territory. However, in May 1989 Vincenzo Puccio, a *capomandamento* (district leader), was killed in Palermo's Ucciardone prison by two cell-mates, both men of honour. The murder was allegedly ordered by Salvatore "Toto" Riina, head of the Corleone family.[16] In another instance, on February 25, 1982, Pietro Marchese, a member of the Ciualli family of Sicily, was stabbed to death in his cell. The order came directly from the Commission, according to Buscetta.[17]

In his testimony before the Pennsylvania Crime Commission in July 1981, Aladena Fratianno provided details as to how murders within the American Cosa Nostra are authorized and carried out. He revealed that the family boss must always consent to any killing; that a family cannot kill a member of another family unless asked to do so by the other family; and that an order to murder someone must be carried out, no matter how close the killer's relationship with the intended victim.[18]

Authorization by the Family Boss

All murder contracts, without exception, must receive the approval of the family boss. As the perpetration of murder carries serious consequences for the security of the family, it is imperative that the boss be aware of it so he can judge whether to authorize the hit. Alphonse D'Arco, a former *caporegime* in the Lucchese family, was appointed acting boss in January 1991 by boss Vittorio Amuso, who was going into hiding to escape an indictment for the murder of an union official. Amuso warned D'Arco that he could not authorize any murder, nor could he allow the admission of new members into the family without Amuso's authorization.[19]

The boss is sovereign in authority and in power over all his family members and associates. Therefore, he can unilaterally order them killed. To murder members affiliated to another Cosa Nostra family, the bosses of both families must approve.[20] Those are the general principles of the code of murder in Cosa Nostra.

Martin Light, a long-time lawyer for the Colombo family, explained to the President's Commission on Organized Crime that when a member has committed a serious offence against a member from another family, he deserves to be punished by death. The offended member must first inform his *caporegime*, the *consigliere* or the underboss about the incident. Messages are then exchanged between the two families by representatives of equal rank to arrange a sit-down. If the member's violation is proven, and if it is serious enough to carry the death sentence, his family, as a courtesy to the requesting family, will take care of the matter by killing the culprit itself.[21]

Killing without permission can bring heat on a family. In the 1950s Anthony Russo, a soldier in the Genovese family, killed a Jewish associate linked to Gerardo Catena, a high-ranking Genovese member. Russo was summoned before Frank Costello and Albert Anastasia for a sit-down. Russo justified his actions by claiming he had received permission from Ruggiero Boiardo, an important *caporegime* who was overseeing rackets for the Genovese family in New Jersey.[22] It was learned, however, that Russo had told Boiardo he had received permission from the Genovese family. Sometime thereafter, Russo was found murdered in his apartment. Russo had both lied and killed without permission. His loss of control posed a security risk to Cosa Nostra.

In another case, John Gotti, the boss of the Gambino family, once warned James Cardinali, a soldier in that family, never to kill somebody without obtaining permission. Cardinali had taken it upon himself to kill Michael Castigliola because the latter had allegedly reported to Gotti that Cardinali was selling drugs. "Never do anything like that again. You come and ask me. You got to post everything with me," said Gotti. Cardinali replied that he knew if he asked first, he would have been refused permission.[23]

During John Gotti's trial in the winter of 1992,[24] Salvatore Gravano, the main witness for the prosecution, told the court he had once had a grudge against Liborio Milito, the owner of a mob-controlled construction business, because Milito was bad-mouthing the family administration and Gotti himself. "My decision was to ask John [Gotti] to kill him. He [Gotti] thought I was right. He gave me permission to take him out."[25] Milito disappeared on March 8, 1988, and was never heard from again.

Previously, in 1982, Gravano had been involved in a murder that had not been authorized by the family boss. Frank Fiala was an independent multi-kilo drug trafficker linked to the Colombian cartels. In spring 1982 he rented a discotheque called the Plaza Suite for one night to throw a huge party for his birthday. The discotheque, located in Brooklyn, was owned by Salvatore Gravano, at that time a soldier in the Gambino family, and by two silent partners from the Genovese and Colombo families. Some time after the party, Fiala, who was a multimillionaire, showed interest in buying the disco and the building it was in. He offered Gravano $1 million for it. After some hesitation, Gravano went along with the deal. A cheque for $100,000 was written as a down payment, to be followed by a cash payment of $650,000 and a cheque for $250,000 at the closing date, set for June 28, 1982.

On June 27, 1982, Gravano was informed that Fiala had started renovations on the building before the last instalment was paid. Gravano rushed to the disco to find Fiala sitting in Gravano's office chair. Fiala aimed an Uzi at Gravano and told him he was a "greaseballs" (old-timer), and that from now on Fiala was the owner of the place. Gravano left the premises, assuredly humiliated. On the same evening, Fiala was shot to death on the street as he walked to the disco.

The killing of Fiala had not been sanctioned by Paul Castellano, as Gravano had not requested permission. Gravano was ordered to meet Castellano to explain his conduct. While Castellano was told the circumstances of Fiala's killing, he reproached Gravano for not having told him about Fiala's intimidation with the Uzi. Castellano would probably have acceded to Gravano's request to kill Fiala, should Gravano have asked. Gravano replied that he did not ask Castellano's permission first because "he did not want any link between us." Castellano allowed that this hit was an "off-the-record move," and reminded Gravano that Cosa Nostra rules are strict. "You won't ever, ever do a piece of work [murder] unless it's approved by me." Gravano's life was spared.[26]

Permission can be given to kill a member who has plotted against the life of another member. In 1959, after Dominick Olivetto declined the leadership of the Philadelphia crime family, two contenders ran for the top position: Dominick Pollina and Angelo Annaloro, better known as Angelo Bruno. Pollina served as acting boss and reputedly conspired to have Bruno killed. Bruno heard about the plot and brought a charge against Pollina before the Commission. The Commission ruled that

Pollina had acted without justification, and Bruno was appointed head of the family. Although Bruno was therefore given a "justified cause" to kill Pollina, he chose not to do so. Pollina finished his criminal career as an inactive member of the family.[27] In this case, had Bruno opted to use violence, it would have been regarded as "legitimate." When violence is not authorized, it is regarded as an act of war.[28]

Killing for Personal Motives or for Remuneration

Cosa Nostra rules forbid its members to kill for personal motives or for profit. A killing must relate to Cosa Nostra business. In a taped conversation between Aladena Fratianno and John Rosselli, both from the Chicago family, Fratianno reminded Rosselli that even a family boss cannot order someone killed for profit. Referring to a plot to kill Fidel Castro, the Cuban leader, with the assistance of the CIA, Fratianno said, "Jesus, Johnny, you can't kill people for the fucking government. You can't even kill people for money. That's against the rules."[29] Rosselli and Sam Giancana, who were part of that plot, were subsequently murdered for their involvement with the CIA and for not having put the case before the Commission.

The rule is not always followed. Luciano Liggio was the first Mafia member to break the rule. In Sicily in August 1958, he killed Dr. Michel Navarra, part of the old guard and the head of the Corleone Mafia. Navarra's murder was committed without the consent of Cosa Nostra. According to Tommaso Buscetta, the murder of Navarra was the beginning of the disintegration of the code of conduct in the Corleone family, later led by Salvatore Riina in the 1980s.[30]

In 1977 Luigi Ronsisvalle, a Sicilian Mafia member from Catania who was living in Brooklyn, was asked by a police officer to have his brother-in-law killed for a fee of $2,000. The man had forced his own wife to have sexual relations with two men in a quittance for a gambling debt. On another occasion, in 1976, Ronsisvalle was contracted to kill a man by the brother of a fourteen-year-old girl who had been raped. Ronsisvalle was arrested and pleaded guilty to the killing. He did six years of a fifteen-year sentence.[31]

Killing a Family Boss

The Commission's Sanction

The killing of the boss of a Cosa Nostra family is certainly one of the most dramatic events to happen in the underworld. It has considerable impact on the family. Following the creation of the Commission in 1931, it was agreed that no family boss would be killed without the consent of the family bosses sitting on the Commission. However, in some instances, the rule was not always observed.

The history of the American Cosa Nostra is filled with sensational killings of its family bosses. The murders of Cosa Nostra bosses such as Giuseppe Masseria (April 15, 1931), Salvatore Maranzano (September, 10, 1931), Vincent Mangano (April 1951), Albert Anastasia (October 25, 1957), Thomas Eboli (July 16, 1972), Carmine Galante (July 12, 1979) and Paul Castellano (December 16, 1985) all occurred in public on the streets of New York. The attempted killings of Frank Costello (May 2, 1957) and Joseph Colombo (June 28, 1971) made headlines as well.[32] The slayings of Albert Anastasia and Paul Castellano, however, had not been approved by the Commission. Nor had the murder of Angelo Bruno, on March 20, 1980.

The Attempted Murder of Frank Costello, May 1957

In 1957 Vito Genovese violated Commission rules when he attempted to kill Frank Costello. Costello had ruled the Genovese family in Genovese's absence, from 1937 until 1946, while Genovese was living in self-imposed exile in Italy to escape a murder charge. Genovese was eventually arrested and brought back to the United States to stand trial for the murder of Ferdinand Boccia, who was killed in 1934. But he managed to have a witness to the killing, Peter LaTempa, murdered. The charge was dismissed. When he resumed the family leadership, Genovese discovered that Costello had enjoyed prestige and popularity during his tenure. Genovese felt that his leadership was threatened.

Late in the evening of May 2, 1957, Genovese soldier Vincent Gigante shot Costello in the lobby of the apartment building where he lived. But Costello turned away from the direction of the shots, and the bullets did not hit any vital organs. Costello was taken to hospital, where he was treated for his wounds. Gigante was arrested and charged with attempted murder. In court, when asked to identify the shooter, Costello, upholding the rule of silence, said Gigante was not the person who had fired the shots. Gigante was released.

Genovese feared that Costello would go before the Commission to request punitive actions against him. Genovese called all the family's *capiregime* for a show of support at his home in Atlantic Highlands, New Jersey. He hoped to use this support to present an air of legitimacy before the Commission. He allegedly told his lieutenants that Costello and Albert Anastasia had been plotting to kill him. Genovese announced that Costello had been deprived of any rank within the family and "put on the shelf."[33] This ban meant that no Cosa Nostra member would be allowed to do business with Costello in the future. Despite being "put on the shelf," Costello did not lose his membership in Cosa Nostra. Genovese confirmed that he was now the head of the family and appointed Gerardo Catena as underboss.[34] Genovese later met in secret with Costello on neutral ground, and they reached an accord: Costello would abandon his charges against Genovese before the Commission and would retire from the family.[35]

The Murder of Albert Anastasia, October 1957

Though no longer threatened by Frank Costello, Genovese feared that the Calabrian-born Albert Anastasia would seek to avenge the attempted murder of his close ally. Genovese concluded a secret pact with Carlo Gambino, at that time underboss to Anastasia, to murder his own boss. Gambino passed the contract to the Profaci family. On October 25, 1957, Anastasia was shot to death while having his hair cut at the Park Sheraton Hotel in Manhattan.

Officially, Anastasia was killed because of his alleged unauthorized incursions in Havana, Cuba. He tried to compete against Santos

Trafficante, boss of the Tampa family, who had several interests in the gaming industry along with Meyer Lansky. Anastasia was also involved in the selling of memberships into Cosa Nostra.

According to author Fred J. Cook, the slaying of Anastasia had an enormous impact on the future of the Cosa Nostra in New York City. It allowed Carlo Gambino to become one of the most powerful Cosa Nostra bosses in the United States for the next two decades; it led to the Apalachin meeting fiasco, during which law enforcement uncovered the interstate dealings of national Cosa Nostra leaders; and it triggered one of the most ferocious rebellions inside the Profaci family, the Gallo-Profaci wars in the early 1960s.[36]

The Murder of Thomas Eboli, July 1972

The murder of Thomas Eboli was sanctioned by the Commission. Eboli, born in a village near Naples in 1911, took command of the Genovese family after Vito Genovese died in February 1969 while serving a fifteen-year jail sentence for drug trafficking. He co-chaired the family with Gerardo Catena. Eboli was later appointed boss of the family when Catena was sent to jail in 1970 for refusing to testify before a grand jury.

Hot-tempered by reputation, Eboli did not make a lot of friends when he sat on the Commission. He lacked tact and would make insulting comments about other members concerning things Genovese had told him in private. Eboli's troubles increased when, in 1971, he introduced a certain Louis Cirillo, a major heroin wholesaler in the United States, to Cosa Nostra circles. Eboli had vouched for Cirillo's trustworthiness. Cirillo persuaded Eboli to borrow $4 million to front an upcoming heroin shipment. The New York families bankrolled the money. The drug deal went sour, and Cirillo was arrested and charged. Following his conviction in April 1972, federal authorities raided Cirillo's home in Bronx and found $1 million in cash.

Eboli was blamed for the loss of the $4 million, particularly by Carlo Gambino. In an unusual action, the Genovese *capiregime* met in March 1972 and voted to remove Eboli from the leadership of the family. Gerardo Catena, with the approval of the Commission, appointed Frank

Tieri, the most senior *caporegime*, head of the family. On July 16 Eboli was shot to death after leaving the apartment of his mistress in the Crown High area of Brooklyn. Police found $2,077 in his pocket.[37]

The Murder of Carmine Galante, July 1979

The killing of Carmine Galante, boss of the Bonanno family, behind a Brooklyn restaurant on July 12, 1979, was a typical Mafia set-up. Two of Galante's most trusted aides and bodyguards, Baldassare Amato and Cesare Bonventre, had left the table where they were all gathered when a hit squad entered the garden and killed the boss. Amato and Bonventre, as it was later discovered, had tipped the hit men to Galante's whereabouts.[38]

Galante was intensely hated by his peers for his aggressive and unfair tactics. A long-time underboss to Joseph Bonanno, he had been released in 1974 from the Lewisburg penitentiary after serving twelve years of a twenty-year sentence for his conviction in 1962 for heroin trafficking.[39] His return to the streets caused a lot of dissatisfaction within the Bonanno family, as it forced Phil Rastelli to step down as acting boss. Galante behaved in an arrogant manner, particularly following Carlo Gambino's death in October 1976, when he pledged to be Gambino's successor as the head of the national Commission. Galante also attempted to revive the infamous "French Connection" heroin smuggling network by recruiting young mafiosi from Sicily known as "Zips." The "Zips" involvement in heroin trafficking caused the Bonanno family to lose its seat on the Commission in the mid-1980s. (The family was allowed back on the Commission when Joseph Massino took over the leadership of the family in 1991.)

The murder of Galante was regarded as an unanimous authorized hit by the New York Commission. Despite the 1966 exile of Joseph Bonanno, some sources allege that Aniello Dellacroce, underboss of the Gambino family, was sent as an emissary on behalf of the Commission to inform Bonanno that Galante was going to be killed. The communication also conveyed a warning message to Bonanno: do not try to take advantage of Galante's downfall by seeking to regain control of the family.

Less than an hour after Galante's execution, Nicholas Marangello and Steve Cannone, underboss and *consigliere* of the Bonanno family, were observed meeting with Aniello Dellacroce at the Ravenite Social Club. Phil Rastelli, then in prison, was later confirmed as the official boss of the Bonanno family, a position he held until his death in June 1991. He was succeeded by Joseph Massino, who is still in charge.

The killing of Galante split the Bonanno family into two factions: *capiregime* Joseph Massino and Dominick Napolitano aligned with Phil Rastelli in one faction; Dominick Trinchera, Philip Giaccone and Anthony Indelicato—who chose to challenge Rastelli's leadership— were in another. On May 5, 1981, Trinchera, Giaccone and Indelicato were summoned to a sit-down, where they were all executed. Their remains were found a few weeks later. Massino and Napolitano ordered the killings.

The Murder of Angelo Bruno, March 1980

It has often been speculated that the murder of Angelo Bruno of Philadelphia on March 20, 1980, was a result of the growth in casinos in New Jersey. But according to informants and law enforcement sources, Bruno was murdered by his own family for several reasons. The younger generation believed Bruno was too passive in letting the Genovese and Gambino families operate in his territory, mainly in Atlantic City. A second reason was that the conservative Bruno had ordered his soldiers to stay in traditional criminal rackets, such as gambling and loansharking, and avoid more lucrative criminal activities such as the drug trade. Third, there had been growing tension between Bruno and his underboss, Phil Testa.[40]

Mob turncoats Thomas Del Giorno and Nicholas Caramandi, both former high-ranking members of the Philadelphia family, testified at several trials that Anthony Caponigro, the family *consigliere*, engineered the plot to kill Bruno. Caponigro was overseeing the northern New Jersey gambling and bookmaking operations for the family. Caponigro is said to have gone to New York to seek the support and permission of Frank Tieri, then head of the Genovese family, and of leaders of the New York Commission for Bruno's murder. Apparently, Tieri led Caponigro to believe that permission was granted.[41] However, the murder was not sanctioned by the Commission. At the time of his death, Bruno was a member of the Commission. The unauthorized killing of Angelo Bruno upset the New York families very much, according to Vincent Cafaro, a former soldier in the Genovese family.[42]

In the following days, Caponigro and Phil Testa met with the administration of the Genovese family to get its blessing for their takeover of the Philadelphia family. Each met Anthony Salerno, the underboss, separately. According to Cafaro, who was close to Salerno, Testa told Salerno that Caponigro had plotted the murder of his boss. Two weeks later, Caponigro was summoned to New York to meet with Vincent Gigante from the Genovese family. In April 1980 Caponigro returned to New York, this time to meet with Dominick Cantarino, a Genovese *caporegime*, in the diamond exchange centre in Manhattan. A few days later, Caponigro's mutilated body was found. He had been shot and stabbed several times. He was the victim of a "triple-cross" orchestrated with Machiavellian precision by the Genovese family.[43]

A year after Bruno's assassination, on March 15, 1981, Phil Testa was killed by a remote-controlled bomb packed with finishing nails that had been placed on the porch of his home. Testa's murder was not sanctioned by the Commission. The Genovese family was placed in charge of conducting an investigation into the killing. Meanwhile, the Commission appointed Nicodemo Scarfo as the new boss of the Philadelphia family. Scarfo was told to find and kill those responsible for Testa's murder. Of the five individuals involved, two were found and killed.

The Murder of Paul Castellano, December 1985

The slaying of Paul Castellano was the last hit of a family boss to take place in New York City. The decision to kill the boss of the Gambino family was reached by a very small number of *capiregime* at the instigation of John Gotti. Castellano had discovered that members of his crime family, and in particular of the John Gotti *regime*, had been pinched by the FBI for heroin trafficking. Castellano wanted to hear the taped conversations that the FBI had released to the prosecution in which drugs were the main topic of discussion between members of the Gotti crew; ". . . he wanted to prove to Neil [Dellacroce] that Angelo [Ruggiero] was in the drug business," Salvatore Gravano later stated on the witness stand. Gotti knew that Castellano would not only have members killed for violating the no-drug dealing rule but would also dismantle Gotti's crew. With the death of underboss Aniello Dellacroce two weeks before his own execution, Castellano lost his firewall against Gotti. Only Dellacroce had the influence to stop Gotti from plotting Castellano's death. Gotti hit first and fast.

According to law enforcement sources and the testimony of Salvatore Gravano at the trial of John Gotti for Castellano's murder in 1992, there were several other reasons Castellano was marked for death. Some felt that, due to his poor health and age (he was seventy at the time of his murder), he would not stand the pressure of the two trials he was facing: a RICO indictment for being part of a criminal organization (the so-called Commission Trial) and an indictment for being part of an international car theft ring. Others feared he would make an agreement with the government to plead guilty to lesser charges and become a witness for the prosecution.

Castellano had also upset the family administration by letting the Genovese family take the initiative in killing Frank Piccolo, a *caporegime* in the Gambino family who had entered into competition with a Genovese *caporegime*. Piccolo was killed just before he was to go on trial in relation to charges of conspiring to extort money. It was felt by Gambino family members that Castellano had "given up" a member to another family, a breach against the Cosa Nostra rule that states that disputes between different families must be settled by a sit-down.[44]

Immediately after the killings of Castellano and his underboss, Thomas Bilotti, Gotti and Salvatore Gravano contacted all the family *capiregime* to inform them of the murders. According to Gravano, ". . . there is a Commission rule about killing the boss. And we broke that rule. And we weren't ever going admit it." Messengers were sent to meet with the other New York families to tell them what had happened. Gravano explained that, as time was running out for Gotti and others, they felt they did not have time to seek permission from the Commission to kill Castellano, since it would require a formal meeting of all New York families. Instead, they contacted the other families before the murders: "It was an off-the-record contact, just to see where and what direction they were going to go."[45]

The Murder of John D'Amato, Spring 1992

The acting boss of the DeCavalcante family, John D'Amato, was killed by members of his own family. D'Amato was alleged to have been engaged in homosexual activities for some time. In 1991 he fled to Florida after he learned that the Ravenite Social Club, the headquarters of the Gambino family, had been bugged by the FBI and that John Gotti had been indicted under the RICO Act. D'Amato had discussed a murder plot with Gotti. The news of D'Amato's homosexuality came from Anthony Capo, a former soldier in the DeCavalcante family, who testified at the May 2003 trial of consigliere Stefano Vitabile and two capiregime charged with ordering the murder of D'Amato. Capo told the court he had learned about D'Amato's sex life from D'Amato's girlfriend. Capo quickly reported the stunning revelation to Vitabile. The DeCavalcante family feared they would lose respect and become the laughing stock of the five New York families, and decided to kill D'Amato right away. "Nobody's gonna respect us if we have a gay homosexual boss sitting down discussing Cosa Nostra business," Capo said to justify the killing.[46] The family wanted the murder to look like a "sneak" killing, one in which no one would take credit.

Impact on the Family

The killing of a Mafia boss is always followed by a series of shock-waves in the family. Whether a boss dies violently or of natural causes, the election of a new boss brings changes within the family's hierarchy. The new boss can promote or demote members of his family. Some capiregime may be asked to step down because they are aging. More killings may follow, such as those of discontented members who refuse to support the new administration. Following Carmine

Galante's murder, there were considerable changes in the upper eche-lons of the family's hierarchy. Nicholas Marangello, who had been slated to be killed, was demoted from underboss to soldier. *Caporegime* Mike Sabella was demoted to soldier. After the murder of Paul Castel-lano, Joseph N. Gallo, the long-time *consigliere* of the Gambino family, was forced to retire, while Anthony Scotto, an influential *caporegime*, was demoted to the rank of soldier. At a 1981 induction ceremony Nicodemo Scarfo elevated Lawrence Merlino and Philip Leonetti from soldier to *caporegime*, and demoted John Cappello and Joseph Scafidi from *caporegime* to soldier.[47]

Protocol requires that other Cosa Nostra families be notified of any changes in the family administration after the death of a boss. Immedi-ately after the election of Gotti, messengers from the Gambino family were sent to notify the other four families of the new boss, underboss and *consigliere*, and to say that these changes had been agreed on by all the *capiregime*. According to Salvatore Gravano, the new Gambino adminis-tration was concerned that it would not be recognized by the other New York families and would thus be prevented from sitting and voting on the Commission. The Gambino family also worried that there would be sanctions against it.[48] But the New York families were receptive to the changes, except for the Genovese family. Its boss, Vincent Gigante, insisted that the Gambino family had broken a rule and would have to answer for that sooner or later.

That payment may have come due on April 13, 1986, when Frank DeCicco, the newly appointed Gambino family underboss, was killed when his car exploded in the Bensonhurst section of Brooklyn.[49] There was speculation that DeCicco had played a role in Castellano's murder by tipping Gotti about when Castellano was to hold a meeting at the Spark's Steak House in Manhattan. But it now seems that the DeCicco slaying was the result of a conspiracy between Vincent Gigante and Anthony Casso, at that time a *caporegime* in the Lucchese family, as the bomb was intended for Gotti.[50] It was well acknowledged that Gigante did not like Gotti's flashy style and brusqueness in his crime business dealings.

Killing a Cosa Nostra Member

Killings within Cosa Nostra are often done with a sense of tradition, but also with a touch of sensationalism. Tradition requires that a killing be prompt and sudden. In the old days, a Mafia tradition prevailed when someone was about to be murdered. His executioners would entertain their victim with a lavish meal and drinks. Many Mafia bosses marked for death have been entertained in this way. The idea is to allay any suspicions the victim might have and set him at ease. He must not be aware he is living the last hours of his life.

The killing of a Cosa Nostra member must be done out of the sight of his relatives. But this policy has been broken often, perhaps because the killers did not hold the victim in high regard, or because they were rushed or because the opportunity to kill the victim came at an unexpected moment. Robert Riccobene, a member of the Philadelphia family, was killed right in front of his mother in December 1983.[51] One can assume that the hit man was not of Italian descent. Worse was the killing in 1969 of Giuseppe Sirchia, a Sicilian Mafia member, as he was met by his wife at the doors of the Ucciardone prison in Palermo. Both died in the hail of bullets.[52]

Perhaps the most sensational killing was that of Joey Gallo, in April 1972 at Umberto's Clam House in the heart of Manhattan's Little Italy. Gallo, a member of the Colombo family, was celebrating his forty-third birthday when he was killed in front of his second wife and her child. Gallo was suspected of plotting the attempted murder of Joseph Colombo in June 1971. Carlo Gambino was reportedly very upset about the "saloon-style" shooting, in that Gallo was killed in front of his family.[53]

Killing a Relative of a Member

In August 1982 the Nicodemo Scarfo family set a precedent by shooting and wounding the father of an informant. It was the first time Cosa Nostra had attempted to kill the relative of an informant. On March 10, 1992, a similar incident occurred with the attempted murder of Peter

Chiodo's sister. Chiodo, a former *caporegime* in the Lucchese family, was himself shot twelve times on May 8, 1991, but survived and became a witness for the prosecution in the trials of several Cosa Nostra members. The accused were involved in the use of rigged bids and labour payoffs to control window-installation contracts with the New York City Housing Authority. The shooting of Chiodo's sister was the "desperate act" of organized-crime leaders who were trying to send the message to their subordinates that it is not a good idea to testify against members of a criminal association. The attempted murder was regarded as motivated by vengeance, rather than as essential to business.[54]

In March 2001 the FBI uncovered a plot to kill the members of Ralph Natale's family, in particular, his son, Frank, and daughter, Vanessa. Natale was the main prosecution witness against Joseph Merlino and six co-defendants, who faced thirty-six charges, including three for murder.[55]

The killing of relatives in reprisal against Cosa Nostra members who broke a rule has been in practise for a long time in Sicily. The most vivid example is probably that of Tommaso Buscetta. Two of his sons and an uncle were killed by the Corleone family, led at that time by Michele Greco. In his autobiography, Buscetta stated: "Cosa Nostra had violated a rule, that mistakes done by the father shall not be passed to children."[56]

Killing Associates and Outsiders

Killings of Cosa Nostra associates and outsiders are strictly controlled in Cosa Nostra. An associate tied to a crime family, particularly if he "belongs" to a member of that family, cannot be killed without the approval of the boss of the family. If the associate belongs to another Cosa Nostra family, approval of that family must be sought first.

Harold Konigsberg, a long-time associate of the New Jersey Bonanno family faction, enraged Anthony Provenzano, a Genovese soldier, over a crap game and Provenzano stabbed him. Konigsberg was connected to Joseph Zicarelli, a Bonanno soldier based in New Jersey. In other words, Konisgberg belonged to Zicarelli and could not be touched. Angelo De Carlo, a Genovese *caporegime* overseeing the interests of the family in

New Jersey, discussed the situation with two other Cosa Nostra members in his office in December 1962. In De Carlo's opinion, Provenzano should have consulted Zicarelli before hurting Konigsberg: "You can't kill nobody without an OK from the boss. Not even a *caporegime* can OK a killing. It's got to be OK'ed by the boss."[57]

The Murder of Charles "Ruby" Stein

The killing, in March 1977, of Charles "Ruby" Stein caused the Gambino family a great deal of concern. Stein ran a million dollars' worth of loan-sharking operations on the West Side of Manhattan, right in the heart of the Gambino family's territory. He was killed by Jimmy Coonan, the leader of the infamous Hell's Kitchen gang known as the Westies. Apparently, several Westies members were indebted to Stein. By killing Stein, Coonan hoped to take over Stein's loansharking operations.

The murder of Ruby Stein infuriated Paul Castellano, boss of the Gambino family, as the other New York families had invested a lot of money in Stein's activities. He summoned Coonan to a restaurant for a sit-down with representatives from the other families. Castellano was eager to know if the Westies were behind Stein's murder and wanted to find out where Stein's black book was. Coonan denied his involvement, on the advice of Roy DeMeo, a Gambino soldier who acted as liaison between the Westies and the Gambinos. Had Coonan admitted to the murder, Castellano would have been forced to reimburse the other New York families the money—capital and interest—they had invested in Stein's operations.[58] Castellano warned Coonan that if any killing was to take place on the West Side, it had to have the approval the Gambino family first: ". . . you and your boys have got to end this wild behavior. From now on, every killing must be authorized."[59]

The Westies then fell under the Gambino family's control. They were allowed to borrow money from the Gambino family at a privileged rate of one percent a week and use the name of the Gambino family in their racketeering activities on the West Side docks. They were permitted to continue with their criminal activities—gambling, extortion, drug trafficking and labour racketeering—provided they paid the Gambino family ten percent of their proceeds.

Some time after this meeting, Castellano was apparently reprimanded by Anthony Salerno, boss of the Genovese family, for having made an alliance with the Westies. Salerno stated that it was against Cosa Nostra's tradition to hire outsiders to commit crimes on behalf of a Cosa Nostra family.[60]

The Case of Jimmy Hoffa

The disappearance of Jimmy Hoffa, the former president of the International Union of Teamsters of America, in July 1975 could only have taken place with the approval of the Cosa Nostra Commission.

After a few years of absence from the labour scene, Hoffa was again seeking the presidency of the international union. In 1971 he had been granted a pardon by President Richard Nixon, after serving almost five years in prison for his 1964 conviction for having misappropriated monies in union pension funds. The presidential pardon was granted under the condition that Hoffa stay away from unions for ten years. Hoffa had cultivated throughout his union career strong links with organized-crime figures. When he was sent to prison in 1967, he was replaced by Frank Fitzsimmons, a less flamboyant leader over whom Cosa Nostra had easy control. But Hoffa made clear his intention not to remain in the shadow for long, and began to fight to regain control of the Teamsters. Hoffa's comeback did not please Cosa Nostra at all. On July 30, 1975, Hoffa received a phone call from someone he trusted to meet with Anthony Giacalone, an influential *caporegime* in the Zerilli family of Detroit, in a restaurant in suburban Detroit. Soon afterwards Hoffa was reported missing and is presumed dead.

Joseph Zerilli, Sicilian in origin, maintained his status as leader of his family by abiding by strict rules for several decades, until his death in October 1977. He had firm control over criminal activities on his territory. In particular, he would not tolerate outsiders committing murders on his territory. If someone was to be murdered in the Detroit area, not only was Zerilli's authorization needed, but only the Zerilli family itself could take care of the matter. Hoffa's disappearance, it can be assumed, was handled entirely by the Detroit family.[61]

Killing on Another Family's Territory

A Cosa Nostra family's territory is sacred. As a matter of protocol, an individual cannot be killed on territory that is under the jurisdiction of a Cosa Nostra family without its approval. Joe Barboza was a hired killer for the Raymond Patriarca family of New England. In the mid-1960s, he was arrested and charged for a murder unrelated to organized crime. Barboza thus became a liability for the Patriarca family. After he was released from jail in October 1975, Barboza went to California to hide, but he was located a year later. The information was relayed to Frank Scibelli, a *caporegime* in the Genovese family, who lived in Massachusetts and had close ties to the Patriarca family. Consultations were held with Jimmy Lanza, the Cosa Nostra boss in San Francisco, for permission to dispatch a hit team to kill Barboza. The contract was performed on February 11, 1976.[62]

The Commission has ruled that no killing of members or individuals with ties to Cosa Nostra are to take place in Las Vegas, Nevada. Its objective was to make Las Vegas a safe and quiet place for gamblers and tourists from across North America and abroad. Robberies, holdups and other acts of violence were practically nonexistent in the city. In April 1953 Louis Strauss, a hustler and heavy gambler with a reputation for manipulating forged dice, blackmailed a Las Vegas casino operator. The operator turned to Nick Licata, a high-ranking Cosa Nostra member in Los Angeles, for help. It was decided that Strauss, also known as "Russian Louis," would be killed. Since Strauss had ties to the Chicago family, permission to kill him had to be sought from that family. The murder contract was authorized on the condition that Strauss would not be killed in Nevada, or at least that his body would be disposed of elsewhere. Strauss was finally lured to California, where he was killed.[63]

In Sicily, the Cupola regulates the use of violence. A murder cannot be carried out without the consent of the family boss of the area where the murder is going to take place. If permission is not sought, it is considered an act of defiance or war. In most cases, the Cupola is properly consulted in advance. In May 1971 Pietro Scaglione, a chief public prosecutor, was killed in a section of Palermo controlled by the boss of the Porto Nuova family, Giuseppe "Pippo" Calò. The murder of Scaglione could not have been done without Calò's authorization, as such a hit inevitably draws police and media attention to the area where it occurred.[64]

Former Sicilian Mafia member Antonino Calderone explained that if an important public figure such as a politician, a police officer or a magistrate has to be killed, the decision must come from the highest level of command of Cosa Nostra.[65] But the rule has been violated several times.[66] In August 1980 the murder of Gaetano Costa, another Sicilian prosecutor, was done without the consent of the Cupola. According to Tommaso Buscetta, the murder was carried out by Stefano Bontate in retaliation for the murder of Giuseppe Di Cristina, the boss of Riesi, a village in the province of Caltanissetta.[67] Di Cristina had been killed in May 1978 in Palermo, in the territory of Mafia boss Salvatore Inzerillo.[68]

The killing of Giuseppe Russo, chief of *carabinieri*, on August 20, 1977, caused a stir inside the Cupola. Russo was executed on the territory of the Corleone family. The leader of the Cupola, Gaetano Badalamenti, had not been informed of the contract, nor had the regional secretary, Giuseppe Calderone. The interregional commission had been set up by Calderone so that the Cupola could ensure better control over decisions made by the families, especially influential families such the Corleonesi.[69] Badalamenti's prestige was severely affected by Russo's assassination.

Killing Law Enforcement Agents and Government Officials

There is an unwritten rule in the underworld that police, prosecutors and anyone working for a federal agency cannot be killed due to the nature of their work or because they are successful in the arrest and conviction of gangsters. Joseph Bonanno pointed out in his autobiography that there was a strict prohibition against harming or killing a police officer. He was considered "the servant of the government and thus was not to be held fully responsible for his actions. He merely had a job to do."[70]

As a rule, the American Cosa Nostra does not use violence against government officials or police officers as often as its Sicilian counterpart. The Sicilian Mafia does not hesitate to strike back in response to state arrests and investigations against the organization. When the Mafia feels threatened, Italian magistrates will be killed. Sometimes, the ordeal is transported outside Sicily, as Antonino Giuffrè, the former *capomafia* of Caccamo, in the province of Trapani, Sicily, told Italian authorities in March 2003. According to the rules of the Sicilian Mafia, if a prosecutor, judge or police officer goes to America and causes damage to the American Cosa Nostra, the boss of the Sicilian province the official comes from has the duty to have him killed. This rule was the explanation for the murder of Giovanni Falcone in May 1992. Falcone had assisted Rudolph Giuliani, at that time a U.S. attorney in Manhattan, in preparing the "Commission Case" against the heads of the five New York families.[71] The rule was explained to Giuffrè by Salvatore Riina before Riina's arrest in January 1993. Giuffrè, wanted since 1994 for his alleged involvement in Falcone's murder, was arrested by the Italian police in April 2002.

The American Cosa Nostra is very cautious about engaging in acts of violence against servants of the state.[72] The case of Thomas C. Dewey, a New York City special prosecutor in the mid-1930s, is interesting. Dewey had been fighting New York's underworld for years and had solid credibility with the public due to his success. In 1935 he tracked down Arthur Flegenheimer, also known as Dutch Schultz. Dewey was about to indict Schultz for his control of the restaurant-protection racket and for murdering one of his enforcers. Rumours came to Salvatore Luciano, the head of the Cosa Nostra Commission, that Schultz was planning to murder Dewey to escape the federal indictments. The Commission, of course, voted unanimously against Schultz's plan. Schultz rejected the Commission's decision and let it be known that he would go ahead with killing Dewey. Schultz's plans were put to an end on October 25, 1935, when he was shot to death in his favourite hangout, the Palace Chop House and Tavern in Newark.

Nevertheless, there have been numerous instances of North American law enforcement officials being killed by members of the underworld.

The first case occurred on October 15, 1890, when the police chief of New Orleans, David Hennessey, was murdered by a group of mafiosi, the Matrangas, that Hennessey had been investigating for some time. Eleven members of the Matranga group were indicted and tried. On March 13, 1891, quite surprisingly, the jury acquitted three of them for lack of sufficient evidence, and the others were cleared of all charges. On hearing the verdict, the citizens of New Orleans were enraged and marched to the city jail, where the prisoners were still being held. The jail guards tried to save their lives by letting them go. But the mob of citizens succeeded in capturing three Matranga members inside the jail who were then killed on the spot; the others were lynched outside.[73]

The second police officer to be murdered while on duty was New York City detective Giuseppe "Joe" Petrosino, the head of the Italian squad set up in 1905. On the orders of the city's police commissioner, Petrosino had been sent to Rome and Palermo to investigate Mafia aliens and to gather intelligence on members of the Black Hand and the Neapolitan Camorra that Petrosino wished to have deported from the United States.[74] Petrosino was killed on March 12, 1909, allegedly by Vito Cascio Ferro, an influential mafioso from Palermo.

In 1963, while incarcerated, Vito Genovese was asked to authorize the use of violence against narcotics agents who were suspected of framing some members of his family. Genovese refused to grant permission. However, violence is often used against law enforcement officers who have double-crossed the organization.[75] When members of the Bonanno family found out in the summer of 1982 that Joseph Pistone was a FBI undercover agent, a $500,000 open contract was immediately issued. But a team of FBI agents knocked on the doors of the New York crime family leaders, warning them that any harm that befell Pistone would bring intense heat on them.[76]

In March 1987 Carmine Persico, serving a hundred-year jail sentence, felt that William Aronwald, a former federal prosecutor in the Justice Department, had "disrespected" organized crime. Holding a grudge, Persico ordered soldier Joel Cacace to murder Aronwald, who had become a defence attorney. Cacace turned the murder contract over to two henchmen, brothers Eddie and Vincent Carini, who mistakenly killed George Aronwald, William's father, an administrative law judge for New York City's Parking Violations Bureau. The terrible blunder outraged the other four New York families. Under intense pressure, Cacace got permission to hire an associate from the Bonanno family and a soldier from the Lucchese family to kill the Carinis. The brothers were later found shot to death in the back seats of separate cars. After attending their funeral, Cacace made arrangements to get rid of the Carinis' killers by recruiting Frank Smith, an associate and drug trafficker. In January 2003 Cacace, by then the acting boss of the Colombo family, was indicted with George Aronwald's murder and conspiracy to kill his son.[77]

In 1988 Michael H. Lloyd, an inmate at the federal penitentiary in Marion, Illinois, sent a letter to Rudolph Giuliani at the U.S. Attorney's office in Manhattan revealing a plot to kill the Assistant District Attorney, Aaron Marcu, who had, with Giuliani, successfully prosecuted Carmine Persico in 1986. Persico had confided to Lloyd his intent to kill Marcu. Persico told Lloyd he chose Marcu as the target rather than Giuliani, as Giuliani was constantly surrounded by heavy protection.[78]

The killing of Everett Hatcher, on February 28, 1989, was one of the most dramatic events ever to happen in New York City. The suspect, Costabile Farace, a twenty-nine-year-old Bonanno wannabe and small-time drug trafficker, shot and killed Hatcher during a routine meeting for a drug deal. Farace believed that Hatcher was a police informant. Hatcher was, in reality, a Drug Enforcement Administration (DEA) undercover special agent posing as a drug-dealing army officer. Hatcher had been investigating a cocaine ring operated by Gerardo Chilli, a *caporegime* in the Bonanno family. On that night, Hatcher met with Farace. Federal backup teams lost sight of Hatcher in traffic. One hour later, the federal agent was found dead in his car, hit by several bullets.

The minute Hatcher's body was discovered, one of the most frantic manhunts in U.S. history began. The Department of Justice offered a reward of $250,000 for information leading to the arrest of Farace. The FBI and the DEA maintained twenty-four-hour surveillance on relatives and friends of Farace. The pressure was intended to hurt the businesses of all the New York Cosa Nostra families. The DEA agents even paid a visit to John Gotti in an attempt to gain his co-operation. But Gotti refused, saying that anyone who would reveal the whereabouts of Farace was not a true wiseguy. At the same time, the Bonanno and Lucchese families engaged in a race to locate Farace. He had become a burden for Cosa Nostra.

Right after the murder, Farace found refuge with the help of his girl-friend, Margaret Chilli, the daughter of Gerardo Chilli, in a house, where he stayed for several weeks. Meanwhile, federal agents arrested Dominick Farace, Costabile's cousin. He agreed to co-operate, telling authorities he had witnessed the murder of Hatcher. Sensing heat, Costabile Farace moved into the Bronx and sought the help of John Petrucelli, a former jail-mate and a soldier in the Lucchese family. In Sep-tember 1989 two members of the Lucchese family learned that Petrucelli was hiding Farace, paid a visit to Petrucelli and ordered him to kill Farace. Astonishingly, Petrucelli refused to obey the order or give any information on Farace. He was found dead within a week. Two Lucchese family members who were suspected of the murder of Petrucelli were arrested not long after. When Farace learned of Petrucelli's fate, he found refuge in a studio in Uptown Manhattan. He lived there until November 17, 1989, when he was lured into a trap and killed in exactly the same way he had killed Hatcher nine months earlier.[79]

Farace had brought too much heat on Cosa Nostra by killing a law enforcement officer. Three crime families were unwillingly drawn into this misdeed: the Colombo family, because Farace was a cousin of Gregory Scarpa Jr.; the Bonanno family, for whom Farace worked as an enforcer; and the Lucchese family, because one of its members hid Farace. It is believed that Anthony Spero, at that time acting boss for the Bonanno family, ordered Gerardo Chilli to kill Farace. The murder con-tract was then passed along to the Lucchese family.

In the early 1990s Anthony Casso, the underboss of the Lucchese fam-ily, planned to kill a federal prosecutor, as well as a federal judge. One of the targets was Charles Rose, District Attorney for the Eastern District of Brooklyn, who was prosecuting Vittorio Amuso, the boss of the Lucchese family, on murder-racketeering charges. The plot was unveiled after an informant told the FBI about Casso's plan. On January 19, 1993, after thirty-two months on the run, Casso was arrested by the FBI. While in custody waiting his trial on multiple murder charges, Casso tried to organize the murder of Eugene H. Nickerson, a federal judge scheduled to preside over his trial. The plot was discovered, and Casso was put into solitary confinement.[80]

And in August 2002 authorities of the Metropolitan Detention Center in Brooklyn put Peter Gotti, the acting boss of the Gambino family, in solitary confinement after it was discovered he had allegedly approved a contract for the murder of a prison warden of the U.S. Medical Center for Federal Prisoners in Springfield, Missouri, where his brother, John, was detained.

Killing Media Reporters

By tradition, members of the press are also protected by the "no-killing" rule. They are considered ordinary citizens by the underworld. However, there have been many cases of journalists who have been assaulted or murdered. In 1925, for instance, Al Capone apologized to a reporter after he had been savagely beaten by members of the Capone gang for having exposed Capone's political alliance in Cicero, Illinois. The journalist, Robert St. John, spent a week in hospital recovering from multiple wounds. Capone allegedly came to the hospital and paid all expenses.[81]

In 1934 and 1935 two journalists were murdered for their crusade against the underworld. Howard Guilford, from Minneapolis, was shot for exposing gambling and vice operations in that city, and Walter W. Liggett was killed for writing about the state governor's alleged affiliation to gangsters. The pair had been tried and acquitted for extortion. They had blackmailed a public figure by threatening to reveal his dubious past.[82]

In 1936 Paul Ricca, a high-ranking member of the Chicago family, wanted to murder Westbrook Pegler, a journalist who was investigating William Bioff's activities as a labour racketeer in Hollywood. Pegler had exposed the takeover of Local 110 of the Motion Picture Operators Union through Bioff, who was associated with Ricca. The Chicago family decided that murdering Pegler would be counterproductive.[83]

In April 1956 Victor Riesel, a journalist specializing in labour activities in New York City, was viciously attacked by a young man who threw sulphuric acid in Riesel's face and eyes, leaving him permanently blind. Riesel was investigating Local 138 of the International Union of Operating Engineers on Long Island for corruption by the Lucchese family. Police investigators learned that John DioGuardi, a *caporegime* in the Lucchese family and a labour racketeer, had ordered the attack. DioGuardi was acquitted of aggravated assault after key witnesses refused to testify against him.

In May 1973 Montreal journalist Jean-Pierre Charbonneau was shot several times by Tony Mucci, at that time a member of the Paolo Violi organization. Charbonneau, who survived the attempt, had been writing penetrating articles on the Cosa Nostra in Montreal.

The killing in June 1976 of Don Bolles, an investigative reporter for the *Arizona Republic* in Phoenix who specialized in organized-crime issues, boomeranged on the underworld. Bolles was fatally wounded by a car bomb after he had published a series of articles denouncing land fraud activities and corruption. In retaliation for Bolles's murder, a team of reporters from across the United States gathered to form the Association of Investigative Reporters and Editors. They undertook "Project Arizona" and revealed what Bolles had found out about organized crime and corruption in that state.[84]

THE USE OF SYMBOLS IN UNDERWORLD KILLINGS

In the world of Cosa Nostra, discretion and efficiency are the rules when carrying out murders. But in many cases, murders will be accompanied with a mark or signs of mutilation on the victim's body. These messages are meant for, and understood by, members of Cosa Nostra.[85]

In Sicily, mutilation was practised primarily by rural mafiosi. A victim suspected of talking to the police would have his tongue cut out or would be found with a stone inserted in his mouth, indicating that he had committed an act of *infamita*. A hand cut off and placed on the chest of the victim meant he was a *scassapagghiari*, or small thief, who was denied permission to operate by the local Mafia. Genitals cut off and placed inside the victim's mouth meant he had raped or tried to have sexual intercourse with the wife or sister of a man of honour.[86]

In North America, symbolism is not as prevalent. Most gangland murders occur in cities, and members of crime families are usually shot on the street. However, there have been instances of bodily mutilation. Giuseppe "Joe" Petrosino, the first Italian member of the New York City Police, became interested in Italian organized crime in 1895, when he was assigned to investigate a type of murder case commonly known as the "barrel murder." This gruesome method of killing always bore the same pattern: the victim was stabbed or shot, then stuffed in a barrel that was left in a noticeable place. The brutality that accompanied the murder was typical of the Mafia. The victim's throat was slit from ear to ear and the neck trussed to the knees. The victim was usually viciously beaten until all his bones were broken. The cruelty of the murder was meant to send a message to anyone who refused to comply. The neck-to-knees bondage was the Mafia's signature of an execution.[87]

In 1938 Anthony "Nino" Colombo Sr., the father of former boss Joseph Colombo Jr., was found garrotted, with his genitals stuffed in his mouth, in a car in Brooklyn. With him was the body of a woman friend, Christina Oliveri, also strangled. Colombo Sr., although not a made member, had violated a cardinal rule of Cosa Nostra by seducing the wife of a Cosa Nostra member.[88]

In June 1952 James Ammino, a petty thief and an associate of Joey Gallo, stole the crown of diamonds that adorned the statue of the Virgin Mary at the Regina Paci church, located in the Bensenthurst–Bath Beach neighbourhood of Brooklyn. The crown was worth several thousand dollars. When crime leader Joseph Profaci found out about the theft, he became very upset, as he was one of the donors of the crown. He ordered that the crown be returned immediately. The precious ornament was recovered, but three diamonds were missing. The underworld is an intricate network, and information circulates fast. Soon after the crown was returned, the thief was discovered and killed. While everyone in the area knew about the theft, most had no idea of the identity of the thief. When

Ammino's body was discovered, everyone understood that he had been the culprit. His killers had placed a set of rosary beads in a band around his neck.[89]

There were many casualties of the Gallo-Profaci wars of the early 1960s. One of them was the former bodyguard of Larry Gallo, Joseph Gioielli, who had been reported missing. When questioned by police about Gioielli's disappearance, Gallo replied that Gioielli was "at the bottom of the ocean." Gallo acknowledged that he had received a "message": when Gioielli's coat was sent to him, a fish had been placed in an inside pocket. The coat was thrown out the window of a speeding car in front of a candy store that was a Gallo hangout.[90]

Another interesting case is that of Anthony Caponigro and his brother-in-law, Alfred Salerno, who plotted the murder of their boss, Angelo Bruno, in March 1980. Less than a month after Bruno's murder, their naked and mutilated bodies were found in garbage bags. Twenty-dollar bills had been stuffed into their rectums, a Sicilian custom that meant they had become too greedy.[91]

In March 1982, exactly one year after the killing of Phil Testa, the underboss of the Philadelphia family, the body of Rocco Marinucci, who was suspected of murdering Testa, was discovered in a parking lot in Philadelphia. He had been shot several times in the head and chest. Three firecrackers were forced down his throat to symbolize his treachery and to convey that the Philadelphia family knew Marinucci was Testa's killer.[92]

In 1982 the body of Pietro Inzerillo was found in the trunk of a Cadillac in New Jersey. Inzerillo's body was wrapped in a plastic bag, his arms handcuffed behind his back. He had dollars bills stuffed in his mouth and crotch. Those in his mouth symbolized his greed; those at the genitals indicated that he was regarded as less than a man.[93] Inzerillo was part of the infamous "Pizza Connection" led by Sicilian brothers John, Rosario and Giuseppe Gambino, who managed pizza parlours used as fronts for the distribution of heroin.

When Dominick Napolitano's mutilated body was discovered on August 12, 1981, in Staten Island, his hands had been cut off. According to FBI agent Joseph Pistone, the mutilation was meant to tell everyone in the

Bonanno family, as well as the other New York families, that Napolitano had caused a serious security breach to his family, an error that carries the death penalty without trial.[94] Cutting off Napolitano's hands may also have been an attempt to make positive identification impossible.

Challenging the authority of a crime leader can be punished with extreme cruelty. William Petrocelli, an enforcer for the Chicago Outfit, took it upon himself to shake down bookmakers under the false pretext of raising money for the family of an imprisoned enforcer. Boss Joseph Ferriola summoned Petrocelli for an explanation, but Petrocelli refused to show up and told Ferriola to go to hell. In the ordinary world, a person would be fired for such a defiant attitude towards his employer. In the underworld, Ferriola's authority and ability to instil fear were at stake. It was a matter of honour and respect. Petrocelli's body was found atrociously mutilated. According to the autopsy report, his entire face looked as if it had been scorched by a blowtorch.[95] The severity of the mutilation was meant to send a message to everyone that an order issued by a crime boss must be complied with right away.

Despite several warnings, a young thief in Queens, New York, defied Carmine Fatico, a high-ranking member of the Gambino family, by carrying out a string of robberies on Fatico's territory. The man's body was found soon after. He had been so savagely beaten that when investigators found him they thought his head was missing. At the autopsy, the mortician located the head: it had been smashed into the thief's chest cavity.[96]

In August 1990 Bruno Facciola, a soldier for the Lucchese family, was killed in an ambush in Brooklyn. Facciola had gone into hiding after it was learned he was talking to police. Vittorio Amuso, then boss of the family, ordered the killers to stuff a dead canary in Facciola's mouth as a warning that anyone who turns informer will meet a similar fate.[97]

UNDERWORLD FUNERALS

The lives—and deaths—of Mafia leaders hold a certain fascination for the general public, especially when the leaders meet with violent deaths. This fascination is apparent at funeral ceremonies: spectators stand along the streets watching long cortèges of limousines carrying elaborate flower arrangements. The funeral of a Mafia leader often reflects his ostentation and flamboyance. A large number of flowers denotes that the deceased was held in high respect within the underworld, as does having ranking organized-crime figures serve as his pallbearers.

In the early 1920s, when bootlegging wars raged in the streets of Chicago and New York, the funerals of gangsters were sensational and colourful. Racketeers such as Al Capone and gang rivals made daily headlines. Should one of these be killed by a volley of machine-gun bullets, he was given a lavish funeral, often meant as a show of solidarity to convey that the family stood behind the deceased. At that time, funerals were attended not only by relatives and friends of the deceased, but quite often by local politicians and judges. That was the case at the funeral of Frank Capone, elder brother of Al, killed in April 1924 during a gunfight with patrolmen.

The funeral of Frank Yale, shot to death on July 1, 1928, on the orders of Al Capone, was one of the most pompous ever held in New York City. Yale's casket was said to have cost $15,000. There were $37,000 worth of floral arrangements, among which was a floral clock set to 4:10, Yale's time of death. The massive attendance seemed to confer a tacit approval of the deceased's life. But the funeral was also an opportunity to watch other members of the underworld come to pay their respects.

Nowadays, some relatives and close friends of the deceased, as well as underworld figures from other crime families, do not attend funerals, as they are aware they will be photographed by police. Funerals of mobsters also attract fewer curious onlookers. The public has come to disapprove of the moral depravity of the mafiosi lifestyle, an opinion reinforced by the Roman Catholic Church's refusal to celebrate funeral masses for many Mafia leaders. Carlo Gambino, who died of natural causes in October 1976, was allowed a funeral mass in Brooklyn, but Carmine Galante (1979), Paul Castellano (1985) and John Gotti (2002) were all denied a religious service. "We are not able to grant a liturgical service in the church because of the scandal that would ensue," said a spokesman for the Roman Catholic Archidiocese of New York, of Carmine Galante. It was the first time since the slaying of Albert

Anastasia, who was also denied a funeral mass and was not buried in consecrated ground, that the Catholic Church took this position.[98]

In the case of Castellano, the Church allowed a private religious memorial service to be held by an auxiliary bishop of the archdiocese of New York, but without the presence of Castellano's body. Moreover, Castellano was buried in a nondenominational cemetery, allegedly at the family's request. The Diocese of Brooklyn took a similar position following the death of John Gotti, who died of cancer in June 2002, while serving a life sentence. The Church granted permission to a priest to celebrate a private prayer of the last rites at the funeral home where Gotti was resting. Gotti was buried in St. John Cemetery in Queens, beside his son Frank, who had died in March 1980, at the age of twelve, when he was accidentally hit by a car. Gotti's funeral lived up to his image: flamboyant and pompous. It included a thirteen-mile parade with twenty limousines carrying floral arrangements. Behind the hearse carrying the bronze casket were twenty-one limousines for family and friends.[99]

Although the funeral in January 1980 of Michael Racco, a baker in Toronto and boss of the 'Ndrangheta, was modest, with only four black cars carrying floral tributes, the tradition of elaborate Mafia funerals prevails in Canada as well. The funerals of Montreal bosses Paolo Violi, murdered in January 1978, and Vincenzo Cotroni, who died of natural causes in September 1984, were unsurpassed for their grandiosity and spectacle. About thirty Cadillacs were used to carry floral arrangements from families across Canada, the United States and Italy in tribute to the violent passing of Violi. At Cotroni's similarly lavish funeral, a fanfare started the procession, playing Chopin's *Marche Funèbre*. The funeral in March 1987 of Giacomo Luppino, one of the last "old-style Mafia dons" in Canada, was also impressive, featuring a 130-car procession and hundreds of mourners. Luppino, who was Paolo Violi's father-in-law, had for several decades led the 'Ndrangheta in Hamilton. While Violi, Cotroni and Luppino were all permitted religious ceremonies, Buffalo family representative John Papalia, who was fatally shot in Hamilton in May 1997, was refused a full funeral mass by the Catholic Diocese of Hamilton because of "his association with the underworld."[100]

Afterword

For the last ten years, the Federal Bureau of Investigation has been successful in tracking Cosa Nostra families throughout the United States. Dozens of ranking members have been convicted under the Racketeering Influenced and Corrupt Organizations Act (RICO) with the assistance of informants, undercover agents, grand juries and court-authorized wiretaps. The myth of invincibility that surrounded Cosa Nostra for so long has been torn off.

In an unprecedented move against the Bonnano family, the United States attorney in Brooklyn unsealed several federal indictments against the administration of the Bonanno family, in particular against its leader, Joseph Massino. The first blow came on January 9, 2003, when Massino was charged for the murder of Dominick Napolitano, killed in August 1981 as punishment for having introduced an FBI undercover agent into the Bonanno family. Then, in August 2003, Massino was indicted for several murders, among them that of Gerlando Sciascia, another *caporegime* in the family. Sciascia was the liaison between New York and the Sicilian organization in Montreal. Finally, on January 20, 2004, The United States Department of Justice issued a warrant for the arrest of Vito Rizzuto, the alleged leader of the Montreal Sicilian Mafia, for allegedly participating in the murders of three *capiregime* of the Bonanno family in May 1981. Rizzuto is currently detained, awaiting his extradition hearing. These indictments are all based on statements made by the former Bonanno underboss Salvatore Vitale, Massino's brother-in-law, who was himself charged with murder and had agreed to co-operate with the authorities.

For the first time in the history of the American Cosa Nostra, all five bosses of the New York families are incarcerated or awaiting trial.

The American Cosa Nostra seems to have reached a plateau in its development and expansion. Its influence and prestige have decreased considerably since the early 1980s. Several factors may have contributed to this deterioration. One has been the successful investigations and prosecutions against the heads of Cosa Nostra families. A second is certainly the creation, in 1970, of the Witness Security Program, which paved the way for snitches. Rather than face a life sentence, a Cosa Nostra member can testify against his family in return for a lighter sentence.

The disintegration of Cosa Nostra may have begun after the Apalachin meeting in 1957, with the admission of members from the second and third generation of Italian-Americans. These new recruits were born and raised with American values. They joined Cosa Nostra not because it was an "Honoured Society," but because it represented an opportunity to get rich quickly. They were not motivated by the traditional values of loyalty and mutual aid that hold Mafia members together. When they were caught by the law, many of these recruits told everything they knew, expecting to plead guilty to a lesser charge or receive a light sentence.

These betrayals have caused a great deal of instability inside Cosa Nostra families, especially in New York City, the seat of the American Cosa Nostra. While the Sicilian Mafia has gone through the same judiciary battle with the Italian state, it has nevertheless succeeded in maintaining continuity in the pursuit of its criminal operations by making the necessary replacements of members in key positions. But for the American Cosa Nostra, finding new blood represents a significant challenge. On many occasions, valuable candidates have declined leadership positions because they did not want to be exposed to constant surveillance from law enforcement. They felt that, sooner or later, they would be struck with a racketeering indictment that could lead them, if convicted, to a long prison sentence. This explains why it has been difficult for the Gambino family to elect a new boss since the arrest of Peter Gotti in June 2002.

Today, the American Cosa Nostra does not enjoy a monopoly in the conduct of major criminal operations. While it remains an influential organization for its ability to infiltrate legitimate markets such as catering, garbage hauling, fish markets and waterfronts, Cosa Nostra must now compete with an emerging breed of Russian, Hispanic, Asian and Albanese organized-crime groups and South American drug cartels. These groups have broken free of the ghettos and have taken advantage of the multiple setbacks suffered by Cosa Nostra. They have the capabilities and resources to create serious competition in areas of crime where Cosa Nostra used to be dominant. Moreover, they do not care about rules and protocols. Their primary goal is to respond to a demand for illicit goods and services.

To survive in the coming years, the new generation of Cosa Nostra members must adjust to constant changes in technology. Moreover, they must return to the traditional values that have been the essence of the Mafia's longstanding stature. As noted by a Sicilian prosecutor in Palermo, "Cosa Nostra is like a living body. If it is injured in any part, it can cauterize it immediately and regenerate its tissues."[1] Each time Cosa Nostra has gone through a difficult period, it has always managed to rebound and adapt—but always through adherence to its code: secrecy, discipline and respect.

Endnotes

Chapter 1: The Birth of a National Criminal Organization

1 Marie-Anne Matard-Bonucci, *Histoire de la mafia*, Questions au XXe siècle (Brussels: Éditions Complexe, 1994), pp. 28–29. See also Gaia Servadio, *Mafioso: A History of the Mafia from Its Origins to the Present Day* (London: Secker and Warburg Ltd., 1976), pp. 3–18.

2 Of all the Italian criminal organizations in existence in Italy, the Sicilian Mafia is one of the oldest and most powerful, after the Camorra (which originated in Naples in the province of Campania in the early nineteenth century); the 'Ndrangheta (which developed in the province of Calabria in the early nineteenth century); and the Sacra Unita Corona (Sacred United Crown, which developed in the province of Puglia in the early 1980s).

3 Henner Hess, *Mafia and Mafiosi: The Structure of Power*, trans. Ewald Osers (Lexington, MA: Saxon House/Lexington Books, D.C. Heath, 1973), p. 156.

4 Arrigo Petacco, *Joe Petrosino* (New York: Macmillan Publishing Co., Inc., 1974), p. 15.

5 Ibid., p. 18.

6 Ibid., p. 30.

7 Ibid., p. 33.

8 David L. Chandler, *Brothers in Blood: The Rise of the Criminal Brotherhoods* (New York: E.P. Dutton and Co., 1975), p. 72.

9 Michele Pantaleone, *The Mafia and Politics: The Definitive Story of the Mafia* (New York: Coward-McCann, 1966), p. 48.

10 Chandler, *Brothers in Blood*, p. 57.

11 Ibid., p. 136.

12 Stephen Fox, *Blood and Power: Organized Crime in Twentieth-Century America* (New York: William Morrow and Co., 1989), p. 40.

13 Chandler, *Brothers in Blood*, p. 131.

14 Joseph Bonanno with Sergio Salli, *A Man of Honor: The Autobiography of Joseph Bonanno* (New York: Simon & Schuster, 1983), pp. 84–85.

15 Norman Lewis, *The Honoured Society: The Mafia Conspiracy Observed* (Middlesex, England: Penguin Books, 1972), p. 36.

16 August Bequai, *Organized Crime: The Fifth Estate* (Lexington, MA: Lexington Books, D.C. Heath and Co., 1979), p. 36.

17 Peter Maas, *The Valachi Papers* (New York: Bantam Books, 1968), pp. 91–92.

18 Nick Gentile, *Vita di capomafia* (Rome: Editori Riuniti, 1963), pp. 109–10.

19 Bonanno, *Man of Honor*, pp. 84–85.

20 U.S. Senate Permanent Subcommittee on Investigations of the Committee on Government Operations, *Organized Crime and Illicit Traffic in Narcotics*, 88th Cong., 1st sess., part 1, 1 October 1963, pp. 215–16; Bonanno, *Man of Honor*, pp. 124–25; John H. Davis, *Mafia Dynasty: The Rise and Fall of the Gambino Crime Family* (New York: HarperCollins Publishers, 1993), p. 38; Maas, *Valachi Papers*, pp. 106–7; Donald R. Cressey, *Theft of the Nation: The Structure and Operation of Organized Crime in America* (New York: Harper and Row, 1969), pp. 41–42.

21 Humbert S. Nelli, *The Business of Crime: Italians and Syndicate Crime in the United States* (New York: Oxford University Press, 1976), pp. 204–6.

22 Chandler, *Brothers in Blood*, p. 156.

23 *New York Herald Tribune*, 12 September 1931.

24 Bonanno, *Man of Honor*, pp. 128–29.

25 Robert Lacey, *Little Man: Meyer Lansky and the Gangster Life* (New York: Little, Brown and Co., 1991), p. 67.

26 Frederic D. Homer, *Guns and Garlic: Myths and Realties of Organized Crime* (West Lafayette, IN: Perdue University Studies, 1974), pp. 39–40. Maranzano's killers were hired from Philadelphia, Baltimore, Boston and Toledo.

27 Nelli, *Business of Crime*, p. 180.

28 Senate Permanent Subcommittee, *Organized Crime and Illicit Traffic in Narcotics*, p. 238.

29 Nelli, *Business of Crime*, pp. 207–10; Richard Hammer, *Gangland U.S.A.: The Making of the Mob, Part I* (Chicago: Playboy Press, 1975), pp. 149–51. Bonanno mentions that his cousin, Stefano Magaddino, got a seat on the national Commission.

30 Hammer, *Gangland U.S.A.*, p. 150.

31 Davis, *Mafia Dynasty*, pp. 42–43.

32 Tony Sciacca, *Luciano: The Man Who Modernized the American Mafia* (New York: Pinnacle Books, 1975), p. 106.

33 Cressey, *Theft of the Nation*, p. 45.

34 Maas, *Valachi Papers*, p. 120; Sciacca, *Luciano*, p. 106.

35 Hammer, *Gangland U.S.A.*, pp. 149–51.

36 Kenneth Allsop, *The Bootleggers: The Story of Prohibition* (New Rochelle, NY: Arlington House, 1968), p. 37.

37 Gus Tyler, *Organized Crime in America: A Book of Readings* (Ann Arbor: University of Michigan Press, 1967), pp. 227–28.

38 Chandler, *Brothers in Blood*, pp. 164–66; Davis, *Mafia Dynasty*, pp. 52–53.

39 Joseph L. Albini, *The American Mafia: Genesis of a Legend* (New York: Meredith Corp., 1971), p. 248.

40 Fred D. Pasley, *Al Capone: The Biography of a Self-Made Man* (New York: Garden City Publishing Company, 1930), pp. 143–44.

41 Cressey, *Theft of the Nation*, p. 38.

42 The Unione Siciliana was founded in Chicago around 1895. It was a fraternal organization whose objectives were "the voluntary and charitable benevolence and assistance of a member towards the other in cases of sickness." Its founder was Mike Merlo, who was president until his death of natural causes in September 1924. He would be succeeded by six other presidents from 1924 to 1929. All were killed in gangland fashion. By the 1920s, the Unione Siciliana had thirty-eight branches, with about 40,000 members in New York City, St. Louis, Detroit, Pittsburgh, Cleveland and Philadelphia. During Prohibition, Chicago gangsters, through Al Capone, tried to gain control of the Unione Siciliana for their own illicit activities by having their representatives elected to high offices in the organization. Following Merlo's peaceful leadership, Antonio Lombardo was, with the support of the Capone gang, elected president in November 1925. His successor was Pasquale Lolardo, killed in 1929. Capone's enemy Joseph Aiello, the sixth president in nine years, was slain in 1930 in the midst of the Castellammarese Wars. Aiello was succeeded by Phil D'Andrea, Capone's financial manager.

43 Rick Porrello, *The Rise and Fall of the Cleveland Mafia* (Fort Lee, NJ: Barricade Books, 1995), pp. 86–96; see also Cressey, *Theft of the Nation*, p. 38; Chandler, *Brothers in Blood*, pp. 137–38; Nelli, *Business of Crime*, p. 213; Martin Short, *Crime Inc.: The Story of Organized Crime* (London: Methuen London, 1984), pp. 33, 169; James Neff, *Mobbed Up: Jackie Presser's High-Wire Life in the Teamsters, the Mafia, and the F.B.I.* (New York: The Atlantic Monthly Press, 1989), p. 13.

44 Mark A. Stuart, *Gangster #2: Longy Zwillman: The Man Who Invented Organized Crime* (Secaucus, NJ: Lyle Stuart, 1985), pp. 71–77.

45 Virgil W. Peterson, *The Mob: 200 Years of Organized Crime in New York* (Ottawa, IL: Green Hill Publishers, 1983), pp. 158–59; Denis Eisenberg, Uri Dan and Eli Landau, *Meyer Lansky* (New York: Paddington Press, 1979), pp. 144–45.

46 John Kobler, *Capone: The Life and World of Al Capone* (Greenwich, CT: Fawcett Publications, 1972), p. 245.

47 Ibid., p. 247.

48 George Wolf with Joseph Dimona, *Frank Costello: Prime Minister of the Underworld* (New York: Bantam Books, 1975), p. 79.

49 Henry A. Zeiger, *Frank Costello* (New York: Berkley Medallion Books, 1974), p. 32.

50 Fred J. Cook, *Mafia!* (Greenwich, CT: Fawcett Publications, 1973), p. 70; Stuart, *Gangster #2*, pp. 71–77.

51 Nelli, *Business of Crime*, p. 214.

52 Peterson, *The Mob*, p. 229; Cressey, *Theft of the Nation*, pp. 49–53; Nelli, *Business of Crime*, pp. 216–17; Howard Abadinsky, *Organized Crime: A Comprehensive Reference to the Laws and Strategies for Preventing and Combatting Organized Crime* (Boston: Allyn and Bacon, 1981), pp. 100–101; Sid Feder and Joesten Joachim, *The Luciano Story* (New York: Award Books, 1972), p. 66.

53 Burton B. Turkus and Sid Feder, *Murder Inc.: The Story of "The Syndicate"* (New York: Manor Books, 1972), p. 86.

54 For more on the Apalachin meeting investigations, see Senate Hearings before the Select Committee, *On Improper Activities in the Labor or Management Field*, 85th Cong., 2nd sess., part 32, 1958.

55 State of New York, Executive Department, Office of the Commissioner of Investigation, *Report of the Activities and Associations of Persons Identified as Present at the Residence of Joseph Barbara Sr., at Apalachin, New York, on November 14, 1957, and the Reasons for their Presence*, submitted to His Excellency Averell Harriman, Governor of the State of New York, by Arthur L. Reuter, Acting Commissioner of Investigation, April 23, 1958, with appendixes.

56 Pennsylvania Crime Commission, *A Decade of Organized Crime* (1980), p. 60.

57 "If Montreal Gets Its Casinos Expect the Mafia to Be There," *Hamilton Spectator*, 6 June 1970.

58 Ovid Demaris, *The Boardwalk Jungle* (New York: Bantam Books, 1986), p. 46.

59 Valachi, at the time of his appearance before the Senate Subcommittee, was serving a twenty-year jail sentence for heroin trafficking at the Atlanta federal penitentiary. Not long after his arrival at the prison, Valachi was suspected of being an informant by his boss, Vito Genovese, incarcerated for the same reasons. On June 22, 1962, Valachi killed an inmate he had mistaken for Joseph DiPalermo, a drug trafficker. He thought he had been assigned to kill him on Genovese orders. Valachi agreed to co-operate in return for protection, and pleaded guilty to a second-degree murder charge. He later met with FBI agents, who debriefed him. He died in 1971 in a federal institution in El Paso, Texas.

60 Senate Permanent Subcommittee, *Organized Crime and Illicit Traffic in Narcotics*, pp. 80, 121.

61 Cressey, *Theft of the Nation*, p. 21.

62 Ibid., p. 23.

63 Senate Permanent Subcommittee, *Organized Crime and Illicit Traffic in Narcotics*, p. 121.

64 Nelli, *Business of Crime*, p. 210.

65 Vincent Teresa with Thomas C. Renner, *My Life in the Mafia* (Greenwich, CT: Fawcett Publications, 1973), pp. 95–96.

66 U.S. Senate Permanent Subcommittee on Investigations of the Committee on Governmental Affairs, *Organized Crime and Use of Violence*, 96th Cong., 2nd sess., part 1, 1 May 1980, p. 208.

67 Ovid Demaris, *The Last Mafioso: The Treacherous World of Jimmy Fratianno* (New York: Times Books, 1981), p. 9.

68 Henry A. Zeiger, *The Jersey Mob* (Scarborough, ON: Signet Books, The New American Library of Canada, 1975), p. 152.

69 Pino Arlacchi, *Buscetta. La Mafia par l'un des siens*, trans. Éric Jozsef (Paris: Éditions du Félin, 1996), p. 29.

70 Pino Arlacchi, *Les hommes du déshonneur. La stupéfiante confession du repenti Antonino Calderone*, trans. Françoise Brun (Paris: Éditions Albin Michel, 1992), p. 79.

Chapter 2: The Structure and Organization of Cosa Nostra

1 U.S. Senate Committee on the Judiciary, *Organized Crime in America*, 98th Congress, 1st sess., part 1, 27 January 1983, pp. 42–43.

2 Historians and law enforcement agencies have continued to refer to the five New York families by the names of their bosses at the time of the October 1963 testimony of Joseph Valachi. The only exception is the Profaci family, which has been referred to as the Colombo family since its leader, Joseph Colombo, became publicly known from his association with the Italian Civil Rights League.

3 Donald R. Cressey, *Theft of the Nation: The Structure and Operation of Organized Crime in America* (New York: Harper and Row, 1969), pp. 110–11.

4 Ovid Demaris, *The Last Mafioso: The Treacherous World of Jimmy Fratianno* (New York: Times Books, 1981), pp. 18–19.

5 This information was obtained from historical documents, Cosa Nostra members, informants, undercover actions, wiretaps and surveillance. See Committee on the Judiciary, *Organized Crime in America*, p. 64.

6 U.S. Senate Permanent Subcommittee on Investigations of the Committee on Governmental Affairs, *Organized Crime and Use of Violence*, 96th Cong., 2nd sess., part 1, 28 April 1980, p. 114.

7 Joseph Bonanno with Sergio Salli, *A Man of Honor: The Autobiography of Joseph Bonanno* (New York: Simon & Schuster, 1983), pp. 227–28.

8 Ibid., pp. 228–29.

9 Annelise Graebner Anderson, *The Business of Organized Crime: A Cosa Nostra Family* (Stanford, CA: Hoover Institute Press, Stanford University, 1980), p. 23.

10 Demaris, *Last Mafioso*, p. 294.

11 Joseph D. Pistone with Richard Woodley, *Donnie Brasco: My Undercover Life in the Mafia* (New York: The New American Library, 1987), p. 304.

12 Joseph Cantalupo and Thomas C. Renner, *Body Mike: An Unsparing Exposé by the Mafia Insider Who Turned on the Mob* (New York: Villard Books, 1990), pp. 84–85.

13 Mark H. Haller, *Life Under Bruno: The Economics of an Organized Crime Family*, report for the Pennsylvania Crime Commission (July 1991), p. 22; Donald Cox,

Mafia Wipeout: How the Feds Put Away an Entire Mob Family (New York: Shapolsky Publishers, 1989), pp. 23–28.

14 Gerard O'Neil and Dick Leher, *The Underboss: The Rise and Fall of a Mafia Family* (New York: St. Martin's Press, 1989), p. 272.

15 Pennsylvania Crime Commission, *Organized Crime in Pennsylvania: A Decade of Change* (1990), pp. 105, 139. Bufalino died in February 1994, at the age of ninety-one. In the early 2000s, authorities reported that the Bufalino family had resumed its activities and was reported to have a membership of about fifteen made members.

16 James B. Jacobs, Christopher Panarella and Jay Worthington, *Busting Mob: United States v. Cosa Nostra* (New York: New York University Press, 1994), pp. 79–89.

17 Selwyn Raab, "Mob's Commission No Longer Meeting, as Families Weaken," *New York Times*, 27 April 1998, p. B1.

18 Jerry Capeci, "Commission Meets Again," *This Week in Gang Land*, www.gang-landnews.com, 18 May 2000; Jerry Capeci, "Mafia Ambassador or Deadbeat," *This Week in Gang Land*, www.ganglandnews.com, 12 December 2002.

19 Robert M. Lombardo, "The Social Organization of Organized Crime in Chicago," *Journal of Contemporary Justice* 10, no. 4 (December 1994): 290–313.

20 Centro Impastato di Documentazione, www.centroimpastato.it; Marcelle Padovani, *Les dernières années de la Mafia* (Paris: Collection Folio/Actuel, Gallimard, 1987), pp. 71–72.

21 Marshall B. Clinard and Richard Quinney, *Criminal Behavior Systems: A Typology*, 2nd ed. (New York: Holt, Rinehart and Winston, 1973), p. 229.

22 Pennsylvania Crime Commission, *Organized Crime in Pennsylvania*, p. 101.

23 U.S. Senate Permanent Subcommittee on Investigations of the Committee on Government Operations, *Organized Crime and Illicit Traffic in Narcotics*, 88th Cong., 1st sess., part 1, 1 October 1963, p. 195.

24 Gentile immigrated to the United States in the late 1920s and joined the family of Vincent Mangano. In 1937 he returned to Sicily to escape arrest for a drug trafficking charge. He later wrote his memoirs, *Vita di capomafia*, which were released in 1963.

25 Humbert S. Nelli, *The Business of Crime: Italians and Syndicate Crime in the United States* (New York: Oxford University Press, 1976), pp. 211–12; Anderson, *Business of Organized Crime*, p. 15.

26 Anderson, *Business of Organized Crime*, p. 35.

27 Bonanno, *Man of Honor*, p. 123.

28 President's Commission on Organized Crime, THE IMPACT: *Organized Crime Today*, Report to the President and the Attorney General, April 1986, p. 44.

29 Ralph Salerno and John S. Tompkins, *The Crime Confederation: Cosa Nostra and Allied Operations in Organized Crime* (New York: Popular Library, 1969), pp. 124–25.

30 Paul S. Meskil, *The Luparelli Tapes* (New York: Playboy Press, 1976), p. 121.

31 Raimondo Catanzaro, "Cosche—Cosa Nostra: la structure organisationnelle de la criminalité mafieuse en Sicile," *Cultures et Conflits* 3 (Fall 1991): 6.

32 Bonanno, *Man of Honor*, pp. 147–48; Ralph Blumenthal and John Miller, *The Gotti Tapes* (New York: Times Books, Random House, 1992), p. 202.

33 Bill Bonanno, *Bound by Honor: A Mafioso's Story* (New York: St. Martin's Press, 1999), pp. 55, 74.

34 Pino Arlacchi, *Les hommes du déshonneur. La stupéfiante confession du repenti Antonino Calderone*, trans. Françoise Brun (Paris: Éditions Albin Michel, 1992), p. 42.

35 George Anastasia, *The Goodfella Tapes* (New York: Avon Books, 1998), p. 31. Sodano was murdered in 1996.

36 Selwyn Raab, "Chips off the Old Cell Block," *New York Times*, 17 June 2000, p. B1.

37 On July 20, 2001, Merlino was acquitted of three murder charges, but was found guilty on twenty counts of extortion, illegal bookmaking and receiving stolen property. He was sentenced to a fourteen-year jail term.

38 George Anastasia, "I Made Myself Boss," *Philadelphia Inquirer*, 11 April 2001.

39 Celeste A. Morello, *Before Bruno: The History of the Philadelphia Mafia, Book 1: 1880–1931* (n.p.: Jefferies and Manz, 2000), p. 98.

40 U.S. Senate Permanent Subcommittee on Investigations of the Committee on Governmental Affairs, *Organized Crime: 25 Years After Valachi*, 100th Cong., 2nd sess., testimony of Vincent Cafaro, 22 April 1988, p. 223.

41 In January 2002 Gigante was charged, along with his son, Andrew, with obstructing justice by feigning insanity to avoid criminal prosecution. Further, he and other members of the Genovese family were charged with infiltration of the waterfront in the New York region and in Miami, financial fraud, extortion, stock fraud and money laundering.

42 Cressey, *Theft of the Nation*, p. 113.

43 Bonanno, *Man of Honor*, p. 160.

44 Cressey, *Theft of the Nation*, p. 113.

45 William Brashler, *The Don: The Life and Death of Sam Giancana* (New York: Harper and Row, 1977), p. 171.

46 Henry A. Zeiger, *Sam the Plumber: One Year in the Life of a Cosa Nostra Boss* (Bergenfield, NJ: The New American Library, Times Mirror, 1972), pp. 268–69.

47 Vincent Teresa, "A Mafioso Cases the Mafia Craze," in *The Crime Society: Organized Crime and Corruption in America*, eds. Francis A.J. Ianni and Elizabeth Reuss-Ianni (New York: Median Books, The New American Library, 1976), p. 152.

48 John H. Davis, *Mafia Dynasty: The Rise and Fall of the Gambino Crime Family* (New York: HarperCollins Publishers, 1993), pp. 144–45.

49 Michele Pantaleone, *The Mafia and Politics: The Definitive Story of the Mafia* (New York: Coward-McCann, 1966), p. 229.

50 Pennsylvania Crime Commission, 1990 Report, A Decade of Change, p. 105.
51 Pistone and Woodley, Donnie Brasco, pp. 260–61.
52 Cantalupo and Renner, Body Mike, p. 175.
53 Michael J. Zuckerman, Vengeance Is Mine (New York: Collier Macmillan Publishers, 1987), pp. 284–85.
54 Nicholas Gage, Mafia, U.S.A. (New York: Dell Books, 1972), p. 177; Joseph Salerno and Stephen J. Rivele, The Plumber: The True Story of How One Good Man Helped Destroy the Entire Philadelphia Mafia (New York: Knightsbridge Publishers, 1990), p. 18.
55 Cressey, Theft of the Nation, pp. 219–20.
56 Brashler, The Don, pp. 158, 258–59.
57 William F. Roemer Jr., Roemer: Man Against the Mob: The Inside Story of How the FBI Cracked the Chicago Mob by the Agent Who Led the Attack (New York: Donald I. Fine, 1989), pp. 263–65.
58 Brashler, The Don, pp. 258–59.
59 Pistone and Woodley, Donnie Brasco, p. 182.
60 Claire Sterling, Octopus: The Long Reach of the International Sicilian Mafia (New York: W.W. Norton & Co., 1990), p. 247.
61 Pistone and Woodley, Donnie Brasco, pp. 207–8.
62 Cressey, Theft of the Nation, p. 113.
63 Pennsylvania Crime Commission, Annual Report (April 1981), p. 10.
64 Salerno and Tompkins, Crime Federation, p. 94; Meskil, Luparelli Tapes, pp. 82–83.
65 Cressey, Theft of the Nation, p. 113; Anderson, Business of Organized Crime, p. 34.
66 Meskil, Luparelli Tapes, pp. 82–83.
67 President's Commission, IMPACT, p. 314.
68 Arlacchi, Hommes du déshonneur, p. 44.
69 Cressey, Theft of the Nation, p. 114.
70 Pistone and Woodley, Donnie Brasco, p. 304.
71 Salerno and Rivele, Plumber, p. 23.
72 Cressey, Theft of the Nation, p. 114.
73 United States v. Badalamenti, 84 CR 236 SDNY (1987), trial transcript, testimony of Tommaso Buscetta, cited in Jacobs, Panarella and Worthington, Busting Mob, p. 154.
74 Salerno and Tompkins, Crime Federation, pp. 94–95.
75 Senate Permanent Subcommittee on Investigations of the Committee on Governmental Affairs, Organized Crime: 25 Years After Valachi, p. 253.
76 Joseph D. Pistone, The Ceremony: The Mafia Initiation Tapes (New York: Dell Books, 1992), p. 63.
77 Joseph F. O'Brien and Andris Kurins, Boss of Bosses: The Fall of the Godfather: The FBI and Paul Castellano (New York: Simon & Schuster, 1991), p. 78.
78 Anderson, Business of Organized Crime, pp. 34, 35.
79 Blumenthal and Miller, Gotti Tapes, pp. 195, 199–200.

80 John Cummings and Ernest Volkman, *Goombata: The Improbable Rise and Fall of John Gotti and His Gang* (Boston: Little, Brown and Co., 1990), pp. 229–30.

81 In 1987 Gallo was sentenced to ten years in prison for bribery. He died of natural causes in 1995.

82 Cummings and Volkman, *Goombata*, p. 230.

83 Cressey, *Theft of the Nation*, pp. 114–15.

84 Gene Mustain and Jerry Capeci, *Mob Star: The Story of John Gotti* (New York: Franklin Watts, 1988), pp. 19–20.

85 Demaris, *Last Mafioso*, p. 68; Howard Abadinsky, *The Criminal Elite: Professional and Organized Crime* (Westport, CT: Greenwood Press, 1983), p. 96.

86 Cummings and Volkman, *Goombata*, p. 231.

87 O'Brien and Kurins, *Boss of Bosses*, p. 79.

88 President's Commission, IMPACT, p. 313.

89 Gene Mustain and Jerry Capeci, *Murder Machine: A True Story of Murders, Madness, and the Mafia* (New York: Dutton Books, 1992), pp. 138, 198.

90 Pistone and Woodley, *Donnie Brasco*, pp. 65–66.

91 Mustain and Capeci, *Mob Star*, p. 19.

92 Ibid., p. 212.

93 See Joseph Volz and Peter J. Bridge, *The Mafia Talks* (Greenwich, CT: Fawcett Publications, 1969). DeCavalcante died in February 1997 at the age of eighty-four.

94 Zeiger, *Sam the Plumber*, p. 254.

95 Anderson, *Business of Organized Crime*, p. 31.

96 Cressey, *Theft of the Nation*, p. 115.

97 Meskil, *Luparelli Tapes*, p. 118.

98 Pistone, *Ceremony*, p. 114.

99 Ibid., pp. 63, 85.

100 Cressey, *Theft of the Nation*, p. 114.

101 Anderson, *Business of Organized Crime*, p. 28.

102 Blumenthal and Miller, *The Gotti Tapes*, p. 164. DiBernardo was murdered in June 1986 because he openly disagreed with the proposed selection of Salvatore Gravano as the next underboss of the family following the murder of Frank DeCicco in April 1986. DiBernardo was warned several times to stop voicing his thoughts until John Gotti, then in jail, reached a decision about the appointment. But DiBernardo persisted, infuriating Gotti, who ordered him killed. (Federal Bureau of Investigations, Salvatore Gravano's debriefing, 19 November 1991, www.1.inet.com/donferin/gravano/gravano_50.html.

103 U.S. Senate Permanent Subcommittee on Investigations of the Committee on Governmental Affairs, *Waterfront Corruption*, 97th Cong., 1st sess., testimony of George Wagner, protected witness, 26 February 1981, p. 425.

104 Richard Hammer, *The Vatican Connection* (New York: Holt, Rinehart and Winston, 1982), pp. 3, 43.

105 Watts was sentenced to six years in prison in August 2002 for money laundering.

106 Chandler, *Brothers in Blood*, pp. 198–200.

107 Ibid.

108 *United States v. Bellomo*, United States Court of Appeals for the Second Circuit, August Term, 1998, testimony of Alphonse D'Arco. On October 11, 2002, D'Arco, a former ranking member in the Lucchese family, was sentenced to "time served" after testifying as a government witness for eleven years in several racketeering trials against high-ranking members of the Lucchese and other crime families.

109 Pistone and Woodley, *Donnie Brasco*, p. 48.

110 Anderson, *Business of Organized Crime*, pp. 39–40.

111 U.S. Senate Permanent Subcommittee on Investigations of the Committee on Governmental Affairs, *Profile of Organized Crime: Mid-Atlantic Region*, 98th Cong., 1st sess., 23 February 1983, p. 183.

112 Anderson, *Business of Organized Crime*, p. 40.

113 President's Commission, IMPACT, testimony of Martin Light, 29 January, 1986, pp. 323–24.

114 Ibid.

Chapter 3: Becoming a Made Member

1 Pino Arlacchi, *Les hommes du déshonneur. La stupéfiante confession du repenti Antonino Calderone*, trans. Françoise Brun (Paris: Éditions Albin Michel, 1992), p. 179.

2 Vincent Teresa with Thomas C. Renner, *My Life in the Mafia* (Greenwich, CT: Fawcett Publications, Inc., 1973), p. 96; Joseph Pistone, *The Ceremony: The Mafia Initiation Tapes* (New York: Dell Books, 1992), p. x; Donald R. Cressey, *Theft of the Nation: The Structure and Operation of Organized Crime in America* (New York: Harper and Row, 1969), p. 118; Howard Abadinsky, *The Criminal Elite: Professional and Organized Crime* (Westport, CT: Greenwood Press, 1983), p. 122; Paul S. Meskil, *The Luparelli Tapes* (New York: Playboy Press, 1976), p. 85.

3 Abadinsky, *Criminal Elite*, p. 116.

4 Cressey, *Theft of the Nation*, pp. 151–52.

5 Henry A. Zeiger, *The Jersey Mob* (Scarborough, ON: Signet Books, The New American Library of Canada, 1975), p. 151.

6 Diego Gambetta, *The Sicilian Mafia: The Business of Private Protection* (Cambridge, MA: Harvard University Press, 1996), p. 147.

7 Cressey, *Theft of the Nation*, p. 118.

8 Arlacchi, *Hommes du déshonneur*, p. 247.

9 U.S. Senate Permanent Subcommittee on Investigations of the Committee on Government Operations, *Organized Crime and Illicit Traffic in Narcotics*, 88th Cong., 1st sess., part 1, 9 October 1963, p. 348. See also Ralph Blumenthal and John Miller, *The Gotti Tapes* (New York: Times Books, Random House, 1992),

p. 99; Gene Mustain and Jerry Capeci, *Murder Machine: A True Story of Murder, Madness, and the Mafia* (New York: Dutton Books, 1992), p. 167; Pistone, *Ceremony*, p. 89; Giovanni Falcone and Marcelle Padovani, *Cosa Nostra. Le juge et les "hommes d'honneur,"* 1st ed. (Paris: Austral, 1991), p. 106.

10 Robilotto was killed in 1957 for fear of reprisals following the murder of Albert Anastasia. Valachi identified Robilotto as the one who was given, in October 1951, the contract to kill William Moretti, an influential New Jersey–based *caporegime* in the Genovese family. Moretti was apparently suffering from syphilis, which made him behave in erratic way, putting the security of Cosa Nostra at stake. Moretti's murder was regarded as a "mercy killing," as he enjoyed great respect among his confederates.

11 Office of the Independent Hearing Officer, Laborers' International Union of North America, No. 98–93D, in re John Matassa Jr., affidavit of John J. O'Rourke.

12 Gambetta, *Sicilian Mafia*, p. 118

13 Cressey, *Theft of the Nation*, p. 118

14 John Cummings and Ernest Volkman, *Goombata: The Improbable Rise and Fall of John Gotti and His Gang* (Boston: Little, Brown and Co., 1990), p. 69.

15 U.S. Senate Permanent Subcommittee on Investigations of the Committee on Governmental Affairs, *Organized Crime: 25 Years After Valachi*, 100th Cong., 2nd sess., testimony of Tommaso Buscetta, 11 April 1988, p. 50.

16 Francis A.J. Ianni, "New Mafia: Black, Hispanic and Italian Style," in *The Crime Society: Organized Crime and Corruption in America*, eds. Francis A.J. Ianni and Elizabeth Reuss-Ianni (New York: Median Books, The New American Library, 1976), p. 129.

17 Howard Abadinsky, *Organized Crime: A Comprehensive Reference to the Laws and Strategies for Preventing and Combatting Organized Crime* (Boston: Allyn and Bacon, 1981), pp. 19–20.

18 Ralph Salerno and John S. Tompkins, *The Crime Confederation: Cosa Nostra and Allied Operations in Organized Crime* (New York: Popular Library, 1969), pp. 96–107; Cummings and Volkman, *Goombata*, p. 62.

19 Salerno and Tompkins, *Crime Confederation*, pp. 105–6.

20 Ibid.

21 Arlacchi, *Hommes du déshonneur*, p. 248.

22 Meskil, *Luparelli Tapes*, p. 71.

23 Annelise Graebner Anderson, *The Business of Organized Crime: A Cosa Nostra Family* (Stanford: Hoover Institute Press, Stanford University, 1980), pp. 18–19.

24 Cummings and Volkman, *Goombata*, p. 73.

25 Zeiger, *Jersey Mob*, p. 150.

26 Ibid., p. 155.

27 Ibid., p. 150.

28 Spero, age seventy-two, was tried in March and April 2001 and was found

guilty of Gulino's murder and two others he had ordered. He was sentenced to life imprisonment in April 2002.

29 Senate Permanent Subcommittee, *Organized Crime: 25 Years After Valachi*, testimony of Tommaso Buscetta, 11 April 1988, p. 50.

30 Greg B. Smith, "Big Fish Is Spilling," *New York Daily News*, 12 May 2003.

31 Peter Maas, *Underboss: Sammy the Bull Gravano's Story of Life in the Mafia* (New York: HarperPerennial, 1999), p. 46.

32 Michael Franzese and Dary Matera, *Quitting the Mob* (New York: Harper Paperback, April 1993), p. 129.

33 George Anastasia, "Natale Gives an Insider's View of the 'Dark Side,'" *Philadelphia Inquirer*, 10 April 2001.

34 Howard Abadinsky, "The McDonald's-ization of the Mafia," in *Organized Crime in America: Concepts and Controversies*, ed. Timothy S. Bynum, Issues in Crime and Justice, vol. 1 (Monsey, NY: Willow Tree Press, 1987), p. 45.

35 Joseph D. Pistone with Richard Woodley, *Donnie Brasco: My Undercover Life in the Mafia* (New York: The New American Library, 1987), pp. 365, 369. On February 18, 1982, Anthony Mirra, a soldier in the Bonanno family, was killed for the same reason.

36 Senate Permanent Subcommittee, *Organized Crime: 25 Years After Valachi*, testimony of Joseph Pistone, 22 April 1988, pp. 203, 210.

37 *United States v. Bellomo*, United States Court of Appeals for the Second Circuit, August Term, 1998, testimony of Alphonse D'Arco. Circulating the names of prospective candidates is also practised among the Hells Angels. As well as names, the pictures of all candidates are circulated to the worldwide Hells Angels chapters for scrutiny, and to determine if any of the prospects is a police informant.

38 Giuseppe Alongi, *La Mafia, Fattori—Manifestazioni—Rimedi*, new ed. (Palermo: Ristampo dell'edizionne di Palermo, 1904; Bologna: Arnaldo Forni Editore, 1977), p. 281.

39 Eric J. Hobsbawm, *Primitive Rebels: Studies in Archaic Forms of Social Movement in the 19th and 20th Centuries* (New York: The Norton Library, W.W. Norton and Co., 1965), pp. 34–35. See also Giuseppe Alongi, *La camorra. Studio di Sociologia criminale* (Torino, 1890), p. 41.

40 Falcone and Padovani, *Cosa Nostra*, pp. 103–5.

41 Letizia Paoli, "The Integration of the Italian Crime Scene," *European Journal of Crime, Criminal Law and Criminal Justice* 2 (1996): 131.

42 Blumenthal and Miller, *Gotti Tapes*, pp. 143–46; Fred J. Cook, *Mafia!* (Greenwich, CT: Fawcett Publications, 1973), p. 33; Ovid Demaris, *The Lucky Luciano Story* (New York: Belmont Tower Books, 1974), pp. 26–27; Ovid Demaris, *The Last Mafioso: The Treacherous World of Jimmy Fratianno* (New York: Times Books, 1981), pp. 3–4, 325–26; Meskil, *Luparelli Tapes*, p. 123; Tim Shawcross and Martin Young, *Men of Honour: The Confessions of Tommaso Buscetta* (London: Collins, 1987), pp. 34–35; Claire Sterling, *Octopus: The Long*

Reach of the International Sicilian Mafia (New York: W.W. Norton & Co., 1990), pp. 72–73.

43 Cummings and Volkman, *Goombata*, p. 101; Donald Cox, *Mafia Wipeout: How the Feds Put Away an Entire Mob Family* (New York: Shapolsky Publishers, 1989), pp. xii-xiii.

44 Pistone, *Ceremony*, pp. x-xi.

45 Cox, *Mafia Wipeout*, p. 283.

46 Senate Permanent Subcommittee, *Organized Crime and Illicit Traffic in Narcotics*, 1 October 1963, p. 183.

47 Ibid., pp. 183–85. The practice of counting off fingers still occurs in initiation ceremonies in New York City and Boston, particularly in the Patriarca family. See also Pistone, *Ceremony*, pp. 52, 72, 80, 92; Salvatore Bonanno talks about the counting of numbers when he was initiated in Bill Bonanno, *Bound by Honor, A Mafioso's Story* (New York: St. Martin's Press, 1999), p. 17.

48 *United States v. Salerno*, 85 CR 139 SDNY (1985), testimony of Angelo Lonardo, cited in James B. Jacobs, Christopher Panarella and Jay Worthington, *Busting Mob: United States v. Cosa Nostra* (New York: New York University Press, 1994), p. 119.

49 Pistone, *Ceremony*, pp. 48–53.

50 *United States v. Francis P. Salemme, et al.* Cr. No. 94-10287-MLW; *United States v. John Martorano*, Cr. No. 97-10009.

51 Fresolone's assistance to authorities gave birth to "Operation Broadsword," which lasted from 1988 until August 1990, after which Fresolone was withdrawn from the undercover operation. Soon after, forty-one members and associates of the Scarfo, DeCavalcante, Gambino, Lucchese, Genovese and Colombo families were arrested and charged for various racketeering activities. Fresolone died on March 15, 2002, of natural causes. See George Fresolone and Robert J. Wagman, *Blood Oath: The Heroic Story of a Gangster Turned Government Agent Who Brought Down One of America's Most Powerful Mob Families* (New York: Simon & Schuster, 1994).

52 Jerry Capeci, "New Jersey Family Is Second Class," *This Week in Gang Land*, www.ganglandnews.com, 12 June 2003.

53 Jerry Capeci, "No Longer Garden State Farmers," *This Week in Gang Land*, www.ganglandnews.com, 28 June 2001.

54 Jerry Capeci, "The Toilet Bowl Gangster," *This Week in Gang Land*, www.ganglandnews.com, 2 November 1998.

55 Arlacchi, *Hommes du déshonneur*, p. 83.

56 Abadinsky, *Criminal Elite*, p. 116.

57 *R. v. Francesco Caccamo*, Supreme Court of Canada, on appeal from the Court of Appeal of Ontario, Part II, evidence, filed on 27 November, 1973.

58 Pistone and Woodley, *Donnie Brasco*, p. 64.

59 Ibid., pp. 64–65.

60 Ibid., p. 36.

61 Mark H. Haller, *Life Under Bruno: The Economics of an Organized Crime Family*, report for the Pennsylvania Crime Commission (July 1991), p. 5.

62 Abadinsky, "McDonald's-ization," pp. 46, 47–8; Cressey, *Theft of the Nation*, p. 117; Salerno and Tompkins, *Crime Confederation*, p. 101.

63 Nicholas Pileggi, *Wiseguy: Life in a Mafia Family* (New York: Simon & Schuster, 1985), pp. 39–40.

64 Zeiger, *Jersey Mob*, p. 149.

65 Pennsylvania Crime Commission, *1983 Report*, p. 27.

66 Senate Permanent Subcommittee, *Organized Crime: 25 Years After Valachi*, testimony of Tommaso Buscetta, 11 April 1988, p. 51.

67 Corrado Stajano, *Mafia. L'atto d'accusa dei giudici di Palermo* (Rome: Editori Riuniti, 1986), p. 47.

68 Abadinsky, "McDonald's-ization," p. 47.

69 Ibid., p. 46.

70 Michael J. Zuckerman, *Vengeance Is Mine* (New York: Collier Macmillan Publishers, 1987), pp. 84–85.

71 U.S. Senate Permanent Subcommittee on Investigations of the Committee on Governmental Affairs, *Organized Crime and Use of Violence*, 96th Cong., 2nd sess., part 1, 28 April 1980, p. 98.

72 U.S. Senate Permanent Subcommittee on Investigations of the Committee on Governmental Affairs, *Waterfront Corruption*, 97th Cong., 1st sess., 26 February 1981, p. 350.

73 Abadinsky, *Criminal Elite*, pp. 118–19.

74 The FBI defines a made member as a person who has participated in a formalized ceremony, has the right to share in the profits of the crime family and is allowed to develop his own criminal ventures, in which he sets the rules and conditions of his deals for the associates who work for him.

   The FBI determines whether an individual is a made member based on an identification by other members of Cosa Nostra. Two known made members must be heard discussing a third person as a made member either on a wiretap or in the presence of an undercover FBI agent. This information is counterchecked with other data, such as records, wiretaps and microphones (body packs) that informants wear to gather information. (*Waterfront Corruption*, Hearings before the U.S. Senate Permanent Subcommittee on Investigations of the Committee on Governmental Affairs, 97th Cong., 1st sess., 18 February, 1981, testimony of George Wagner, protected witness, p. 109; U.S. Senate Permanent Subcommittee, *Organized Crime and Use of Violence*, p. 91.)

75 Senate Permanent Subcommittee, *Organized Crime and Illicit Traffic in Narcotics*, 8 October 1963, p. 297.

76 Peter Maas, *The Valachi Papers* (New York: Bantam Books, 1968), p. 262.

77 Nicholas Gage, *The Mafia Is Not an Equal Opportunity Employer* (New York: Dell Books, 1972), p. 42; Joseph Salerno and Stephen J. Rivele, *The Plumber: The True*

Story of How One Good Man Helped Destroy the Entire Philadelphia Mafia (New York: Knightsbridge Publishers, 1990), p. 18.

78 Demaris, *Last Mafioso*, p. 391.

79 Al Guart, "Mafia: Help Wanted," *New York Post*, 19 May 2002.

80 *United States v. Salerno*, 85 CR 139 SDNY (1985), testimony of Angelo Lonardo, cited in Jacobs, Panarella and Worthington, *Busting Mob*, p. 111.

81 Senate Permanent Subcommittee, *Organized Crime and Illicit Traffic in Narcotics*, 9 October 1963, p. 367.

82 Salerno and Tompkins, *Crime Confederation*, pp. 125–26.

83 Demaris, *Last Mafioso*, pp. 119–20; Zuckerman, *Vengeance Is Mine*, p. 138.

84 Joseph Cantalupo and Thomas C. Renner, *Body Mike: An Unsparing Exposé by the Mafia Insider Who Turned on the Mob* (New York: Villard Books, 1990), p. 46.

85 Gene Mustain and Jerry Capeci, *Mob Star: The Story of John Gotti* (New York: Franklin Watts, 1988), p. 122.

86 Shawcross and Young, *Men of Honour*, p. 61.

87 Blumenthal and Miller, *Gotti Tapes*, pp. 139–40.

Chapter 4: The Code of Conduct

1 Ralph Salerno and John S. Tompkins, *The Crime Confederation: Cosa Nostra and Allied Operations in Organized Crime* (New York: Popular Library, 1969), p. 114.

2 Joseph D. Pistone, *The Ceremony: The Mafia Initiation Tapes* (New York: Dell Books, 1992), p. 113.

3 Pino Arlacchi, *Buscetta. La Mafia par l'un des siens*, trans. Éric Jozsef (Paris: Éditions du Félin, 1996), pp. 93–94.

4 Giovanni Falcone and Marcelle Padovani, *Cosa Nostra. Le juge et les "hommes d'honneur,"* 1st ed. (Paris: Austral, 1991), p. 51.

5 U.S. Senate Permanent Subcommittee on Investigations of the Committee on Governmental Affairs, *Organized Crime: 25 Years After Valachi*, 100th Cong., 2nd sess., testimony of Joseph Pistone, 22 April 1988, p. 204.

6 Corrado Stajano, *Mafia. L'atto d'accusa dei giudici di Palermo* (Rome: Editori Riuniti, 1986), p. 44.

7 *United States v. Badalamenti*, 84 CR 236 SDNY (1987), trial transcript, testimony of Tommaso Buscetta, cited in James B. Jacobs, Christopher Panarella and Jay Worthington, *Busting Mob: United States v. Cosa Nostra* (New York: New York University Press, 1994), p. 152.

8 Letizia Paoli, *Fratelli di Mafia: Cosa Nostra e 'Ndrangheta* (Bologna: Il Mulino, 2000), p. 136.

9 Stajano, *Mafia*, p. 48.

10 Joseph D. Pistone with Richard Woodley, *Donnie Brasco: My Undercover Life in the Mafia* (New York, The New American Library, 1987), p. 206.

11 *United States v. Vittorio Amuso*, United States Court of Appeals for the Second Circuit, 21 F. 3d 1251 (1994).

12 Federal Bureau of Investigations, Salvatore Gravano's debriefing, 15 November 1991, www.1.1net.com/donferin/gravano/gravano_50. html.

13 Ralph Blumenthal, *Last Days of the Sicilians: At War with the Mafia: The F.B.I. Assault on the Pizza Connection* (New York: Times Books, 1988), pp. 301–2.

14 Fred D. Pasley, *Al Capone: The Biography of a Self-Made Man* (New York: Garden City Publishing Company, 1930), p. 232.

15 Jerry Capeci, "Mob Capo: I'm retired," *This Week in Gang Land*, www.gangland-news.com, 14 September 2000.

16 "Il cassiere di Cosa Nostra: 'Mi dissocio ma non mi pento,'" *La Repubblica*, 25 September 2001, p. 29.

17 Jerry Capeci, *This Week in Gang Land*, www.ganglandnews.com, 20 December 2001 and 27 December 2001.

18 John Marsulli, "Chin Set to Admit Mob Exists," *New York Daily News*, 22 August 2002.

19 Pistone, *Ceremony*, pp. 76, 87–88.

20 Kenneth Allsop, *The Bootleggers: The Story of Prohibition* (New Rochelle, NY: Arlington House, 1968), p. 271.

21 Donald R. Cressey, *Theft of the Nation: The Structure and Operation of Organized Crime in America* (New York: Harper and Row, 1969), p. 186.

22 Stafano, *Mafia*, pp. 43–44.

23 Salerno and Tompkins, *The Crime Confederation*, pp. 127–28.

24 Ibid., pp. 123–24.

25 According to Antonino Giuffrè, a Sicilian Cosa Nostra member who was arrested in April 2002 by Italian police, members of the Bonanno family were sent to Trapani, Sicily, during the 1990s to be taught "Mafia lessons." American Cosa Nostra bosses apparently felt frustrated by the lack of professionalism displayed by aspiring successors.

26 J.M. Lawrence, "Mafia Ain't What It Used to Be," *Boston Herald*, 23 September 2002.

27 George Anastasia, *The Goodfella Tapes* (New York: Avon Books, 1998), p. 20.

28 Donald Cox, *Mafia Wipeout: How the Feds Put Away an Entire Mob Family* (New York: Shapolsky Publishers, 1989), p. 11.

29 Joseph F. O'Brien and Andris Kurins, *Boss of Bosses: The Fall of the Godfather: The FBI and Paul Castellano* (New York: Simon & Schuster, 1991), pp. 20–21.

30 Cox, *Mafia Wipeout*, p. 351.

31 The Peter Principle was explained for the first time in a book dealing with the management of human resources within an enterprise (Dr. Laurence J. Peter and Raymond Hull, *The Peter Principle* [London: Pan Books, 1970]). The theory is that a person who is successful at one job gets promoted to another. The process continues until the person cannot handle the new job, as that person has reached his or her level of incompetence.

32 O'Brien and Kurins, *Boss of Bosses*, pp. 276–77.

33 Pistone, *Ceremony*, pp. 107–8.

34 Quebec Police Commission, Commission of Inquiry into Organized Crime, Project "Benoit," conversation of 21 May 1972, exhibit 1176, filed before the Commission on 23 November 1975, p. 29.

35 Gene Mustain and Jerry Capeci, *Mob Star: The Story of John Gotti* (New York: Franklin Watts, 1988), pp. 117–18.

36 Ernest Volkman, *Gangbusters: The Destruction of America's Last Great Mafia Dynasty* (New York: Avon Books, 1999), p. 184.

37 Joseph Cantalupo and Thomas C. Renner, *Body Mike: An Unsparing Exposé by the Mafia Insider Who Turned on the Mob* (New York: Villard Books, 1990), p. 87.

38 Rosalie Bonanno with Beverly Donofrio, *Mafia Marriage: My Story* (New York: William Morrow and Company, 1990), p. 62.

39 Salerno and Tompkins, *Crime Confederation*, p. 93.

40 Giuseppe Alongi, *La Mafia, Fattori—Manifestazioni—Rimedi*, new ed. (Palermo: Ristampo dell'edizionne di Palermo, 1904; Bologna: Arnaldo Forni Editore, 1977), p. 280.

41 Antonino Cutrera, *La Mafia e i Mafiosi: origini e manifestazioni, studio di sociologio criminale* (Palermo, 1900), p. 177, quoted in Robert T. Anderson, "From Mafia to Cosa Nostra," *The American Journal of Sociology* 71 (November 1965): 302.

42 Francis A.J. Ianni, "New Mafia: Black, Hispanic and Italian Styles," in *The Crime Society: Organized Crime and Corruption in America*, eds. Francis A.J. Ianni and Elizabeth Reuss-Ianni (New York: Median Books, The New American Library, 1976), p. 137.

43 Ianni, "New Mafia," p. 139.

44 Cressey, *Theft of the Nation*, pp. 174–75.

45 John Cummings and Ernest Volkman, *Goombata: The Improbable Rise and Fall of John Gotti and His Gang* (Boston: Little, Brown and Co., 1990), pp. 68–69.

46 Joseph L. Albini, *The American Mafia: Genesis of a Legend* (New York: Meredith Corp., 1971), pp. 269, 272–73.

47 Cressey, *Theft of the Nation*, pp. 166–67.

48 Frederic D. Homer, *Guns and Garlic: Myths and Realties of Organized Crime* (West Lafayette, IN: Perdue University Studies, 1974), p. 139.

49 Marie-Anne Matard-Bonucci, *Histoire de la mafia*, Questions au XXᵉ siècle (Brussels: Éditions Complexe, 1994), p. 122.

50 Volkman, *Gangbusters*, p. 229.

51 In 1987 Scarfo was charged and convicted of conspiracy and racketeering. He is currently serving fourteen- and fifty-five-year consecutive sentences. In March 1997, after a second trial, he was acquitted of the 1985 murder of Frank D'Alfonso, a South Philadelphia bookmaker.

52 Cox, *Mafia Wipeout*, p. 34.

53 Senate Permanent Subcommittee, *Organized Crime: 25 Years After Valachi*, statement of the Pennsylvania Crime Commission, 15 April 1988, p. 630.

54 Homer, *Guns and Garlic*, p. 110.
55 Carl Sifakis, *The Mafia Encyclopedia* (New York: Facts on Files Publications, 1987), pp. 78–79.
56 Ibid., p. 297.
57 Office of the United States Attorney for the Eastern District of New York, press release, 16 October 2003.

Chapter 5: Rules of Conduct

1 Joseph D. Pistone, *The Ceremony: The Mafia Initiation Tapes* (New York: Dell Books, 1992), pp. 57–61, 97–100, conversation recorded on 29 October 1989, at 34 Guild Street, Medford, MA.
2 Ibid.
3 *United States v. Badalamenti*, 84 CR 236 SDNY (1987), trial transcript, testimony of Tommaso Buscetta, cited in James B. Jacobs, Christopher Panarella and Jay Worthington, *Busting Mob: United States v. Cosa Nostra* (New York: New York University Press, 1994), p. 152.
4 Pistone, *Ceremony*, p. 60.
5 Pistone, *Ceremony*, p. 77.
6 Henry A. Ziegler, *Sam the Plumber: One Year in the Life of a Cosa Nostra Boss* (Bergenfield, NJ: The New American Library, Times Mirror, 1972), p. 46.
7 Gerard O'Neil and Dick Leher, *The Underboss: The Rise and Fall of a Mafia Family* (New York: St. Martin Press, 1989), p. 258.
8 Ralph Blumenthal and John Miller, *The Gotti Tapes* (New York: Times Books, Random House, 1992), p. 44.
9 Henry A. Zeiger, *Sam the Plumber: One Year in the Life of a Cosa Nostra Boss* (Bergenfield, NJ: The New American Library, Times Mirror, 1972), p. 254.
10 Peter Maas, *Underboss: Sammy the Bull Gravano's Story of Life in the Mafia* (New York: HarperPerennial, 1999), p. 88.
11 Strollo was suspected to have encouraged the Gallo brothers to rebel against their boss, Joseph Profaci, in early 1962. Strollo's alleged involvement in heroin trafficking is another explanation for his murder.
12 In 1963 the Caruana and Cuntrera families from Siciliana, Sicily, were given permission by the Cupola to establish a family in Caracas, Venezuela. They had fled Sicily to escape a massive Italian police manhunt following a car explosion that killed seven *carabinieri* in Ciaculli, Sicily, in 1963. The Caruanas and Cuntreras immigrated to Montreal, where they set up a drug trafficking pipeline from Europe to North America. Later, they moved to Caracas.
13 Joseph Bonanno with Sergio Salli, *A Man of Honor: The Autobiography of Joseph Bonanno* (New York: Simon & Schuster, 1983), p. 157.
14 John Cummings and Ernest Volkman, *Goombata: The Improbable Rise and Fall of John Gotti and His Gang* (Boston: Little, Brown and Co., 1990), p. 237.

15 Mark H. Haller, *Life Under Bruno: The Economics of an Organized Crime Family*, report for the Pennsylvania Crime Commission (July 1991), p. 7.

16 Humbert S. Nelli, *The Business of Crime: Italians and Syndicate Crime in the United States* (New York: Oxford University Press, 1976), p. 15.

17 Ibid., pp. 15–16.

18 Pino Arlacchi, *Les hommes du déshonneur. La stupéfiante confession du repenti Antonino Calderone*, trans. Françoise Brun (Paris: Éditions Albin Michel, 1992), p. 167.

19 Pistone, *Ceremony*, pp. 118–22.

20 Cummings and Volkman, *Goombata*, p. 238.

21 Joseph D. Pistone with Richard Woodley, *Donnie Brasco: My Undercover Life in the Mafia* (New York: The New American Library, 1987), pp. 66–67.

22 Ovid Demaris, *The Boardwalk Jungle* (New York: Bantam Books, 1986), p. 349.

23 Thomas L. Jones, "A Death in the Family: The Killing of Michael Pappadio," www.BostonMafia.com, January 2002.

24 Haller, *Life Under Bruno*, pp. 6–7.

25 Jerry Capeci, "Commission Meets Again," *This Week in Gang Land*, www.ganglandnews.com, 18 May 2000.

26 Haller, *Life Under Bruno*, p. 17.

27 Donald R. Cressey, *Theft of the Nation: The Structure and Operation of Organized Crime in America* (New York: Harper and Row, 1969), p. 118.

28 Bonanno with Salli, *Man of Honor*, p. 79.

29 Pistone and Woodley, *Donnie Brasco*, pp. 65, 210.

30 Quebec Police Commission, *Organized Crime and the World of Business*, report of the Commission of Inquiry on Organized Crime and Recommendations, 1977, pp. 100–101.

31 Arlacchi, *Hommes du déshonneur*, pp. 79–80.

32 Paul S. Meskil, *Don Carlo: Boss of Bosses* (Toronto: Popular Library, 1973), pp. 109–10.

33 Nicholas Gage, *The Mafia Is Not an Equal Opportunity Employer* (New York: Dell Books, 1972), pp. 141–42.

34 Ralph Salerno and John S. Tompkins, *The Crime Confederation: Cosa Nostra and Allied Operations in Organized Crime* (New York: Popular Library, 1969), p. 121.

35 T.J. English, *The Westies: Inside the Hell's Kitchen Irish Mob* (New York: G.P. Putnam's Sons, 1990), pp. 34–35.

36 Ibid., p. 53.

37 Gene Mustain and Jerry Capeci, *Mob Star: The Story of John Gotti* (New York: Franklin Watts, 1988), p. 121.

38 For more on the Gallo-Profaci War, see Raymond Martin, *Revolt in the Mafia* (New York: Duell Storn and Pearce, Publishers, 1963); Vincent Teresa and Thomas C. Renner, *My Life in the Mafia* (Greenwich, CT: Fawcett Publications, 1973), pp. 91–94; Paul S. Meskil, *The Luparelli Tapes* (New York: Playboy Press, 1976), pp. 87–93, 232–33.

39 Mario Mori, "The Sicilian Mafia," *Atti del 1° Seminario Europeo "Falcone One" sulla Criminalità Organizzata*, Rome, 26–27 April 1995.

40 Arlacchi, *Hommes du déshonneur*, pp. 26, 154; Giovanni Falcone and Marcelle Padovani, *Cosa Nostra. Le juge et les "hommes d'honneur,"* 1st ed. (Paris: Austral, 1991), p. 98.

41 Arlacchi, *Hommes du déshonneur*, p. 158.

42 Ibid., p. 26.

43 Peter Maas, *The Valachi Papers* (New York: Bantam Books, 1968), p. 207.

44 Bonanno with Salli, *Man of Honor*, pp. 154–55. Salvatore Bonanno relates an incident in which Albert Anastasia slapped Carlo Gambino in the face for allegedly having bungled an assignment. See also Bill Bonanno, *Bound by Honor: A Mafioso's Story* (New York: St. Martin's Press, 1999), pp. 54–55.

45 Howard Abadinsky, *The Criminal Elite: Professional and Organized Crime* (Westport, CT: Greenwood Press, 1983), p. 120.

46 Mustain and Capeci, *Mob Star*, p. 92.

47 Zeiger, *Sam the Plumber*, pp. 242, 244.

48 Blumenthal and Miller, *Gotti Tapes*, pp. 248–52.

49 Gene Mustain and Jerry Capeci, *Murder Machine: A True Story of Murder, Madness, and the Mafia* (New York: Dutton Books, 1992), pp. 102–3.

50 Donald R. Cressey, *Criminal Organization* (New York: Harper and Row, 1972), p. 58.

51 Ernest Volkman, *Gangbusters: The Destruction of America's Last Great Mafia Dynasty* (New York: Avon Books, 1999), p. 288.

52 Paul S. Meskil, *Luparelli Tapes*, pp. 166–67.

53 Joseph F. O'Brien and Andris Kurins, *Boss of Bosses: The Fall of the Godfather: The FBI and Paul Castellano* (New York: Simon & Schuster, 1991), p. 202.

54 English, *Westies*, p. 185.

55 Henry A. Zeiger, *The Jersey Mob* (Scarborough, ON: Signet Books, The New American Library of Canada, 1975), pp. 91–92.

56 U.S. Senate Permanent Subcommittee on Investigations of the Committee on Governmental Affairs, *Organized Crime and Use of Violence*, 96th Cong., 2nd sess., part 1, 29 April 1980, p. 101.

57 Paul S. Meskil, *Don Carlo*, pp. 194–95.

58 Ibid., pp. 195–96.

59 U.S. House Select Committee on Assassinations, *Investigation of the Assassination of President John F. Kennedy*, 95th Cong., 2nd sess., vol. IX, appendix, Staff and Consultants Reports on Organized Crime, March 1979, p. 31.

60 John H. Davis, *Mafia Kingfish: Carlos Marcello and the Assassination of John F. Kennedy* (New York: Signet Book, The New American Library, 1989), p. 357.

61 O'Neil and Leher, *Underboss*, p. 5.

62 William Brashler, *The Don: The Life and Death of Sam Giancana* (New York: Harper and Row, 1977), pp. 189–90.

63 Maas, *Valachi Papers*, p. 210; Meskil, *Luparelli Tapes*, p. 137; Mustain and Capeci, *Mob Star*, pp. 9, 121; English, *Westies*, p. 176.

64 Pistone and Woodley, *Donnie Brasco*, p. 102.
65 Jerry Capeci, "My Son, the Dummy Don," *This Week in Gang Land*, www.gang-landnews.com, 8 July 1999.
66 Blumenthal and Miller, *Gotti Tapes*, pp. 286–87; Federal Bureau of Investigations, Salvatore Gravano's debriefing, 20 November 1991, www.1.1net.com/donferin/gravano/gravano_50.html.
67 Pistone, *Ceremony*, pp. 100–101.
68 Salerno and Tomkins, *Crime Confederation*, p. 119.
69 President's Commission on Organized Crime, THE IMPACT: *Organized Crime Today*, Report to the President and the Attorney General, April 1986, p. 400; Bonanno with Salli, *Man of Honor*, p. 154.
70 Meskil, *Don Carlo*, p. 194.
71 Volkman, *Gangbusters*, p. 224.
72 Zeiger, *Sam the Plumber*, p. 262.
73 Meskil, *Don Carlo*, pp. 122–23.
74 Pino Arlacchi, *Buscetta. La Mafia par l'un des siens*, trans. Éric Jozsef (Paris: Éditions du Félin, 1996), pp. 74–75.
75 Falcone and Padovani, *Cosa Nostra*, p. 82.
76 Meskil, *Don Carlo*, pp. 188–89.
77 Tim Shawcross and Martin Young, *Men of Honour: The Confessions of Tommaso Buscetta* (London: Collins, 1987), pp. 279–80.
78 Mustain and Capeci, *Mob Star*, pp. 116–17.
79 William F. Roemer Jr., *Accardo: The Genuine Godfather* (New York: Ivy Books, Ballantine Books, 1995), p. 270.
80 In March 1932 Genovese had Anna Pitillo's husband, Gerardo Vernotico, murdered so he could marry her.
81 Salerno and Tomkins, *Crime Confederation*, p. 119.
82 U.S. Senate Select Committee on Improper Activities in the Labor or Management Field, *Hearings Before the Select Committee on Improper Activities in the Labor or Management Field*, 85th Cong., 2nd sess., part 32, 1 July 1958, pp. 12252–56.
83 Rosalie's uncle, Joseph Profaci, was the leader of one of the five New York families from 1931 until his death in June 1962.
84 Rosalie Bonanno with Beverly Donofrio, *Mafia Marriage: My Story* (New York: William Morrow and Company, 1990), pp. 77, 143, 218–19.
85 Cummings and Volkman, *Goombata*, p. 64.
86 Gage, *Mafia Is Not An Equal Opportunity Employer*, pp. 122–24.
87 Celestine Bohlen, "As Omertà Crumbles, the Mafia Changes the Rules," *New York Times*, 1 October 1995.
88 Ovid Demaris, *The Last Mafioso: The Treacherous World of Jimmy Fratianno* (New York: Times Books, 1981), p. 98.
89 Abadinsky, *Criminal Elite*, pp. 158–59.
90 Arlacchi, *Hommes du déshonneur*, pp. 28–29.

91 U.S. Senate Permanent Subcommittee on Investigations of the Committee on Governmental Affairs, *Waterfront Corruption*, 97th Cong., 1st sess., 26 February 1981, p. 352.

92 Pistone, *Ceremony*, pp. 126–27.

93 Frederic Sondern Jr., *Brotherhood of Evil: The Mafia* (New York: Manor Books, 1972), pp. 106–7.

94 Maas, *Valachi Papers*, p. 163.

95 Ibid., pp. 46–47.

96 Pistone and Woodley, *Donnie Brasco*, p. 117.

97 Joseph Salerno and Stephen J. Rivele, *The Plumber: The True Story of How One Good Man Helped Destroy the Entire Philadelphia Mafia* (New York: Knightsbridge Publishers, 1990), p. 35.

98 Volkman, *Gangbusters*, pp. 230, 320.

99 Daniel R. Wolf, *The Rebels: A Brotherhood of Outlaw Bikers* (Toronto: University of Toronto Press, 1991), pp. 75–77.

100 Salerno and Tompkins, *Crime Confederation*, pp. 150–51.

101 Stephen Fox, *Blood and Power: Organized Crime in Twentieth-Century America* (New York: William Morrow and Co., 1989), pp. 96–98.

102 Donald Cox, *Mafia Wipeout: How the Feds Put Away an Entire Mob Family* (New York: Shapolsky Publishers, 1989), pp. 15–16.

103 Senate Permanent Subcommittee, *Waterfront Corruption*, pp. 377–78.

104 Cox, *Mafia Wipeout*, p. 68.

105 Pistone and Woodley, *Donnie Brasco*, p. 187.

106 After it was discovered that Pistone was an undercover agent, the FBI immediately arrested Ruggiero for his own safety, as the Bonanno family was about to issue a contract on his life.

107 Pistone and Woodley, *Donnie Brasco*, pp. 310, 327.

108 Blumenthal and Miller, *Gotti Tapes*, p. 140.

109 Nicholas Pileggi, *Wiseguy: Life in a Mafia Family* (New York: Simon & Schuster, 1985), p. 55.

110 Pistone and Woodley, *Donnie Brasco*, p. 101.

111 Haller, *Life Under Bruno*, p. 7.

112 Pistone and Woodley, *Donnie Brasco*, p. 117.

113 Zeiger, *Sam the Plumber*, p. 33.

114 Pileggi, *Wiseguy*, pp. 85–86.

115 Cressey, *Theft of the Nation*, p. 212.

116 U.S. Senate Permanent Subcommittee on Investigations of the Committee on Governmental Affairs, *Profile of Organized Crime: Great Lakes Region*, 98th Cong., 2nd sess., 25 January 1984, p. 46.

117 Zeiger, *Jersey Mob*, pp. 201–2.

118 Zeiger, *Sam the Plumber*, pp. 23–24.

119 Ibid., p. 72.

120 According to the President's Commission on Organized Crime (in 1986), since the 1950s, Cosa Nostra has controlled the leaders of the nation's largest union, the International Brotherhood of Teamsters (IBT), primarily through the office of the president. It exerted influence on at least thirty-eight of the largest locals and a joint council in Chicago, Cleveland, New Jersey, New York, Philadelphia, St. Louis and other major cities. From 1952 to 1985 there have been five IBT presidents. The first, Dave Beck, was convicted in 1959 for violating federal income tax laws. His successor, James R. "Jimmy" Hoffa, was convicted of jury tampering in 1964, and disappeared in July 1975. The next president, Frank Fitzsimmons, was not indicted during his tenure and died a natural death in office in 1981. It has not been clearly established by law enforcement whether Fitzsimmons had links to Cosa Nostra figures. His successor, Roy L. Williams, was president from 1981 until 1983. He was convicted of conspiracy to attempt to bribe a U.S. senator. The next president was Jackie Presser. Cosa Nostra has been attracted to the IBT because IBT oversees hundreds of individual benefit funds, including the Central States Pension Fund, which generates significant monies from the dues paid by its 1.6 million members. (President's Commission on Organized Crime, Report to the President and the Attorney General, THE EDGE: *Organized Crime, Business, and Labor Unions*, March 1986.)

121 James Neff, *Mobbed Up: Jackie Presser's High-Wire Life in the Teamsters, the Mafia, and the FBI* (New York: The Atlantic Monthly Press, 1989), p. 307.

122 O'Neil and Leher, *Underboss*, p. 238.

123 Frederic D. Homer, *Guns and Garlic: Myths and Realties of Organized Crime* (West Lafayette, IN: Perdue University Studies, 1974), p. 98.

124 Abadinsky, *Criminal Elite*, p. 106; Joseph L. Albini, *The American Mafia: Genesis of a Legend* (New York: Meredith Corp., 1971), p. 301.

125 Charles Rappleye and Ed Becker, *All-American Mafioso: The Johnny Rosselli Story* (New York: Doubleday, 1991), p. 83.

126 Howard Abadinsky, *Organized Crime: A Comprehensive Reference to the Laws and Strategies for Preventing and Combatting Organized Crime* (Boston: Allyn and Bacon, 1981), pp. 53–54.

127 U.S. Senate Permanent Subcommittee on Investigations of the Committee on Governmental Affairs, *Profile of Organized Crime: Mid-Atlantic Region*, 98th Cong., 1st sess., 15 February 1983, pp. 98–99. See also U.S. Senate Committee on the Judiciary, *Organized Crime in America*, 98th Cong., 1st sess., part 1, 16 February 1983, pp. 147–48.

128 In December 2000 the Satan's Choice chapters were all absorbed by the Hells Angels.

129 Paul Volpe, a high-ranking member of the Joseph Todaro family, was killed in November 1983. By tradition, the Buffalo family has jurisdiction in the southern part of Ontario, including Toronto, Hamilton and Niagara Falls. Volpe

had made considerable investments in real estate for speculation purposes in Atlantic City, with Angelo Bruno's permission. With the expected opening of five new casinos in Atlantic City, real estate and land values increased sharply. For some reason, Volpe's business dealings irritated certain members of the Bruno organization, who complained about Volpe to the Buffalo family. It was later learned that Volpe did not have permission from Buffalo to do business in Atlantic City.

Chapter 6: Territories and Areas of Jurisdiction

1 Pennsylvania Crime Commission, *Organized Crime in Pennsylvania: A Decade of Change* (1990), p. 116.

2 John Cummings and Ernest Volkman, *Goombata: The Improbable Rise and Fall of John Gotti and His Gang* (Boston: Little, Brown and Co., 1990), pp. 239–40.

3 Henry A. Zeiger, *Sam the Plumber: One Year in the Life of a Cosa Nostra Boss* (Bergenfield, NJ: The New American Library, Times Mirror, 1972), p. 49.

4 Joseph D. Pistone with Richard Woodley, *Donnie Brasco: My Undercover Life in the Mafia* (New York: The New American Library, 1987), pp. 142–43, 151–53, 174, 196.

5 Howard Abadinsky, "The McDonald's-ization of the Mafia," in *Organized Crime in America: Concepts and Controversies*, ed. Timothy S. Bynum, Issues in Crime and Justice, vol. 1 (Monsey, NY: Willow Tree Press, 1987), pp. 49–50.

6 Ovid Demaris, *The Last Mafioso: The Treacherous World of Jimmy Fratianno* (New York: Times Books, 1981), pp. 345–46.

7 Ovid Demaris, *The Boardwalk Jungle* (New York: Bantam Books, 1986), pp. 126–30.

8 Cummings and Volkman, *Goombata*, pp. 252–53.

9 Henry A. Zeiger, *The Jersey Mob* (Scarborough, ON: Signet Books, The New American Library of Canada, 1975), pp. 172–73.

10 Cummings and Volkman, *Goombata*, pp. 91–92.

11 Donald R. Cressey, *Theft of the Nation: The Structure and Operation of Organized Crime in America* (New York: Harper and Row, 1969), p. 148.

12 Ibid., p. 149.

13 Howard Abadinsky, *The Criminal Elite: Professional and Organized Crime* (Westport, CT: Greenwood Press, 1983), pp. 96–97.

14 U.S. Senate Committee on the Judiciary, *Organized Crime in America*, 98th Cong., 1st sess., part 1, 16 February 1983, pp. 136–37.

15 Ibid., p. 137.

16 United States District Court, Southern District of New York, *United States of America and Robert B. Reich, Secretary of the United States Department of Labor, Plaintiffs-against-Mason Tenders District Council of Greater New York, et al., Defendants,* declaration of Alphonse D'Arco, 94 Civ. 6487 (RWS), 5 October 1994.

17 Senate Committee, *Organized Crime in America*, p. 137.

18 Ibid., pp. 139–40.

19 Ibid., pp. 140–41.

20 In September 2003, Riggi was sentenced to ten years for the murder of a businessman in 1989, as a favour to John Gotti.

21 Senate Committee, *Organized Crime in America*, pp. 141–42.

22 Alan A. Block and Frank R. Scarpitti, *Poisoning for Profit: The Mafia and Toxic Waste in America* (New York: Morrow and Co., 1985), p. 118.

23 U.S. Senate Permanent Subcommittee on Investigations of the Committee on Government Operations, *Organized Crime and Illicit Traffic in Narcotics*, 88th Cong., 1st sess., part 1, 27 September 1963, p. 117.

24 President's Commission on Organized Crime, *Organized Crime and Heroin Trafficking*, Record of Hearing V, testimony of Leroy Barnes, Miami, 20–21 February 1985, pp. 215–16.

25 Ibid.

26 Robert Lombardo, "Organized Crime and the Concept of Community" (Chicago: University of Illinois at Chicago Circle, Department of Sociology, 1979), cited in Abadinsky, *Criminal Elite*, p. 146.

27 David E. Kaplan and Alec Dubro, *Yakuza: The Explosive Account of Japan's Criminal Underworld* (Reading, MA: Addison-Wesley Publishing Company, 1983), pp. 263–64.

28 Pennsylvania Crime Commission, *Organized Crime in Pennsylvania*, p. 153. Joseph Bruno is not related to Angelo Bruno, murdered in March 1980.

29 Joseph Salerno and Stephen J. Rivele, *The Plumber: The True Story of How One Good Man Helped Destroy the Entire Philadelphia Mafia* (New York: Knightsbridge Publishers, 1990), pp. 15–16.

30 Ibid., p. 18; Mark H. Haller, *Life Under Bruno: The Economics of an Organized Crime Family*, report for the Pennsylvania Crime Commission (July 1991), p. 14.

31 Haller, *Life Under Bruno*, p. 7.

32 Senate Permanent Subcommittee, *Organized Crime and Illicit Traffic in Narcotics*, 9 October 1963, p. 367.

33 James Neff, *Mobbed Up: Jackie Presser's High-Wire Life in the Teamsters, the Mafia, and the FBI* (New York: The Atlantic Monthly Press, 1989), pp. 198–99.

34 U.S. Senate Permanent Subcommittee on Investigations of the Committee on Governmental Affairs, *Organized Crime and Use of Violence*. 96th Cong., 2nd sess., part 1, 29 April 1980, p. 164.

35 William F. Roemer Jr., *Roemer: Man Against the Mob: The Inside Story of How the FBI Cracked the Chicago Mob by the Agent Who Led the Attack* (New York: Donald I. Fine, 1989), p. 138.

36 Senate Permanent Subcommittee, *Organized Crime and Use of Violence*, p. 109.

37 U.S. Senate Permanent Subcommittee on Investigations of the Committee on Governmental Affairs, *Organized Criminal Activities in South Florida*, 96th Cong., 2nd sess., part 3, 25 October 1978, pp. 755–61.

38 Demaris, *Boardwalk Jungle*, pp. 71–72.

39 Another motive for Bruno's murder is that he allegedly refused to trade joint ventures in Florida for some in Atlantic City with Cosa Nostra boss Santos Trafficante; see Ralph Blumenthal, *Last Days of the Sicilians: At War with the Mafia: The FBI Assault on the Pizza Connection* (New York: Times Books, 1988), p. 44.

40 U.S. Senate Permanent Subcommittee on Investigations of the Committee on Governmental Affairs, *Hotel Employees and Restaurant Employees International Union*, 97th Cong., 2nd sess., part 1, 22 June 1982, p. 30.

41 David L. Chandler, *Brothers in Blood: The Rise of the Criminal Brotherhoods* (New York: E.P. Dutton and Co., 1975), p. 174; U.S. House Select Committee on Assassinations, *Investigation of the Assassination of President John F. Kennedy*, 95th Cong., 2nd sess., vol. IX, appendix, Staff and Consultants Reports on Organized Crime, March 1979, pp. 66–67.

42 Roemer, *Roemer*, pp. 27–28.

43 U.S. Senate Permanent Subcommittee on Investigations of the Committee on Governmental Affairs, *Organized Crime: 25 Years After Valachi*, 100th Cong., 2nd sess., testimony of Angelo Lonardo, 15 April 1988, p. 88.

44 Sean M. McWeeney, "The Sicilian Mafia and Its Impact on the United States," *FBI Law Enforcement Bulletin* 56, no. 2 (February 1987). The provision of "soggiorno obbligatorio" was repealed in 1999 and replaced by lengthy prison sentences.

45 Tim Shawcross and Martin Young, *Men of Honour: The Confessions of Tommaso Buscetta* (London: Collins, 1987), pp. 78, 83.

46 President's Commission on Organized Crime, THE IMPACT: *Organized Crime Today*, Report to the President and the Attorney General, April 1986, p. 56.

47 Claire Sterling, *Octopus: The Long Reach of the International Sicilian Mafia* (New York: W.W. Norton & Co., 1990), pp. 240–41, 245–46.

48 Quebec Police Commission, Commission of Inquiry into Organized Crime, Project "Benoit," conversation of 22 April 1974, exhibit 540, filed before the commission on 23 November 1975, pp. 30–32.

Chapter 7: Rules Regarding Criminal Activities

1 Thomas Cupples and David Kauzlarich, "La Cosa Nostra in Philadelphia: A Functionalist Perspective," *Criminal Organizations* 11, Nos. 1 & 2 (1997), p. 18.

2 New York State Organized Task Force, *Corruption and Racketeering in the New York City Construction Industry*, Final Report (New York: New York University Press, 1990), pp. 75–76. For more comprehensive and detailed descriptions of Cosa Nostra criminal activities, see David L. Herbert and Howard Tritt, *Corporations of Corruption: A Systematic Study of Organized Crime* (Springfield, IL: Charles C. Thomas, Publisher, 1984), pp. 36–64; The Chicago Crime Commission, A

Study of Organized Crime in Illinois (Chicago: IIT Research Institute and the Chicago Crime Commission, 1971), pp. 146–53, 172–79.

3 President's Commission on Organized Crime, THE IMPACT: *Organized Crime Today*, Report to the President and the Attorney General, April 1986, pp. 45–47.

4 Mark H. Haller, *Life Under Bruno: The Economics of an Organized Crime Family*, report to the Pennsylvania Crime Commission, July 1991, p. 23.

5 Peter Maas, *The Valachi Papers* (New York: Bantam Books, 1968), pp. 132, 134, 136.

6 Nicholas Pileggi, *Wiseguy: Life in a Mafia Family* (New York: Simon & Schuster, 1985), p. 226.

7 The "numbers" business, or "policy," is a very lucrative illegal gambling activity. A series of numbers from 000 to 999 are bet on sport events such as races or boxing, or on legal lotteries. For example, if the number picked is 739, it can pay up to $700 for a one dollar bet. "In the game of numbers, a player selects a number between 0 and 999 in a three-digit system. The winning combination will be based for example on results of daily horse races or on stock market quotations which are used to determine the winning number. The payoff is typically $600 for each dollar bet" (Herbert and Tritt, *Corporations of Corruption*, pp. 46–47).

8 Annelise Graebner Anderson, *The Business of Organized Crime: A Cosa Nostra Family* (Stanford: Hoover Institute Press, Stanford University, 1980), p. 37.

9 Pileggi, *Wiseguy*, pp. 217–18.

10 Jerry Capeci and Gene Mustain, *Gotti: Rise and Fall* (New York: Onyx Books, 1996), p. 116.

11 Pennsylvania Crime Commission, *Organized Crime in Pennsylvania: A Decade of Change* (1990), p. 157; Donald Cox, *Mafia Wipeout: How the Feds Put Away an Entire Mob Family* (New York: Shapolsky Publishers, 1989), p. 258.

12 Ronald Koziol and John O'Brien, "Rent-a-Racket is Mob's New Plan to Make Cash, Avoid Law," *Chicago Tribune*, 29 November 1982.

13 "Something Fishy in Chicago," *Time*, 7 August 1978, p. 19. See also William F. Roemer Jr. *Accardo: The Genuine Godfather* (New York: Ivy Books, Ballantine Books, 1995), p. 9.

14 President's Commission on Organized Crime, *Organized Crime and Gambling*, Record of Hearing VII, New York, 24 June 1985, pp. 69–70, 105–6, 143–44.

15 U.S. Senate Permanent Subcommittee on Investigations of the Committee on Governmental Affairs, *Profile of Organized Crime: Great Lakes Region*, 98th Cong., 2nd sess., 31 January 1984, p. 209.

16 Claire Sterling, *Octopus: The Long Reach of the International Sicilian Mafia* (New York: W.W. Norton & Co., 1990), p. 86.

17 U.S. Senate Permanent Subcommittee on Investigations of the Committee on Governmental Affairs, *Organized Crime: 25 Years After Valachi*, 100th Cong., 2nd sess., 11 April 1988, p. 80.

18 Maas, *Valachi Papers*, pp. 245–46.

19 Sterling, *Octopus*, p. 83.

20 Diego Gambetta, *The Sicilian Mafia: The Business of Private Protection* (Cambridge, MA: Harvard University Press, 1996), p. 238.

21 U.S. Senate Permanent Subcommittee on Investigations of the Committee on Government Operations, *Organized Crime and Illicit Traffic in Narcotics*, 88th Cong., 1st sess., part 1, 9 October 1963, pp. 319–20.

22 Ibid., p. 320.

23 Ibid., pp. 320–21.

24 Ibid., p. 322.

25 Nicholas Gage, *The Mafia Is Not an Equal Opportunity Employer* (New York: Dell Books, 1972), pp. 167–68.

26 John Cummings and Ernest Volkman, *Goombata: The Improbable Rise and Fall of John Gotti and His Gang* (Boston: Little, Brown and Co., 1990), p. 78.

27 Gene Mustain and Jerry Capeci, *Mob Star: The Story of John Gotti* (New York: Franklin Watts, 1988), p. 16.

28 Joseph F. O'Brien and Andris Kurins, *Boss of Bosses: The Fall of the Godfather: The FBI and Paul Castellano* (New York: Simon & Schuster, 1991), p. 134.

29 Gene Mustain and Jerry Capeci, *Murder Machine: A True Story of Murder, Madness, and the Mafia* (New York: Dutton Books, 1992), p. 119.

30 This edict did not prevent Roy DeMeo from being initiated as a made member sometime after. DeMeo was involved in marijuana and cocaine trafficking.

31 O'Brien and Kurins, *Boss of Bosses*, p. 148.

32 Ralph Blumenthal and John Miller, *The Gotti Tapes* (New York: Times Books, Random House, 1992), p. 149.

33 Tim Shawcross and Martin Young, *Men of Honour: The Confessions of Tommaso Buscetta* (London: Collins, 1987), pp. 292–93.

34 John H. Davis, *Mafia Dynasty: The Rise and Fall of the Gambino Crime Family* (New York: HarperCollins Publishers, 1993), p. 186.

35 Davis, *Mafia Dynasty*, p. 207. See also Capeci and Mustain, *Gotti: Rise and Fall*, p. 97.

36 Cummings and Volkman, *Goombata*, p. 185.

37 Cummings and Volkman, *Goombata*, pp. 185–86.

38 John Gotti died on June 10, 2002, after serving eleven years in prison.

39 Patrice O'Shaughnessy, "Meet Boss Zeke," *New York Daily News*, 17 June 2002, p. 6.

40 Ministero dell' Interno, Direzione Investigativa Antimafia, *Activities and Results*, second half of the year 1999, Italy.

41 Mustain and Capeci, *Mob Star*, p. 86.

42 Blumenthal and Miller, *Gotti Tapes*, p. 147.

43 Haller, *Life Under Bruno*, p. 6.

44 Vincent Teresa with Thomas C. Renner, *My Life in the Mafia* (Greenwich, CT: Fawcett Publications, 1973), p. 99. Al Capone's involvement in prostitution was one of the reasons he was refused membership in Cosa Nostra in 1931.

45 United States v. Salerno, 85 CR 139 SDNY (1985), testimony of Angelo Lonardo, cited in James B. Jacobs, Christopher Panarella and Jay Worthington, *Busting Mob: United States v. Cosa Nostra* (New York: New York University Press, 1994), p. 118.

46 Pino Arlacchi, *Les hommes du déshonneur. La stupéfiante confession du repenti Antonino Calderone*, trans. Françoise Brun (Paris: Éditions Albin Michel, 1992), pp. 25, 166.

47 President's Commission on Organized Crime, *Organized Crime and Heroin Trafficking*, Record of Hearing V, Miami, 20 February 1985, p. 118.

48 Senate Permanent Subcommittee, *Organized Crime and Illicit Traffic in Narcotics*, 2 October 1963, pp. 241–42.

49 Anderson, *Business of Organized Crime*, pp. 27–28.

Chapter 8: The Judicial System of Cosa Nostra

1 Donald R. Cressey, *Theft of the Nation: The Structure and Operation of Organized Crime in America* (New York: Harper and Row, 1969), pp. 203–4.

2 Ibid., p. 203.

3 Ibid., pp. 203–4.

4 Gilbert Cordeau, "Les homicides entre délinquants: une analyse des conflits qui provoquent des règlements de comptes," *Criminologie*, vol. XXII, no. 2 (Montreal: Presses de l'Université de Montréal, 1989), pp. 24–25.

5 Peter Reuter, *Disorganized Crime: Illegal Markets and the Mafia* (Cambridge, MA: MIT Press, 1984), p. 158.

6 Ibid., pp. 165–66, 216 n35.

7 Cressey, *Theft of the Nation*, p. 210.

8 Ibid.

9 Ibid., p. 211.

10 Howard Abadinsky, *The Criminal Elite: Professional and Organized Crime* (Westport, CT: Greenwood Press, 1983), pp. 153–54, 155–56.

11 Joseph Volz and Peter J. Bridge, *The Mafia Talks* (Greenwich, CT: Fawcett Publications, 1969), p. 17.

12 Cressey, *Theft of the Nation*, p. 207.

13 Peter Diapoulos and Steven Linakis, *The Sixth Family* (New York: Bantam Books, 1977), p. 27.

14 Peter Maas, *The Valachi Papers* (New York: Bantam Books, 1968), pp. 211–12.

15 Ibid., p. 214.

16 Ralph Salerno and John S. Tompkins, *The Crime Confederation: Cosa Nostra and Allied Operations in Organized Crime* (New York: Popular Library, 1969), pp. 126–27.

17 President's Commission on Organized Crime, THE IMPACT: *Organized Crime Today*, Report to the President and the Attorney General, testimony of Martin Light, April 1986, pp. 316–18.

18 Both San Felice and Roselle were murdered, San Felice in 1978 and Roselle in 1980.

19 Alan A. Block and Frank R. Scarpitti, *Poisoning for Profit: The Mafia and Toxic Waste in America* (New York: Morrow and Co., 1985), p. 234.

20 Charles Grutzner, "Organized Crime and the Businessman," in *The Crime Establishment: Organized Crime and American Society*, ed. John E. Conklin (Englewood Cliffs, NJ: Prentice-Hall, 1973), p. 109.

21 Cressey, *Theft of the Nation*, pp. 207–8.

22 Henry A. Zeiger, *Sam the Plumber: One Year in the Life of a Cosa Nostra Boss* (Bergenfield, NJ: The New American Library, Times Mirror, 1972), pp. 260–62.

23 Paul S. Meskil, *Don Carlo: Boss of Bosses* (Toronto: Popular Library, 1973), p. 190.

24 Maas, *Valachi Papers*, p. 259.

25 Pennsylvania Crime Commission, *Organized Crime in Pennsylvania: A Decade of Change* (1990), p. 154.

26 Salerno and Tompkins, *Crime Confederation*, pp. 124–25; see also Montana's testimony in U.S. Senate Select Committee, *On Improper Activities in the Labor or Management Field*, 85th Cong., 2nd sess., part 32, testimony of John C. Montana, 1 July 1958, pp. 12, 293–321.

27 Salerno and Tompkins, *Crime Conferderation*, pp. 124–25; Meskil, *Don Carlo*, pp. 84–85.

28 For more on Joseph Bonanno's history, see Joseph Bonanno with Sergio Salli, *A Man of Honor: The Autobiography of Joseph Bonanno* (New York: Simon & Schuster, 1983); Gay Talese, *Honor Thy Father* (Greenwich, CT: Fawcett Publications, 1972); Bill Bonanno, *Bound by Honor: A Mafioso's Story* (New York: St. Martin's Press, 1999).

29 Bill Bonanno, *Bound by Honor*, p. 129.

30 Michael J. Zuckerman, *Vengeance Is Mine* (New York: Collier Macmillan Publishers, 1987), p. 109.

31 Fabrizio Calvi, *L'Europe des parrains. La Mafia à l'assaut de l'Europe* (Paris: Grasset, 1993), p. 164.

Chapter 9: The Code of Murder

1 John H. Davis, *Mafia Dynasty: The Rise and Fall of the Gambino Crime Family* (New York: HarperCollins Publishers, 1993), p. 206.

2 Gus Tyler, *Organized Crime in America: A Book of Readings* (Ann Arbor: Ann Arbor Paperbacks, University of Michigan Press, 1967), p. 231.

3 Gaia Servadio, *Mafioso: A History of the Mafia from Its Origins to the Present Day* (London: Secker and Warburg, 1976), p. 27.

4 Henner Hess, *Mafia and Mafiosi: The Structure of Power*, trans. Ewald Osers (Lexington, MA: Saxon House/Lexington Books, D.C. Heath, 1973), p. 104.

5 Tim Shawcross and Martin Young, *Men of Honour: The Confessions of Tommaso Buscetta* (London: Collins, 1987), p. 149.

6 Peter Maas, *The Valachi Papers* (New York: Bantam Books, 1968), p. 44; Ralph Blumenthal and John Miller, *The Gotti Tapes* (New York: Times Books, Random House, 1992), p. 153; Michael J. Zuckerman, *Vengeance Is Mine* (New York: Collier Macmillan Publishers, 1987), p. 101.

7 U.S. Senate Permanent Subcommittee on Investigations of the Committee on Government Operations, *Organized Crime and Illicit Traffic in Narcotics*, 88th Cong., 1st sess., part 1, 1 October 1963, pp. 192–93.

8 Peter Maas, *Underboss: Sammy the Bull Gravano's Story of Life in the Mafia* (New York: HarperPerennial, 1999), p. 250.

9 Tyler, *Organized Crime in America*, pp. 229–31.

10 Unfortunately, errors often occur, and innocent citizens get killed. The shooting of four men in the Neopolitan Noodle, a restaurant in Upper Manhattan frequented by members of the Colombo family, is certainly the most horrifying example. In August 1972 four kosher-meat dealers were sitting at the bar. A member of the Brooklyn Gallo faction spotted the four men, and mistakenly thought them to be members of the Colombo family. The man left the restaurant and informed the Gallo clan, which was looking to revenge the death of its leader, Joey Gallo, killed four months earlier. Half an hour later, a gunman entered the restaurant and fired shots, killing two of the men and wounding the other two.

11 U.S. Senate Permanent Subcommittee on Investigations of the Committee on Governmental Affairs, *Organized Crime and Use of Violence*, 96th Cong., 2nd sess., part 1, 29 April 1980, p. 97.

12 President's Commission on Organized Crime, *Organized Crime and Gambling*, Record of Hearing VII, New York, 24 June 1985, p. 154.

13 Donald R. Cressey, *Theft of the Nation: The Structure and Operation of Organized Crime in America* (New York: Harper and Row, 1969), p. 32.

14 Claire Sterling, *Octopus: The Long Reach of the International Sicilian Mafia* (New York: W.W. Norton & Co., 1990), pp. 73–74.

15 Pino Arlacchi, *Les hommes du déshonneur. La stupéfiante confession du repenti Antonino Calderone*, trans. Françoise Brun (Paris: Éditions Albin Michel, 1992), p. 195.

16 Alexander Stille, *Excellent Cadavers: The Mafia and the Death of the First Italian Republic* (New York: Pantheon Books, 1995), pp. 307–8.

17 Corrado Stajano, *Mafia. L'atto d'accusa dei giudici di Palermo* (Rome: Editori Riuniti, 1986), p. 47.

18 Pennsylvania Crime Commission, *Health Care Fraud: A Rising Threat*, testimony of Aladena Fratianno, 28 July 1981, p. 42.

19 *United States v. Bellomo*, U.S. Court of Appeals for the Second Circuit, August Term, 1998.

20 Howard Abadinsky, *The Criminal Elite: Professional and Organized Crime* (Westport, CT: Greenwood Press, 1983), pp. 160–61.

21 President's Commission on Organized Crime, THE IMPACT: *Organized Crime Today*, Report to the President and the Attorney General, April 1986, pp. 319–20.

22 Henry A. Zeiger, *The Jersey Mob* (Scarborough, ON: Signet Books, The New American Library of Canada, 1975), p. 180.

23 Gene Mustain and Jerry Capeci, *Mob Star: The Story of John Gotti* (New York: Franklin Watts, 1988), p. 143.

24 In December 1990 Gotti, Frank Locascio and Thomas Gambino were charged with thirteen counts of racketeering under the RICO Act for having conducted a criminal enterprise through a pattern of criminal activity. The trial began in February 1992 and lasted six weeks. The main government prosecution witness was Salvatore Gravano, who was initially charged along with Gotti but later turned against his boss. On April 2, 1992, Gotti was found guilty of the murders of Paul Castellano, Thomas Bilotti, Robert DiBernardo, Liborio Milito and Louis DiBono. On June 23, 1992, he was sentenced to life imprisonment without parole.

25 *United States v. John Gotti, Salvatore Gravano, Frank Locascio, Thomas Gambino*, U.S. District Court, Eastern District of New York, RICO Indictment, testimony of Salvatore Gravano, 21 January–23 June 1992.

26 Maas, *Underboss*, pp. 140–50; See also Federal Bureau of Investigation, Salvatore Gravano's debriefing, 14 November 1991, www.1.1net.com/ don-ferin/gravano/gravano_50.html.

27 Pennsylvania Crime Commission, *Organized Crime in Pennsylvania: A Decade of Change* (1990), p. 153.

28 Annelise Graebner Anderson, *The Business of Organized Crime: A Cosa Nostra Family* (Stanford, CA: Hoover Institute Press, Stanford University, 1980), pp. 45–46.

29 Abadinsky, *Criminal Elite*, p. 152. Rosselli's body was found in August 1976. He was scheduled to appear before the U.S. Senate Select Committee on Intelligence Activities of CIA.

30 Fabrizio Calvi, *La vie quotidienne de la Mafia de 1950 à nos jours*, trans. Mario Fusco (Paris: Hachette, 1986), pp. 66–67.

31 Ralph Blumenthal, *Last Days of the Sicilians: At War with the Mafia: The FBI Assault on the Pizza Connection* (New York: Times Books, 1988), p. 20.

32 Colombo, who sustained severe brain damage from the gunshots, died seven years later, in May 1978, at age fifty-four.

33 U.S. Senate Permanent Subcommittee on Investigations of the Committee on Government Operations, *Organized Crime and Illicit Traffic in Narcotics*, United States Senate, 88th Cong., 1st sess., part 1, 9 October 1963, p. 348. According to Valachi, Costello was later "reinstated" in the Genovese family.

34 Salvatore Luciano, the founder of that family, had been deported to Italy from the United States in February 1946. Luciano, who had been sentenced in June

1936 to thirty years minimum and fifty years maximum for compulsory prostitution, saw his sentence commuted following his co-operation with the U.S. Naval Intelligence Services in helping American authorities to prevent acts of sabotage on the New York waterfronts. For more on Luciano's participation with the Allied Forces during the Second World War, see Rodney Campbell, *The Luciano Project: The Secret Wartime Collaboration of the Mafia and the U.S. Navy* (New York: McGraw-Hill Books, 1977).

35 Richard Hammer, *Hoodlum Empire: The Survival of the Syndicate, Part II* (Chicago: Playboy Press, 1975), pp. 113–14. Costello died of natural causes in February 1973 at the age of eighty-two.

36 Fred J. Cook, *Mafia!* (Greenwich, CT: Fawcett Publications, 1973), pp. 187–90.

37 Paul S. Meskil, *Don Carlo: Boss of Bosses* (Toronto: Popular Library, 1973), pp. 224–31.

38 Bonventre disappeared in April 1984. His dismembered body was discovered in a glue barrel. In August 2003, Joseph Massino, the boss of the Bonanno family, was charged by the U.S. authorities with the murder of Bonventre.

39 In 1974 a contract to kill Galante was allegedly issued by Carlo Gambino to a Gambino faction in Connecticut. In 1977 Galante returned to prison for a parole violation. He was put in solitary confinement for his own protection (*New York Post*, 20 July 1979).

40 Pennsylvania Crime Commission, *Organized Crime in Pennsylvania*, p. 153.

41 Donald Cox, *Mafia Wipeout: How the Feds Put Away an Entire Mob Family* (New York: Shapolsky Publishers, 1989), p. 29.

42 U.S. Senate Permanent Subcommittee on Investigations of the Committee on Governmental Affairs, *Organized Crime: 25 Years After Valachi*, 100th Cong., 2nd sess., testimony of Vincent Cafaro, 29 April 1988, pp. 233–36.

43 Cox, *Mafia Wipeout*, p. 30.

44 "Condolences Are Called for Frank Piccolo," *Organized Crime Digest* 2, no. 9 (September 1981): 9.

45 *United States v. John Gotti, Salvatore Gravano, Frank Locascio, Thomas Gambino*, testimony of Salvatore Gravano. In 1994, as a reward for his testimony against Gotti, Gravano was given a lenient sentence of five years for the nineteen murders to which he had confessed. After his release, Gravano left the Witness Protection Program and settled in Arizona, where he became involved in selling ecstasy. He and his wife, son and daughter were arrested in February 2000. Gravano's arrest saved his life, as the administration of the Gambino family had sent a hit team to Arizona in late 1999 to set up and kill the former underboss. In September 2002 Gravano pleaded guilty to leading a drug ring that distributed and sold ecstasy in Arizona and in New York City and was sentenced to a twenty-year jail term. In August 2003, Gravano was charged for being an accomplice in the 1980 killing of a New York City police officer.

46 John Lehmann, "Mobster Sleeps with the Swishes," *New York Post*, 1 May 2003.

47 State of New Jersey, Commission of Investigation, *Organized Crime in Bars, Part II* (1993).

48 Ibid.

49 The use of explosives in the DeCicco murder violated a Commission edict that prohibited the use of explosives, for public safety.

50 Ernest Volkman, *Gangbusters: The Destruction of America's Last Great Mafia Dynasty* (New York: Avon Books, 1999), p. 225.

51 Joseph Salerno and Stephen J. Rivele, *The Plumber: The True Story of How One Good Man Helped Destroy the Entire Philadelphia Mafia* (New York: Knightsbridge Publishers, 1990), p. 151.

52 Shawcross and Young, *Men of Honour*, p. 69.

53 Thomas Plate, "The Mafia at War," *New York* magazine, 1972, p. 79.

54 James Bennet, "Sister of a Mob Informant Is Shot, Apparently as Mafia Vengeance," *New York Times*, 11 March 1992.

55 Kitty Caparella, "Natale: My Wife, 2 Kids Threatened," *Philadelphia Daily News*, 13 April 2001.

56 Pino Arlacchi, *Buscetta. La Mafia par l'un des siens*, trans. Éric Jozsef (Paris: Éditions du Félin, 1996), p. 27.

57 Jonathan Kwitny, *Vicious Circle: The Mafia in the Marketplace* (New York: W.W. Norton & Co., 1979), pp. 60–61.

58 Gene Mustain and Jerry Capeci, *Murder Machine: A True Story of Murder, Madness, and the Mafia* (New York: Dutton Books, 1992), pp. 142–43.

59 T.J. English, *The Westies. Inside the Hell's Kitchen Irish Mob* (New York: G.P. Putnam's Sons, 1990), p. 175.

60 John H. Davis, *Mafia Dynasty: The Rise and Fall of the Gambino Crime Family* (New York: HarperCollins Publishers, 1993), p. 292.

61 Carl Sifakis, *The Mafia Encyclopedia* (New York: Facts on Files Publications, 1987), p. 352.

62 Ovid Demaris, *The Last Mafioso: The Treacherous World of Jimmy Fratianno* (New York: Times Books, 1981), pp. 309–10.

63 Ibid., p. 66.

64 Shawcross and Young, *Men of Honour*, p. 115.

65 Arlacchi, *Hommes du déshonneur*, pp. 45–46.

66 Diego Gambetta, *The Sicilian Mafia: The Business of Private Protection* (Cambridge, MA: Harvard University Press, 1996), p. 114.

67 Blumenthal, *Last Days of the Sicilians*, p. 112.

68 Sterling, *Octopus*, p. 208.

69 Arlacchi, *Hommes du déshonneur*, pp. 282–83.

70 Joseph Bonanno with Sergio Salli, *A Man of Honor: The Autobiography of Joseph Bonanno* (New York: Simon & Schuster, 1983), p. 156.

71 According to Vincent Palermo, a former member of the DeCavalcante family who turned informant, the Gambino family once considered having Giuliani murdered.

72 Senate Permanent Subcommittee, *Organized Crime and Use of Violence*, p. 93.

73 For more on the Hennessey murder, see Richard Gambino, *Vendetta* (Garden City, NY: Doubleday and Co., 1977).

74 Arrigo Petacco, *Joe Petrosino* (New York: Macmillan Publishing Co., 1974), pp. 70–71, 147.

75 U.S. House Select Committee on Assassinations, *Investigation of the Assassination of President John F. Kennedy*, 95th Cong., 2nd sess., vol. IX, appendix, Staff and Consultants Reports on Organized Crime, March 1979, p. 44.

76 Joseph D. Pistone with Richard Woodley, *Donnie Brasco: My Undercover Life in the Mafia* (New York: The New American Library, 1987), pp. 367–68.

77 William Glaberson, "Tangled Tale of Botched Hit Is Detailed in an Indictment," *New York Times*, 23 January 2003.

78 Tom Robbins, "The Con and the Mayor," *Village Voice*, 26 July 2000.

79 Eric Pooley, "Death of a Hood," *New York* magazine, 29 January 1990, pp. 26–33.

80 In March 1994 Casso pleaded guilty to eleven murder charges in exchange for a lenient sentence. He then became a government witness in other mob trials. In August 1997 the government withdrew Casso as a co-operating witness after it was discovered that he had been involved in a series of crimes in prison. Moreover, he was accused of providing false information to the prosecution. Casso is now serving a life sentence without parole.

81 John Kobler, *Capone: The Life and World of Al Capone* (Greenwich, CT: Fawcett Publications, 1972), p. 144.

82 Stephen Fox, *Blood and Power: Organized Crime in Twentieth-Century America* (New York: William Morrow and Co., 1989), p. 274.

83 William F. Roemer Jr., *Accardo: The Genuine Godfather* (New York: Ivy Books, 1995), p. 85.

84 See Michael F. Wendland, *The Arizona Project: How a Team of Investigative Reporters Got Revenge on Deadline* (Kansas City: Sheed Andrews and McMell, 1977).

85 Giovanni Falcone and Marcelle Padovani, *Cosa Nostra. Le juge et les "hommes d'honneur,"* 1st ed. (Paris: Austral, 1991), p. 28.

86 Servadio, *Mafioso*, p. 27.

87 David L. Chandler, *Brothers in Blood: The Rise of the Criminal Brotherhoods* (New York: E.P. Dutton and Co., 1975), pp. 112, 115.

88 Nicholas Gage, *The Mafia Is Not an Equal Opportunity Employer* (New York: Dell Books, 1972), p. 124.

89 Raymond Martin, *Revolt in the Mafia* (New York: Duell Storn and Pearce, Publishers, 1963), p. 69.

90 Ibid., p. 161.

91 Salerno and Rivele, *Plumber*, p. 84.

92 Ibid., p. 117.

93 Sterling, *Octopus*, p. 209.

94 Pistone with Woodley, *Donnie Brasco*, p. 370.

95 Abadinsky, *Criminal Elite*, p. 103.

96 John Cummings and Ernest Volkman, *Goombata: The Improbable Rise and Fall of John Gotti and His Gang* (Boston: Little, Brown and Co., 1990), p. 61.

97 Michel Marriott, "Mob Witness Talks of Murder as Management Tool," *New York Times*, 28 May 1992.

98 Robert D. McFadden, "Archidiocese Denies Request for Galante Funeral Mass," *New York Times*, 16 July 1979; Alan Feuer, "Diocese of Brooklyn Denies Mass for Gotti," *New York Times*, 13 June 2002.

99 Al Guart, Lisa Pulitzer and Andy Geller, "Fans of Dead Don Mob His Burial Rites in Queens Spectacular," *New York Post*, 16 June 2002.

100 Catherine Wheeler, "Catholic Bishop Respects Church Mass for Mafia Boss," *Hamilton Spectator*, 4 June 1997.

Afterword

1 Giancarlo Caselli, "The Criminal Phenomenon in Italy. Illegal Activities, Threats and Contrasting Strategies," *Atti del 1° Seminario Europeo "Falcone One" sulla Criminalità Organizzata*, Rome, 26–28 April 1995.

Glossary

associate: A person who works for a specific crime family but is not an official member.

"books": A term used to describe membership in Cosa Nostra. When "books" are opened, it means that Cosa Nostra is recruiting new members. When "books" are closed, the families will not be admitting new members for a certain period of time.

borgata: Literally means a section of town; a borough. This is another name for an American Cosa Nostra family.

capo (plural capi): Head or boss of a Cosa Nostra family. This person is chosen by all the capiregime (section leaders) of a family.

Capo di tutti capi: "Boss of all bosses." This position was eliminated after the Commission was created in 1931.

capodecina (plural capidecina): "Chief of ten." This person can also be referred to as caporegime, a section leader or lieutenant.

capomandamento (plural capimandamento): A Sicilian Mafia member elected by a family to represent one or more families at the Provincial Commission. Also known as "district leader."

caporegime (plural capiregime): A section leader or lieutenant of a regime—a group of ten or more soldiers.

Commission: Also known as Commissione, this is the highest ruling body of American Cosa Nostra. It arbitrates disputes to maintain stability among Cosa Nostra families.

consigliere (plural consiglieri): An advisor or counselor. He settles disputes between soldiers and upper-echelon family members and advises the boss.

Cosa Nostra: The crime organization. Literally "Our Thing" or "This Thing of Ours."

cosca (plural cosche): A Sicilian crime family.

crew: A group that is composed of soldiers (made members) and associates (non-members). Each crew has its own specialization, or area of criminal activity. See also regime.

cupola: The Sicilian Cosa Nostra's Commission.

gombah: A made member who acts as "godfather" to a newly made member.

hit: An underworld murder. Also called "contract" or "assignment." Members will also use the expressions "do a piece of work," "whack somebody" or "clip a guy."

made member: A person who is officially inducted into a crime family. This person is referred to as a "Man of Honour" in Sicily.

'Ndrangheta: Name for the Calabrese Mafia.

pentito (plural pentiti): A Mafia member who has decided to collaborate with authorities.

pizzu: Literally means the beak of a small bird. Paying the pizzu, or "wetting the beak," is an expression used when a Mafia boss asks someone to make an obligatory payment.

posato: A Sicilian Cosa Nostra member who has been permanently or temporarily expelled from the organization.

Rabbi: A person who acts as a representative for an associate (a non-member who works for the Mafia) during a dispute.

regime: A group of Cosa Nostra soldiers presided over by a caporegime or lieutenant.

reggènte: This term is used by the Sicilian Mafia to describe someone who temporarily holds a high-ranking position on behalf of another Cosa Nostra member.

sit-down: A meeting convened between two or more members to settle a dispute.

soldato: Soldier. This member holds the lowest position in the crime family. He has between 10 and 15 associates working for him.

sottocapo: Underboss. He is the second in command of a crime family.

Index